THE DYNAMICS OF
POLYANDRY

THE DYNAMICS OF
POLYANDRY

*Kinship, Domesticity, and Population
on the Tibetan Border*

Nancy E. Levine

The University of Chicago Press
Chicago and London

Nancy E. Levine is associate professor of anthropology at the University of California, Los Angeles.

The University of Chicago Press, Chicago 60637
The University of Chicago Press, Ltd., London
© 1988 by The University of Chicago
All rights reserved. Published 1988
Printed in the United States of America

97 96 95 94 93 92 91 90 89 88   5 4 3 2 1

Library of Congress Cataloging-in-Publication Data

Levine, Nancy E.
  The Dynamics of polyandry : kinship, domesticity, and population
on the Tibetan border / Nancy E. Levine.
      p.   cm.
  Bibliography: p.
  Includes index.
  ISBN 0-226-47568-9.   ISBN 0-226-47569-7 (pbk.)
  1. Nyinba (Nepalese people)—Social life and customs.   2. Kinship—
Nepal.   3. Polyandry—Nepal.   I. Title.
DS493.9.N92L48   1988
306.8'08991495—dc 19   87-34478
                                                                            CIP

In memory of Anna Bradburd Leopold

Contents

Tables

Illustrations

Preface

This is a book about polyandry as it is practiced among the Nyinba, a culturally Tibetan group resident in Northwestern Nepal. It uses ethnographic data to explore polyandry's cultural and social parameters and the multiplex factors that enter into individuals' decisions to remain in their polyandrous marriages or, as rarely happens, to dissolve them. This leads to a critique of arguments that find a determinant materialist logic in polyandry and seek its causes in exogenous circumstances.

When I first went to Nepal in 1973, it was not to study polyandry specifically, but to carry out general ethnographic research. At the time, only the barest outlines of Tibetan culture and social structure were known, and basic information seemed to be the critical need. My study of Nyinba, who may be the most polyandrous of Tibetan groups in Nepal, also was the outcome of chance. Originally I had intended to work in an area more easily accessible from Kathmandu. This plan, however, changed after I spoke to Christoph von Fürer-Haimendorf of the School of Oriental and African Studies in London, where I had enrolled to study Tibetan. He had just returned from a tour of Humla district in the distant Karnali Zone of Northwestern Nepal, an area previously closed to foreign researchers and ethnographically unknown. Fürer-Haimendorf suggested that I work among the Nyinba, because, he explained, they seemed to be extremely interesting and they still were quite traditional—and, an added advantage, they lived in an area of great natural beauty. I was convinced, took down the names of villages he described as most promising, made a copy of his map and left for Nepal a few weeks later.

In 1973 the only airstrip in the entire Karnali Zone was more than a week's walk from the Nyinba region. I will never forget my first journey there and the impoverished villages I passed along the way. Humla is one of the poorest districts in Nepal, and its people have among the smallest per capita holdings and the largest food deficits of any in the country. The road wound along cramped lanes between tiny houses, all jammed together, many of them in disrepair; it was springtime, people were hungry and, lacking food for themselves, had none for sale. When I finally reached Trangshod, the first Nyinba village on the main road, there was a dramatic change in scene. The road suddenly widened; it was better maintained, lined by fruit trees in bloom, and bordered by broad, carefully terraced fields. From a distance, the houses seemed large and the village well planned; as I drew closer the houses appeared even more substantial and imposing—each looked like a small, self-contained fort. I had arrived on the eve of the annual ancestor celebration and promptly was invited to attend. There were enormous baskets of fried bread, casks of beer, and pots of curd and milk, all of which was freely shared with me. This extraordinary wealth in a difficult environment owes much to the system of polyandry, as I was to find out, and to other practices that moderate village growth.

Polyandry, the simultaneous marriage of two or more men to a single woman, is cross-culturally rare and has been little studied. In most kinship texts, it stands as little more than a footnote underpinned by exotic and androcentric biases. In the Tibetan case, polyandry has been explained away as an adaptation born of necessity and individual self-interest: a strategy for conserving resources and limiting population in a resource-scarce environment and a custom readily abandoned once economic conditions improve. I have, however, found this view to be misleading. Nyinba polyandry is fraternal; it unites men who are brothers, and it is expected that brothers will share sexual and reproductive interests in a single woman throughout their lives. Fraternal solidarity in many areas of life, including matters sexual, is very deeply engrained. This became apparent early in my fieldwork when I overheard a discussion of two brothers who met one night outside the home of a common girl friend. The two simply decided to consult one another in future and coordinate their visits. Nyinba thought it appropriate for brothers to share lovers as they share wives. I found the absence of jealousy surprising, although later, after I had more opportunity to observe polyandrous marriages, it became unremarkable to me as well. Polyandry thus affects interpersonal relationships in marriage and in family life; it also is associated with a unique household system, supports a special type of domestic economy, and has a major impact on village political organization.

My research among the Nyinba was conducted in two phases. The first phase involved an extended period of traditional anthropological fieldwork between May 1973 and June 1975. During this period, I was able to spend approximately eighteen months in Nyinba villages; the remaining time was spent on the road—traveling to and from Kathmandu to renew my visa and visiting other Humla communities. I was nevertheless fortunate in finding Nyinba friends to accompany me on most of these journeys. The second phase of research lasted from October 1982 to December 1983 and involved a larger, comparative study of seven communities in Humla district. During this time, I spent approximately four months in Nyinba villages and also managed to take Nyinba companions to my new research sites.

The first period of research provided the data for my doctoral dissertation, which was submitted to the Department of Anthropology of the University of Rochester in 1977. Some of the materials used in the dissertation are incorporated here with data gathered during my second term of field research. Some of the earlier arguments also prefigure those developed in this book. At the time the dissertation was written, there were far fewer published accounts of Tibetan society, and little of the available material on Tibetan polyandry was drawn from modern anthropological fieldwork. In the last decade, Nepalese and Tibetan studies have expanded greatly, and now many more published studies and unpublished dissertations are available. Over this period as well, the arguments on Tibetan polyandry have sharpened, and anthropologists have come increasingly to portray it as an institution shaped by a dominant economic rationale.

I embarked upon my second period of field research in order to collect fuller demographic and economic data and to survey a larger number of individuals than I had managed to in my predoctoral research. If anything, my second stay among the Nyinba brought home to me the salience of kinship commitments in the conduct of polyandrous marriages. During the earlier period, my primary friends were young people of approximately my age, who were newly married or about to be married. By the second period, my friends' marriages were firmly established, each had several young children, and all had experienced the satisfactions and frustrations associated with family life generally and polyandrous family life particularly. At the same time, their parents, who also were closely associated with me, had begun to cede their authority and had assumed the role of indulgent grandparents, while my friends' grandparents had mostly retired from active life. Other anthropologists have attested to the value of long-term field research. In my case, I found it to provide a richer view of Nyinba marital, family, and social life and a fuller understanding of cycles of domestic development and changes over the life course.

Research in an area so difficult of access over so long a period of time depends in a major way on external sources of financial support. My doctoral dissertation research was made possible by a Graduate Research Grant from the National Science Foundation (SOC 73-05709). A fellowship from the National Institute of Mental Health (1F01 MH55 787-01) provided additional support during the second year of research and during the period of write-up at the School of Oriental and African Studies and the University of Rochester. Subsequent research was supported by a National Science Foundation Research Grant (BNS 81-16829) and by a Research Grant from the Population Council (CP84.09A/CP85.22A). I would like to express my thanks to these three institutions for their generous support. In addition I must thank the University of California, Los Angeles, for annual grants in support of research assistance and for funding a trip to Nepal in 1981 to plan for the second period of research.

Thanks also are due to a number of persons who provided encouragement, advice, and useful criticism of the manuscript at various stages: Sharman Babior, Anthony T. Carter, Karen Casper, Christoph von Fürer-Haimendorf, Grace Harris, Allen Johnson, Hilda Kuper, Robert Merrill, Kathryn Moran, Nazif Shahrani, and Joan Silk. The greatest debt of all is owed to my husband, Tahir Ali, for his detailed comments on early drafts of the manuscript and for his interest throughout the years it was in progress.

In Nepal, I was affiliated with the Research Centre for Nepal and Asian Studies (RCNAS) of Tribhuvan University, without whose help it would have been difficult to secure permission to work in so remote an area. I am particularly grateful to a number of Nepalese social scientists: Professor Dor Bahadur Bista, Dr. Harka Gurung, Dr. Navin Kumar Rai, and Dr. B. Prakash Upreti, who encouraged my research and who offered me a fuller picture of the special problems of Humla district.

Most of all I have to thank the Nyinba, for their tolerance of my presence, often uninvited, at their weddings, ceremonies, and funerals and for their extraordinary warmth and hospitality, which continued during serious food shortages in 1983. There is no measuring my gratitude to the family at Khor Gompa, especially to Tagpa Chodun and Nagderma, who treated me as one of their own children, and to their son Tshewang, who has acted as my research assistant for over a decade now. I also must thank my cook, Bum Dorje, who traveled throughout Humla with me, and Tsebal Lhamo, for her help in administering questionnaires during the second period of field research. Finally, I must single out Kunka Sendrup, Tshering Chombel, Dhami Mangal, and Jampal Sonam for the knowledge of their villages that they freely shared with me. There are many other individuals I could name; I hope to thank them in person before too many years have passed. I hope that they appreciate this book, for it is Nyinba most of all for whom it has been written.

I will close with two final notes on the book. The first concerns orthography. I have chosen to spell Tibetan terms used in the Nyinba dialect as they sounded to me and in a way that I hope will facilitate more accurate pronunciation by English speakers. The first time each new word appears, I have added its classical Tibetan spelling in parentheses, following the system of transliteration established by Wylie (1959). In giving the occasional Nepali words that Nyinba use, I have followed Turner's (1966) spellings and system of transliteration. This and capsule definitions of key terms can be found in the glossary at the end of the book. The names of individuals, households, and places have been disguised in the descriptions of particular events. Village names are accurately given, except where such an identification might create political difficulties for villagers or where an individual might be easily identified and embarrassed by the circumstances detailed.

Part 1
Introduction

1
Cultural Models and the Dynamics of Social Structure

Nyinba are ethnic Tibetans whose ancestors entered the remote and rugged Himalayan borderlands of Northwestern Nepal centuries ago. The area they settled is enclosed by mountain chains to the north and cut by major river systems to the south, and the community has remained small and self-contained. In 1983, it included approximately 1,330 men and women living in four villages situated amidst farmlands on a series of gently sloping, south-facing valleys. While these villages may be distinctive in many ways, what seems most unusual about the Nyinba is their system of fraternal polyandry. Every man who has brothers—with the rarest of exceptions—marries polyandrously, and virtually all the brothers remain in intact, fraternally polyandrous marriages throughout their lives.

The management of sexual relationships in polyandry may be the focus of exotic preoccupations, although in practice it is relatively unproblematic. Far more profound are polyandry's effects on the domestic order and on closely articulated spheres of cultural and social life. Thus, as we might expect, the presence of more men than women in polyandrous marriages affects day-to-day interpersonal dynamics. What might be less obvious is the impact gender imbalances have on the management of the domestic economy. The solution among the Nyinba is for men to specialize in diverse subsistence activities, including long-distance trade, while their wives supervise agriculture in the village. This division of labor, in turn, refracts upon cultural constructions of gender.

As we also might expect, the linkage of brothers in marriage and their lifelong co-residence are associated with special systems of property inheritance and succession to positions of household authority. The presumption of lifelong fraternal unity also means that partition is restricted, and this produces households which are large and complex in composition. Because partition is rare, village size remains relatively stable and becomes a matter of collective concern and collective regulation. This, finally, has an impact on village growth.

This briefest of summaries only touches on a few of the cultural and social entailments of fraternally polyandrous marriage. Despite structural and systemic complexities, the subject of polyandry has tended to motivate narrowly conceived analytical treatments and single-cause explanations. Polyandry also has come to be understood primarily in terms of an analytical calculus of individual, or collective, economic, and demographic advantages. Certain of its consequences—constraining population growth and preventing land fragmentation in particular—have been read as its causes, just as the high sex ratios common in polyandrous systems once were seen as the force that induced men to band together in their marriages. In the Nyinba case, the predominance of men seems to be the outcome of gender preferences: parental concerns about the limited marital chances of daughters and associated patterns of differential child care. There also have been theorists who tried to explain polyandry in terms of affective relations between brothers, but this is far less commonly found.

The emphasis on explaining polyandry in itself seems the product of androcentric and exotic biases. As Berreman points out, we find little need for explanations of monogamy, which seems regarded "as expectable (even moral)," or of polygyny, which may be seen as "reasonable (even enviable)," while polyandry is, "perhaps especially to the male eye, problematic" (Berreman 1980:378). One might dismiss these views as relics from an earlier stage in the discipline's development. Nevertheless, texts still in use refer to men's natural "predispositions" for polygyny and their "deeply polygynous tendencies" (Lévi-Strauss 1969:38; Linton 1968:285).

Surely the features of polyandry characteristically seen as problematic tell more about our own cultural preoccupations than about the world of our subjects. For one example, polyandry is seen as requiring men to relinquish exclusive control over their wives' sexual and childbearing capacities—which we presume is something men otherwise would wish and enforce. For a second example, polyandry is presumed to require a certain degree of sexual abnegation from men—this is purely on logical grounds, for we have absolutely no data on the subject. Conversely, polyandrously married women might be expected to benefit from a wealth of sexual attention, although this rarely is even mentioned. In addition, we see polyandry as limiting men's reproductive opportunities, relative, that is, to their counterparts in monogamous and polygynous marriage and, more problematic, obligating them to rear children not their own. The assumption that men necessarily favor their own, over siblings', children is a long-standing one that also has influenced analyses of matrilineal systems—and merits closer, critical attention.

Behavioral ecologists find polyandry problematic for these reasons as well and also find it particularly intriguing because it is so rare—it occurs in a few human societies, in some species of birds, and in at most a few species of mammals—and because it challenges assumptions about the evolution of male and female reproductive strategies. It is true that polyandry involves sharing sexual access to one's wife and thus is likely to reduce the number of children the average man can have. However, it is another matter whether fraternal polyandry practiced in a small population also reduces men's net genetic representation in subsequent generations—a matter I leave for others to resolve.

Here my concern lies with the quality of polyandrous marital and familial relationships and with their consequences for sociocultural systems and village population. Before we can begin to understand polyandry's consequences, we must consider its contexts, and this calls for a somewhat different way of looking at marriage, parenthood, family life, sexual relations, and gender than we may be accustomed to. It is simplest to begin with an illustration, and I have selected for this a household that displays the diversity and complexity of polyandrous arrangements. Members of this household have experienced the range of problems that beset polyandrous marriages, yet have managed to transcend them. The household remains unified and today exemplifies the domestic harmony that Nyinba individually find so admirable and wish for themselves.

The Dynamics of a Polyandrous Marriage

In 1983, the largest Nyinba household numbered eighteen men and women of three generations. The most-senior generation included three polyandrously married brothers, who ranged in age from fifty-two to sixty, and their common wife, who was fifty-nine at the time. Living with them were five of their sons, aged twenty to forty, and their sons' wife, who then was thirty-five. The other household members included one unmarried teenaged daughter, three grandsons, and four granddaughters. These men had another son who had partitioned fifteen years earlier and three other daughters who were married and living with their husbands.

In Nyinba polyandrous households, the eldest brother holds a certain authority in domestic affairs and initially a certain precedence in marriage. This gives him the opportunity to father most of the children born in the marriage's early years. Nor is this a trivial matter, for Nyinba try to determine the paternity of children produced in polyandrous unions, and men place great value on having sons considered their own. In the case of the senior generation, the eldest brother was quite mild and good-natured and made little attempt to lead his family or monopolize the common wife. Nonetheless, he is supposed to have fathered the three older sons and also the youngest daughter. The second brother is held to have fathered the three younger sons and one of the daughters. Disparities in the circumstances of the youngest brother were marked, for he is believed to be the father of two daughters only. He viewed his lack of sons as a great disappointment and an issue for complaint, and this was a chronic source of tension in the family.

In 1983, however, the marriage of the sons' generation was considered a model of all such marriages can and should be. The eldest brother was hardworking, extraordinarily skilled at trade, and adept at local politics. Although still relatively young, he had assumed much of the responsibility for household leadership. And despite having—or so people said—the closest and most affectionate relationship with the common wife, he had ceded priority in sexual rights to his younger brothers many years previously. He usually spent the night alone or romancing village girl friends. While he was held to have fathered the family's eldest son and daughter, all subsequent children were attributed to his younger brothers.

This generation of brothers, however, has not been without its problems. It has undergone one partition and for a brief period became involved in a subsidiary, polygynous marriage that might eventually have led to another partition, had not a tragedy intervened.

Originally, all six brothers lived together. In 1966, however, they partitioned, only two years after they had jointly married. The partition was instigated by the second-eldest brother, Padma, who had declared himself unhappy with the common wife. Whatever marred their relationship or whatever other factors may have led Padma to decide to live apart from his brothers is uncertain. All I know is that Padma had trained to be a Buddhist lama, and the woman he wanted to marry was a former nun. His parents were adamantly opposed to the union, and all his relatives and neighbors tried to convince him to abandon the idea, but he persisted.

Things were at an impasse until Jampal, Padma's only surviving grandfather, intervened. Jampal himself was the youngest of three polyandrously married brothers. He too had been unhappy in his marriage, but had managed to secure his brothers' agreement to a second marriage, a sororally polygynous union with their common wife's sister. Subsidiary polygynous marriages of this kind, which I term "conjoint," are quite rare—they numbered less than 5 percent of marriages during my stay among the Nyinba. When they do occur, sisters are uniformly preferred as co-wives, because they are believed to find it easier to cooperate than unrelated women. In this case, the bonds of sisterhood proved inadequate, and the family was riven by discord. The solution was for Jampal and the second wife to reside separately in an arrangement Nyinba call "living on the side." The rest of the family built them a small house, where they moved and spent the rest of their lives. There they had one son and one daughter. The son was encouraged to marry uxorilocally, to a woman without brothers in another village, and the daughter married three brothers from a well-to-do household in a different village, with great ceremony and at great expense. Jampal, despite his separate residence, continued to participate in the affairs of the larger household and guided household decisions until he died in 1975. And one of the things he did was to invite his grandson Padma and Padma's wife-to-be to move in with him. People say that he was especially sympathetic to Padma because he was his "real"—as they put it—grandfather. That is to say, Jampal is the man reputed to have fathered Padma's reputed father.

Unlike Jampal, however, Padma insisted on a final partition and a separate share of property. This amounted to only one-ninth of the family estate, because the Nyinba allocate property by per stirpes reckoning, and Padma happened to be one of three sons of a man who had three brothers. The consequence is that Padma is extremely poor, and his household is considered among the most marginal economically in the village.

In 1975, one of the remaining five brothers decided to bring another wife home, arguing that they were too many to share a single woman. There was relatively little parental opposition this time. Part of the reason was that the new wife, Yeshi, was by any standards an extraordinary woman. She was beautiful, devout, hardworking, and very bright: despite never having attended school, she had taught herself to read and write Nepali. Yeshi, furthermore, was a sister of the first wife, or, more precisely, the two were *pun,* what I call "household siblings," born of different mothers and fathers in a conjoint marriage. Yeshi and the senior co-wife managed to get along without major incident, and Yeshi rapidly integrated herself into the marriage and established sexual relationships with all her mature husbands. Then tragically she died, little more than a week after giving birth to a daughter. This was in 1976; the household was shaken by her loss, and the brothers vowed they would never marry again. To this day they have not established another conjoint marriage, and they probably will not, since their children now are grown, and their sons have begun their own polyandrous marriage.

Nyinba state that very large sibling groups are more likely to initiate conjoint marriages and more likely to partition, and this case confirms their observations. Yet in spite of the number of brothers involved and the complex interpersonal relationships which we might expect to find among any five co-husbands, the marriage remains undivided and at present stands as the model of fraternal and polyandrous amity. The household has seen only one partition in the past three generations and one period when a brother chose to live apart from the others.

Nyinba marriage must be understood as a system embodying all these possibilities for conjugal groupings and as intersecting, multifaceted relationships which encompass both erotic and economic as well as hierarchical dimensions. Relations between the men can be reduced neither to selfless fraternal altruism and unbroken amity nor to calculative compromises and incalculable hardships from trying to share a single wife. In reality, we find brothers trying as best they can to accommodate to their shared and separate interests in their marriages and children. When problems arise, people attempt to find a solution, best if within the household, and at least within the community; very rarely do men abandon their families and kin in order to emigrate and begin a new life elsewhere.

I have said that this example is illustrative, for it demonstrates the possibilities and problems that can arise in polyandrous marriages. However it should not be taken as representative. The average Nyinba household includes not eighteen people, but seven and one-half. The average marriage includes less than two men because of the numbers of families in which only one son is born or survives to adulthood. The average polyandrous marriage includes fewer than three brothers; and less than 10 percent of marriages include five brothers or more. Polygyny, by contrast, is rare. It is acceptable when the first wife is infertile—which is the case in about 7 percent of present-day marriages—and occurs otherwise only in the most exceptional circumstances: mostly in large, complex households.

This household is equally unrepresentative—and equally illustrative—in features of its economy. It owns twice as much land as the average, and more pack animals than any other, Nyinba household. People describe a direct connection between wealth, household size, and polyandry. First, they say, wealth makes it easier for numbers of people to live together, while poverty creates discontent, exacerbates quarreling, and increases the likelihood of partition. Second, a large household finds it easier to sustain a high standard of living, because numbers of men provide the manpower for diverse economic ventures. This, however, is counteracted by the tendency of men in wealthy households to engage in "marital irresponsibility," as Nyinba put it, referring to their more frequent involvements in subsidiary, conjoint marriages. Once brothers have two wives, they tend to find their conjugal and reproductive interests divided. This then undermines fraternal unity in marriage and increases the risk of partition, which divides household property and alters the balance of village households.

Kinship and the Logic of Polyandry

On occasion I would ask Nyinba, sometimes individually and sometimes in small groups, why their society was polyandrous. A foolish question and always in vain, for it elicited nothing but the same, predictable response: that polyandry was an age-old custom that Nyinba ancestors brought from Tibet. People sometimes took this opportunity to rail against their fellow ethnic Tibetans elsewhere in Nepal who had abandoned polyandry, because, it was said, of their proximity to the capital and the pressures they faced from neighboring Hindu groups. On other occasions, I would ask individuals why they had married polyandrously, but I received answers no less predictable: that this was Nyinba custom, and besides, the marriage had been arranged by their parents. There were other times when people would volunteer observations about polyandry's advantages: how it prevented the dispersion of property and fragmentation of limited landholdings and how it supported a higher standard of living. I also heard men speak of their deep sense of obligation to brothers in polyandry and how they were all "the same." I interpret this as meaning that brothers' interests in polyandry are equated, and that after their parents, men trust their brothers more than anyone else in the world. I overheard women say that having more than one husband gave them a sense of security, for if one died, the others would remain. These statements say little else than that custom is the cause of polyandry and that polyandry is a custom that confers myriad practical advantages. In one sense, they are no more than tautologies expressing a folk notion of cultural determinism, although they also offer a kind of truth.

It seems useless to speculate about origins and causes, and here my concerns lie elsewhere: with understanding the impact of polyandry on people's marriages and their domestic lives and its consequences for related kinship, economic, and political structures. Investigating what people themselves see as significant in intimate interpersonal relationships and their satisfactions and discontents is no easy matter; it is hardly one suited to sampling schemes and questionnaires. Instead I observed family life in as many homes as possible and listened when people began unexpectedly to talk about their lives. It was possible to ask some direct questions, but only of a select number of close friends. On balance, it proved far easier to obtain detailed information on marriages that had broken down, because matters normally private then become public in the search for resolutions.

And what I found was that people characteristically explained the successes and failures of marital and household relationships by the closeness of kin relationships between the persons involved.

For Nyinba, kinship is seen fundamentally as a matter of physical commonality and is understood in terms of a folk theory of human reproduction. Concepts of kin relatedness are given tangible expression in notions about the substance of bone, held to be transmitted from father to child, and that of blood, similarly transmitted from mother to child. Kinship, that is, is conceptualized in a natural idiom and is understood in genealogical terms. Closer kin are considered more similar in bone and blood, with bone seen as playing the greater role in determining character and physical traits. Thus precise genealogical identifications are most important where they would seem most elusive: paternity in polyandrous marriages. Common substance, moreover, validates the conduct of kin relationships and shapes the expectations kin have of one another. The result is that kinship proximity becomes important in securing the mutual commitments of co-husbands in polyandrous marriages and co-wives in polygynous marriages; it seems to be among the strongest motivations for cooperation in large Nyinba households.

In recent decades, kinship studies have been polarized by debates about how such concepts of kinship are best understood. A number of theorists continue to affirm the universality of genealogical notions in reckoning kin relationships. Others, by contrast, argue that such an approach risks superimposing our constructs on those of other societies and suggest that we would do better to examine each kinship system anew—and without presuming human reproduction as its point of reference. This debate has had far-reaching consequences: it has divided approaches to the study of kinship and generated ethnographic accounts markedly different in emphasis, mode of analysis, and the aspects of data described (Keesing 1974:86). Concurrently—and perhaps not adventitiously—the concerns of kinship studies have narrowed, with attention drawn away from kinship as social relationships which cross-cut and come into conflict with one another and which are moderated by other forces in social life. My approach here is deliberately eclectic and, I hope, synthetic, and my analyses have been guided by pragmatic considerations: to follow whatever best aids understanding Nyinba kinship notions and the patterning of their kin relationships.

For Nyinba, these notions about heredity and character also support practices of endogamy and a certain closure against the outside world. Concepts of bone figure in this too and serve as the idiom for a system of hierarchical clanship which is ancestor-based and conceptualized as a line of males over time. This system supports a division of the community into two strata and two separate circles of kin: the higher-ranked descendants of village founders, who are full citizens and landholders, and the lower-ranked descendants of their former slaves. It also supports a closed kinship calculus, which has no place for outsiders and reinforces a stance of ethnic separateness. Ethnic separateness, finally, justifies local and stratum endogamy and restrictions placed upon migration.

Despite this, the community remains incompletely sealed off—there is some emigration, less immigration, and rare intermarriage with other Tibetan-speaking ethnic groups in the district and farther afield. When immigrants manage to enter the community, their incorporation necessitates a reformation of the kinship calculus, although this becomes a process spanning generations.

Culture and Contradiction

The analysis here reverses the order of traditional ethnography. The movement is from internal to external contexts, from cultural models to social structure, and from kinship and politics to economic organization and population. The purpose in this is to explore interactions between understandings of society, social arrangements, and exogenous factors which shape decisions about marriage and family life, which, in turn, contribute to an evolving social system. The arguments unfold through glimpses of social structure and environment as Nyinba themselves represent them, and analyses frequently begin or end with folk or cultural models. By this, I refer to Nyinba descriptions of and attempts to account for their society, their evaluations of people's behavior within it, and their assessments of contexts for action (Holy and Stuchlik 1981; Quinn and Holland 1987; Strathern 1981:296).

Some anthropologists speak of expressed models of this kind as guiding behavior; others argue that they are epiphenomenal and retrospective rationalizations of observable social realities.[1] Nor could the reality be easily ascertainable. Action in the world can influence understandings of the world, just as evaluations of behavior can have their own social consequences (see Quinn and Holland 1987:8–9). Folk models, moreover, are hardly all alike. Some have greater directive force and a greater likelihood

---

[1] The most frequently cited instances of these sorts of arguments can be found in the writings of Lévi-Strauss (1967:273), who stated that conscious models serve not to explain, but rather to perpetuate sociocultural phenomena; in Marxist arguments about "false consciousness"; and in cultural materialism (see Quinn and Holland 1987:5; Strathern 1981:297–98). That similar views come from such different quarters surely reflects the more fundamental "mistrust of subjectivity" common in the social sciences (see Giddens 1979:38).

of shaping experience than others, and different models may frame interpretations and inform explanations of experience in differing ways. We can
compare this with the great variability in observers' models. Certain models
are meant to be generative, while others are primarily interpretive; some
are oriented toward explaining a wide range of phenomena, while others
have a much narrower scope. The fundamental problem with observers'
models is that they are tested against an external logic and risk projecting
their own culture's assessments onto the world being observed.

Actors' models, however, have their own flaws. For Nyinba, they characteristically founder in the tendency to a wholesale literalism which
casts all linkages in metonymic terms and in the preferences for historical frameworks of explanation rather than sociological ones, that is, for
diachronic understandings at the expense of synchronic ones. They also,
unsurprisingly, tend to gloss over paradoxical features of the social system
rather than encompassing contradictions: the incomplete community closure, periodic partitioning in the face of its restriction, inequities in a small
community that prizes egalitarian sociality, the existence of a patronage
system that exploits the powerless and divides the community, and a de-
valuation of women—who are few in number, yet so necessary to household prosperity.

Perhaps my concern with folk models derives from people's own elaboration of them. Nyinba have a number of types of formal narrative, each with
a distinctive style and characteristic themes. Their recitation is the province
of older people, who also are most likely to acquire proficiency in genealogical matters and associated village lore. I have heard elders discuss their
interpretations with one another, in what might be described as an effort to
amplify their knowledge and to develop more comprehensive models. Fortunately they were quite generous in sharing their insights with me and pa-
tient and sometimes even eloquent at it.

Perhaps Nyinba skills at cultural and social exegesis derive from their
own cultural self-consciousness. They are a small, ethnically distinct population living on the very edge of the Indo-Tibetan culture-contact zone. As
a Tibetan people in a predominantly Hindu nation, long subject to Hindu
kingdoms and states, they are sensitive to their minority status. They are,
moreover, middlemen in a complex system of ethnic and regional economic specializations. The extensive routes they travel during the year demand an ability to negotiate in various cultures along the way. Finally, their
own society is internally differentiated between the numerically dominant
citizen-landholders and the politically subordinate former slaves, or freedmen, and the differences are expressed through both cultural and social
forms. The outcome of all this is not quite a cultural relativism, but rather

an appreciation of the variability of social and cultural systems and of their impact upon action.

The major division within Nyinba society raises questions about dual sets of models. Anthropologists tend to find themselves directed toward dominant groups and to be exposed primarily to their ideas. When they do gain access to other groups, this can create problems of how to accommodate sometimes overlapping, sometimes opposed, models of a single social and cultural world. In my case, the fact is that I was identified with the higher-ranking group and found my access to freedmen more limited; my analysis suffers from this. I did observe how relations of dominance and dependence affect social interactions on both sides, but rarely found out how it is interpreted by those subordinate. Gender differentiation was less problematic, since I had access to both men and women and was seen as partisan to neither. In any event, most of the models of significance here are shared by men and women, the exceptions involving understandings of sexual politics, domestic politics, and notions about the value of women's contributions to the household economy. Age is another point of differentiation. The younger, more "modern" men try to portray Nyinba ethnic identity as more Nepali than older men or women do and are more apt to describe clanship and village structure in terms of Nepali categories. However, younger men also defer to their elders in such matters, and those aiming for positions of authority in the community study traditional narratives and assimilate the interpretations of the latter, so that the elders' models dominate and probably will continue to do so in the future.

Another problem in utilizing folk or cultural models is the potential for oversystematization. Accounts one collects in the field are apt to be partial and indexical. To understand them presumes additional cultural knowledge, and to explain them requires filling in the gaps with knowledge which may be tacit, esoteric, or deliberately concealed. This means that each folk model must be supplemented with contexts and commentaries, and for this reason, analysts' renditions of folk accounts inevitably produce what are, no more and no less, models of models (Holy and Stuchlik 1981:23). A careful analysis should make this clear enough—and ideally the different levels and sources of explanation should be identifiable. Where the greater hazards lie, it seems, are in the possibilities for implying fuller integration or elaboration and a greater degree of consensus than actually exist and for merging models that ordinarily are dissociated.[2]

---

[2] As Keesing cautions: "Folk models may by their nature have a partial and situational ad hoc quality, a lack of global systematicity . . . what we take to be folk or cultural models may not exist until our strategies of questioning lead informants to create them; or worse yet, until their responses provide fragments out of which we create them" (1987:383).

For such models cannot be presumed to form a coherent, unified, or uniformly shared system. Some are complementary, others contradictory, reflecting sensitivity to, if incomplete assimilation of, paradoxical ideas, the complexities of social structure, and schisms of interest in the society. Also, some models dominate, reflecting interests or beliefs of those who are dominant; others are muted, reflecting notions of subordinate groups or categories of people. As one example, concepts of descent and alliance provide complementary paradigms for members of the most prestigious households, whereas descendants of recent immigrants and freedmen tend to stress respectable affinal ties over their descent lines. Another feature of Nyinba models is their variform treatment of change. It suffices no more to say that Nyinba see their society as a more-or-less-lasting structure than to say they see it as being in constant flux (cf. Holy and Stuchlik 1981:20). They see flux in stasis and points of stability in the course of change.

Here I differentiate between folk categories, theories, and models. The first are used more for specific concepts, the second for explanatory frameworks, and the third for analogical, heuristic representations of social structure. An example of the first is the construct of the corporate landholding household, known as *trongba;* of the second, various accounts of how villages evolved from a single founding household; and of the third, how village households are commonly described as "split from a single hearth," each depicted at its point of partition as nodes on the village genealogy and each with a relic of a relic of the household god's shrine, the appropriate number of degrees removed from the original. The theories and models chart key features of social relationships as they charter them, so that we can say they have both the "of" and "for" sense so elegantly described by Geertz (1965). Here the intrinsic dual resonance of folk models is doubly significant. This is because they serve as an index to sociocultural change, as they lay the foundations for it; that is to say, they channel new cultural and social patterns as they encode them.[3]

Structural Analysis

Implicit in this discussion is an analytical distinction between culture and social structure. Some theorists prefer to focus on culture as an autonomous sphere for study (Schneider 1976:202), while others suggest that disjunctions between culture and social system support functionalist dualisms (Sahlins 1976:114–15). The problem is that to consider either in isolation

---

[3]The distinction between representational and operational models made by Holy and Stuchlik dichotomizes too much, at the expense of reflexive interactions.

constricts the scope of ethnographic inquiry and sacrifices analytical flexibility. In addition, juxtaposing the two may bring into sharper relief structural incongruities that contribute to social change (Geertz 1957:33). For
kinship studies, the distinction proves particularly useful for directing attention to the interplay between kinship constructs, kinship rules, and associated social processes (Strathern 1973:22).

The concept of domains also proves useful in countering monolithic
views of culture and social structure and as a general counterweight to
functionalist presumptions of systemic coherence and integration. As an
analytical tool, however, this has occasioned criticisms—among them that
domains are bounded arbitrarily, that they falsely divide up the seamless
web of social life, and that they are not universally applicable, having little
relevance in simple hunting-and-gathering societies. The latter is a legitimate criticism, for it is virtually impossible to extricate, for example,
kinship from economic elements in the multiplex social relationships of
such societies. By contrast, in tribal societies, and even more in the peasant societies within state systems that Nyinba typify, domestic, politico-
jural, ritual, and economic relationships and activities are differentiated explicitly in the conduct of social relationships, although they overlap as
well.[4] I find the distinction useful in discovering points of contradiction in
the exercise of social roles and in focusing attention on the intersections
between the different subsystems of social life. At the same time, such dif-
ferentiations also support models in which one subsystem is seen as more
basic and as having a disproportionate effect on the others. This is an issue
of relevance here, for much of the work on Tibet places primary emphasis
upon environmental limitations and economic adaptations and cites these
as explanations for marital and household systems.

Continuity and Change

Structuralist approaches in anthropology have been predicated upon an
absolute distinction between synchronic and diachronic frameworks of explanation. Synchrony in analysis may be a simplification adopted for methodological purposes, but it has dominated structuralist studies and lies at
the source of what Giddens (1979:3) describes as the general repression of
time in social theory. While social anthropologists long have incorporated
a temporal dimension in their analyses—concepts of fission and fusion in

---

[4] Such discriminations find recognition in folk models, although the boundaries and content
of Western and other societies' domains may diverge. The Hindu term *dharma*, or enjoined
religious conduct, suggests a very different partitioning of societal domains, although its closest
Tibetan counterpart, *chos*, may stand closer to Western concepts of religion.

segmentary systems and cycles of domestic development being classic examples—these processes were always comprehended within a framework
of structural continuity (Fortes 1969:81).

Few saw this as a major problem until recent decades. The resulting disciplinary shift to an emphasis on process and the dynamics of social transformations and the growing interest in historical analyses may have myriad
sources, but surely one factor has been the increasing and increasingly dramatic pace of change evident to fieldworkers nowadays, even in the most
isolated societies like that of Nyinba. To take my own example, my first
visit to the Nyinba region in 1973 necessitated more than a week's walk
from the bazaar town of Jumla, the zonal capital. The Jumla airstrip was
little more than a decade old then, and had I wished to visit the region prior
to its construction, I would have had to walk for more than three weeks
from the nearest railhead on the Indian border. In 1982, I was able to fly
directly to Simikot, the district capital, and walk less than three hours
to my village residence. It was not until 1972 that tourists and scholars
were first permitted regularly in the region. By 1982, there were a very few
foreign-funded (and very small-scale) development projects, but still hardly
any outside visitors.

In 1973, Nyinba wore and used clothing and items almost entirely of
their own manufacture. By 1982, they were wearing Western clothing and
using some imported goods. In 1973, no medical care was available, although people were being inoculated for smallpox; in the summer of 1974,
a measles epidemic claimed many children's lives. By my second visit,
there were several health posts in the district, and emergency visits made
by a paramedic managed to stave off the worst effects of another measles
epidemic. At the former time, no Nyinba had progressed beyond the early
primary grades; now there are a handful of high school graduates and a few
children in school in Kathmandu. Changes internal to the sociocultural
system, for example in religious practice, marriage, or household organization, were not so apparent in these nine years, yet surely they too are
under way.

The decades preceding my first visit saw dramatic changes in this region, although we tend to know about only those of wider historical significance. There were the conquests of local petty kingdoms by Nepal in 1789,
wars with Tibet in the eighteenth and nineteenth centuries, the emancipation of household slaves in 1926, and the recent Chinese takeover of Tibet.
Resulting political upheavals in Tibet completely disrupted trading patterns
in the 1960s, and trade still has not returned to any settled state. There
were more gradual changes too, such as the slow decline in profits from the
salt trade in the south and the slow increase in the Nyinba population, with
all the economic and sociocultural changes attendant upon that.

Marxist perspectives may offer one way out of the synchronic-diachronic dilemma. However, they have been and may remain better suited to studies focusing upon conflict and inequality in political systems and transformations in economic systems than for detailed accounts of kinship, families, and the solidary social relationships built around them. Nyinba, and this is a point I stress, is a society based upon kinship, whose members by and large are kin, and the idioms and models for their unity all derive from that fact. Changes in systems of kinship, marriage, and household call for a more dynamic structural anthropology, which more recent ethnographic studies have been working towards.[5]

Changes in population are among the most critical matters. Although the Nyinba population has increased far less than that of most groups in Nepal, it continues to grow, despite the serious economic setbacks of the last several decades. Population growth, moreover, is not uniform. Some clans expand, while others contract; some village sections grow by partition, while others decline because of extinction. Among the questions to be considered here are how people's notions about social structure affect processes of change and the accommodations members of Nyinba villages collectively make to various changes, and how, in turn, these changes may influence cultural models and the patterning of social relations.

A concern with demographic processes directs our attention to the phenomena of continuity in change and change in continuity, to the continual reproduction of a society, both in its membership and in its social structure (Macfarlane 1976:5–6). In this book I am concerned primarily with issues of cultural and social analysis, drawn against the backdrop of a changing village population. In a second study, based on field research among seven communities of diverse ethnic origins living near the Nyinba region, I plan to examine demographic processes in greater detail and to demonstrate how these processes are moderated by culturally specific household systems. Meanwhile, I intend to keep the Nyinba community in view to better chart responses to change over the next several decades.

Fieldwork and Sources of Data

When I first went to Humla, I knew little about the region, beyond the fact that it was extremely poor and undeveloped and suffered chronic food shortages; this meant I would have to bring with me most of the food and all of the goods I would need for two years. This required reserving more than half the space on the small plane that flew twice weekly to the zonal capital. Making such arrangements has become progressively more diffi-

[5] For a recent example, see Moore 1986.

cult with every passing year, due to an increasing demand for seats and
cargo space, without a comparable expansion in air services. I also hired a
Sherpa guide, since Sherpas are famous for organizing expeditions of all
kinds. The experienced Sherpa I chose quit the night before my expedition,
because he had received a more lucrative offer elsewhere. He recom-
mended a cousin in his place. That cousin had never guided anyone anywhere, having spent most of his adult years as a radio repairman in India.
I had no choice, however, so I accepted the replacement. He found my research site to be the most miserable of places, declared the food and living
conditions wretched, and resigned after a few months, although not without making the necessary arrangements for me. It was with his departure
and my complete dependence upon my Nyinba hosts—so many days' walk
from plane or radio communication—that my field research began in
earnest.

I spent the first year of my fieldwork in a large rented room in a village
house. The household in which I lived included three brothers who were
polyandrously married. Polyandry, seen as so exotic in the West, was the
Nyinba norm; after several years of living among polyandrous peoples, it
seems unexceptional to me. During this period, I began making regular
visits to the other Nyinba villages. I established ritual friendships with
three women and one man my age, one in each Nyinba village. I also began visiting elders to record their recollections of the past and to collect
accounts of villagewide genealogical data. The latter were checked against
the household registers I had collected in Kathmandu.

As my fieldwork became more productive, the network of people I consulted spread throughout the community. It seemed better to establish my
own residence, where I could freely reciprocate for the hospitality others
had extended to me. I was offered, rent free, the only unoccupied Nyinba
habitation, a cave shrine which had an attached cooking shed. Caves, as
many Tibetan hermits have found, are quite comfortable places to live,
being cool in summer and warm in winter. This cave had beautiful views of
the Dozam Khola and Karnali River valleys and had its own nearby water
sources. It was also within easy reach of three of the four Nyinba villages
and near a major road, which meant frequent passers-by, who were encouraged to stop for lunch or tea and conversation. For these reasons, I made
the cave my home base during my second field research, seven-and-a-half
years after I first left the Nyinba valleys. Following a brief period of readjustment, things seemingly resumed where they had left off so many
years ago. Being gone seems to have had largely positive effects—worries
about problems I might create had evaporated. I was able to ask questions I
would have been hesitant about before, and this time I spoke to members of

every household in the community, nearly all of whom replied with great grace to detailed questions about their economic circumstances and their lives.

Nyinba and Tibetan Society

I describe the Nyinba as culturally or ethnically Tibetan and a Tibetan society, but it is difficult to say how representative they are of populations in Tibet, or even of Tibetan populations in Nepal. The ethnographies we have on Tibetan speakers derive largely from work with refugees or fieldwork outside political Tibet, and much of this remains in dissertation form. At this point, we can do little more than identify the uniformities in certain aspects of Tibetan life and the diversity and features of regional micro-variation in others.

The major poles and sources of variation are clear enough. First are distinctions between nomadic pastoralists of the "northern plains" and settled agriculturalists of regions where agriculture is feasible (Ekvall 1968). Second are distinctions between West ("Upper") and East ("Lower") Tibet. Third are those between peoples of the central plateau, who seem to be more socioculturally uniform, and "lower valley" peoples, whose societies may be more idiosyncratic. In the past, there were also major class distinctions, with the life of aristocrats differing from that of traders; this, in turn, differed from the life of serfs, which itself varied according to the nature of tenancy arrangements (Carrasco 1959; Goldstein 1971a). Political affiliation makes a difference as well—peoples within the borders of Nepal or India have been subject to different laws and cultural influences than those in Tibet proper.

Nyinba are lower-valley agriculturalists of the West, peasants who long have held rights of ownership over their land, subject to Nepalese laws and taxation schemes. They speak a distinctive dialect of Western Tibetan—and these dialects vary greatly from one mountain valley to the next. Nepali loanwords have entered the dialect, more so than for other Humla Tibetan speakers farther from Nepalese villages, less so than for those in closer proximity. As of this date, I have lived among four of the six Tibetan communities in the district, and would describe the situation there as more variations on common themes than dissimilarities and contrasts. In general, all the communities are more similar to Tibetans of the West than to other ethnic Tibetans of Nepal's East, such as the well-known Sherpa (Fürer-Haimendorf 1964; Ortner 1978).

Nyinba are idiosyncratic, diverging from Tibetan culture, it appears, in their compromise per-stirpes inheritance system, in the circumstances of conjoint marriage, and in the institution of spirit mediumship. Some of these are practices which seem to derive from Nepali influences, and, I should add, the cultural borrowing goes both ways here. But Nyinba arrangements of polyandry, certain features of their system of ranking by descent, and their household system are unequivocally Tibetan. The problem of uniqueness versus generalizability is common to all small-community studies; here it is all the greater because of Nyinba distance from mainstream Tibetan life and their placement within the larger multi-ethnic society of Nepal.

2
Societal Reflexivity:
Narrative Themes
and Orientations

Nyinba understand features of their sociocultural system through their legends, particularly their legends of origin, which trace their ancestors' migrations and the settlement and development of their villages over time. To villagers, these legends offer a kind of history, depicting key events in the past that explain and charter significant aspects of present-day village life. To an observer, the value of such accounts may lie more in their mythic qualities and in their representation of cultural themes and archetypal models of and for social structure. Among the principal emphases of these legends are the rationales for clan and social hierarchies, for village structure and settlement patterns, for relations with neighboring groups, and for the problems of growth and loss in village population. The legends also situate the community within the context of the larger region and its history, which is where I shall begin.

The Nyinba in Time and Place

Nyinba, or the Nyin people, inhabit a series of adjoining valleys east of Simikot, the capital of Humla district in the Karnali Zone of Northwestern Nepal (see figure 2.1). The word *nyin* refers both to daytime and the warm valleys on the south face of mountain slopes, which have longer diurnal exposure to sunshine. This is a name that describes the Nyinba region well. The community is formally known among other Humla Tibetan speakers as Nyin Yul Tshan Zhi, or the four Nyin villages, which include Barkhang, Nyimatang, Todpa, and Trangshod.[1] Each village consists of a cluster of

[1] In Tibet, *tsho* (*tshan*) were small territorial and administrative units which comprised a few contiguous villages (Goldstein 1971a:15).

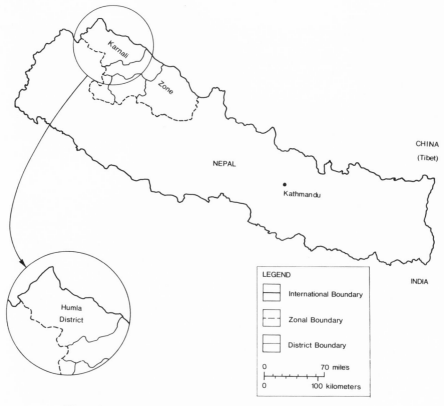

Figure 2.1   Location of Humla District and the Karnali Zone in Nepal

separate settlements: a large core village and one or more small hamlets near distant landholdings. Each village has its own springs and sources of irrigation water and its own collectively held forest and grazing lands. Each also has its own shrines to local deities and its own temples staffed by households of married lamas, for Nyinba are followers of the unreformed, Nyingmapa sect of Tibetan Buddhism. The villages are located several miles apart along steep and rocky trails, and their physical separation supports villagers' sense of uniqueness and separate identity within the Nyinba sphere. These attitudes also are found in milder form among members of the various settlements that make up each village. In figure 2.2 the location of the villages and their hamlets is displayed.

Nyinba villages are situated at a middle range of altitudes for Tibetan groups in the Himalayas. Barkhang is the lowest village, at approximately 9,500 feet, and the highest village is Nyimatang, at nearly 11,000 feet.

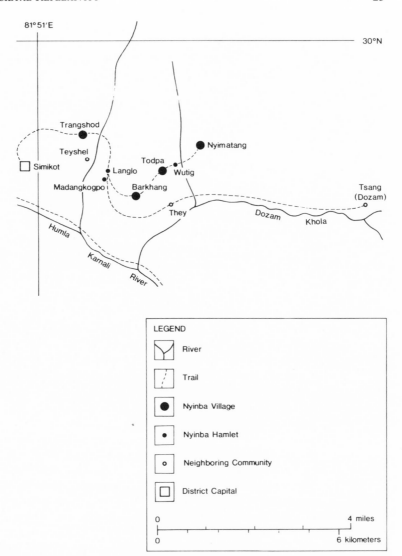

Figure 2.2 Nyinba Villages

Cultivated fields are found above and below these altitudes. Above the fields are fragrant juniper forests alternating with open grasslands. Scattered along the hillside in shady spots ill-suited to agriculture are patches of wild rhododendron and azalea and clusters of pine trees and buckthorn, which produces a sour fruit enjoyed by children in winter. Almost all the land at the very lowest altitudes has been put to agricultural use. The fields are left empty in winter. Most winters see several heavy snowstorms, and this has contributed to the increasing erosion of good farmland. At the very bottom of the valleys run the Karnali River and its tributary the Dozam Khola, whose confluence lies beneath Barkhang village.

The climate is temperate but subject to great diurnal variation due to altitude. Thus the temperature can dip below 0° F on the coldest nights and goes below freezing every night in winter; but it remains very comfortable at midday and afternoon and is surprisingly hot in the direct sun. In summer, the temperature drops as low as 50° F at night and rarely reaches 75° F in the shade, but is unpleasantly hot in the sun. People take advantage of the difference between the temperature in sun and shade and move from one spot to another as the sun moves across the sky. As a result, they can live outdoors virtually year-round, and prefer to. Because Humla is so far west, little of the summer monsoon reaches it, but it is not so arid as the Tibetan plateau which lies within the shadow of the Himalayas. The result is a climate and landscape reminiscent of Europe and unlike that of most of South Asia.

The Nyinba live farther south than most other Tibetan-speaking groups in Humla and on the very edge of the Hindu-Buddhist contact zone. Directly to the west and south and below their villages are Nepali-speaking Hindus of high castes: Thakuri, Chetri, and some Brahmans. Farther west and south live Bura, or Nepalicized Byansi, communities.[2] Nearby to the north are several other Tibetan communities, and Tibetan-speaking transhumant pastoralists camp at the foot of Mount Saipal in summer for the high-altitude grazing. All these peoples speak related dialects of Tibetan; they share a similar Tibetan culture and Tibetan Buddhist religion. This distinguishes them from Hindu Nepali speakers who form the majority in Humla, as in the nation—although the length and ease of contact in Humla has meant considerable mutual cultural interchange. Here, as elsewhere, Tibetans are ranked lower by caste principles than all but the low-occupational Hindu castes; and Humla Tibetans also have a very long history of being politically subject to high-caste Hindus.

The early history of Humla is poorly documented. We have only the names, the rough dates, and few other details of the ruling dynasties. First there were the Mallas, who are thought to have been Indo-European speakers of legendary Khasa ancestry and to have come from the west. By the twelfth century they had extended their rule to West Tibet, and by the thir-

---

[2] These Bura or Byansi cite origins in Indian and Nepalese Darchula to the west. While their legends recount intermarriages with both Nepali and Tibetan speakers in Humla, they are largely Nepalicized Hindus today (Levine 1987).

teenth century, to West Nepal. At its height, their kingdom included Purang, Guge, and possibly Ladakh in the northwest, down through Dullu and Kasikot in the south and east. Historical documents suggest that they even mounted a successful invasion of Kathmandu. While they supported both Buddhism and Hinduism in the earlier years of their rule, they later fell under increasing Hindu influence (Tucci 1956). The stability of that rule may have facilitated and laid the foundations for the forms of trade between Tibet and India that still are carried on today (Fürer-Haimendorf 1975:222–25).

The Malla kingdom collapsed in the late fourteenth century, possibly under the pressures of outside invasions, and splintered into independent chiefdoms. Part of the southern kingdom remained under the control of Malla heirs; other regions came under the control of high-caste Thakuri, and rule of territories in Tibet was assumed by local Tibetan families. Nyinba believe that Humla was controlled by Tibetans for a brief period. Eventually it fell under the rule of Thakuris who formed what came to be known as the Kalyal confederacy (Tucci 1956:106–7, 116–30).

Nyinba hold that their ancestors settled in villages which had been abandoned in the upheavals following the Malla collapse. By this account, they never would have experienced Malla rule. Their legends nevertheless describe it as a time of peace and religious efflorescence. People point to ruins of Buddhist temples in the region, identifiable as Sakya in sect, and attribute them to the Mallas. They also note terracing at high altitudes, well beyond the present-day limits of cultivation, and attribute this to the efforts of prior inhabitants.

Nyinba contrast the golden age of the Buddhist Mallas with the darker times of Kalyal rule. The latter period seems to have been marked by great instability and oppression for Humla's Tibetan inhabitants. One reason was the general high-caste Hindu prejudice against peoples of Tibetan ethnicity. Another was that the Kalyal lords were unable to sustain a strong and unified state. Their rules of inheritance and succession resulted in continual divisions of landholdings, serfs, and free subjects, so that already-small kingdoms grew ever smaller and came to consist of widely dispersed parcels of land.[3] At the same time, individual lords multiplied, and each was relatively weaker. The end result was an expanding confederacy of lords, increasing disunity, and lack of coordination of rule. Nyinba say that their ancestors accepted Kalyal dominion in exchange for rights to land,

---

[3] Stiller regards this as a chronic problem throughout Nepal's petty kingdoms (Stiller 1973:37–46). Appositely, the fragmentation of fiefs is consistent with general Nepali practices of partible inheritance.

and they describe their situation by a term used in Tibet for serfdom (that is, *gzhi-ma;* see Tucci 1956:129). But it was an onerous serfdom and became even harsher over time. The lords were entitled to repossess their serfs' lands; they seized their possessions and food stores at will and imposed very heavy taxes on them. More damaging to cultural traditions, they destroyed local Buddhist temples.

In 1789, the armies of the kingdom of Gorkha conquered independent principalities throughout the western hills, Humla among them. This followed other conquests to the east and completed the political unification of lands that constitute modern Nepal. Within a short time, however, the families of the conquered Kalyal lords had risen to power again. They managed this by becoming advisors to, and winning appointments in, local agencies created by the new national government. Thus Kalyal oppression was renewed and was directed particularly against Nyinba who had aided the Gorkha side. Nyinba claim that during this period Kalyal henchmen murdered strong Nyinba leaders. And as Nepalese government documents from the mid nineteenth century onward attest, there were frequent disturbances centering around Kalyal attempts to seize their former subjects' property and their other "lawless activities" (Regmi Research 1971:66, 211–14).

Legends of Settlement and Growth

Nyinba account for their past history through the medium of formal narratives. These narratives fall into distinct, named genres; each follows a somewhat different convention, and each serves a somewhat different purpose. One such genre is the "chronicles of the years" (*lo-rgyus*), which stands closest to our concept of history in its stress on the presumptively factual. Second are the "hero's tales," which describe the opposition of Nyinba men of superhuman strength (*dpa'-bo*) to the perfidies of Kalyal. Nyinba also are familiar with Tibetan epics, or "legends of the kings" (*rgyal-sgrungs*), such as the famous Gesar saga. These are of less relevance to Humla, but are important in reaffirming ethnic identity. Local Tibetan Buddhist lamas familiar with Tibetan literary works also relate versions of the sacred geographies of nearby pilgrimage places and biographies of religious figures of local interest, often embellishing upon the literary sources to make them more meaningful or to enhance the importance of local sites.[4]

---

[4] For example, there are tales of Padmasambhava's and Milarepa's visits to local sacred spots, although according to Nyinba genealogical lore, their first ancestors would not have arrived in Humla until well after the deaths of these two religious figures. There also are numer-

Here we are interested in the "stories of origin" (*chags-pa'i chags-tshul*), accounts of village settlement and development over time. These detail migrations to the Nyinba region, village foundings, and key events in the village's past. They also relate ancestral pedigrees and explain the evolution of present-day village structure. Finally, each reveals concerns with matters of population. There are, for example, portrayals of the early settlers' struggles to colonize the region, subsequent events of decline and losses of population, and cautions about the importance of regulating village growth. All the legends follow the same general format, the major difference being that some are more fully developed than others. The legends also reflect the Nyinba predilection for explaining culture and social structure in historical terms—a pattern we shall encounter again.[5]

There is no better way to introduce Nyinba society than through their own accounts of it. This is because their narratives about the past offer a reading of current cultural preoccupations. The choice of episodes and the events each legend describes are patently ordered by notions about society in the present—while portraying that present as shaped by events in a reconstructed past. I shall begin with a much-abbreviated summary of one of the more comprehensive origin legends and then turn to a discussion of its social and cultural points of reference.[6]

> In a time of warfare and strife, three sons of a high lord of ancient lineage in Purang (West Tibet) left their home and fled south. They managed to cross only the first of several passes into Nepal before the snows fell and left them stranded in a narrow valley for the winter. They were fortunate, however, because they found a local god who protected them and provided food for them there. In gratitude, they adopted him as the god of their household line (*pho-lha*). In spring, they started south again and stopped in northern Humla. Thereupon the brothers split up. The first joined a Kalyal Thakuri village above Simikot, the second joined a Chetri village within Simikot, and the youngest moved to an uninhabited site to the east, which became the present-day Nyinba village of Todpa. The brothers prospered in their new homes and

---

ous stories detailing the visit of the famed religious teacher Zhabkar Rangdrol (1781–1850). The latter's autobiography does mention a visit to Limi, a community to the north, but only an imagined visit to lower Humla during his meditations (Zhabs-dkar n.d.: 528, 553–54).

[5] Regarding this, the only explanation of my fieldwork that ever gained acceptance was that I was carrying out a historical study. The study of culture and social structure from any other perspective seemingly made no sense, or perhaps Nyinba lack the terms to contextualize it.

[6] This legend has been presented in its entirety elsewhere, in both transliterated Tibetan and translation (Levine 1976).

maintained their relationship, annually meeting to worship and
sacrifice to their common gods. After many years, the eldest
brother in Simikot (or his descendants) came into conflict with the
reigning Kalyal lord. He sought divine counsel, and the portents
led him to Todpa, the home of his agnates. Thereafter, Todpa's
population expanded and divided into three separate villages.
Later, however, there were other troubles created by Kalyal. The
village lost one person after another, and finally only one small
boy was left alive. His family's slaves reared him, and when he
grew up, the headman of Trangshod village gave him his daughter
in marriage. This was the first of many marriages between these
villages. To secure prosperity, the couple sought the advice of
lamas. They sponsored the building of *mani* (prayer) walls, planted
trees at the four corners of the village, and constructed other religious edifices. They then had three sons who fathered innumer-
able descendants. Thus came about the flourishing village of the
present day.

Descent, Status, and Village Membership

At the outset, the legend displays Nyinba concerns with descent and pedigree. The very first sentences establish the pedigree of Todpa's founders
and do so by stating the names (not included here) of the ancestor in Tibet,
his three sons, and the founders of their clan. For Nyinba, pedigree is
based on descent and is denoted by the clan's name, which establishes position in larger, community-wide ranking systems.

Legends such as these offer clan members their only support for status
claims, and the acceptance of their legend by others in the society is all the
support they need. With reference to only a few key details, these legends
are able to establish the clan's rank in its place of origin and fix, relative to
other clans, the time its ancestors settled in the Nyinba region. Hereditary
rank—which follows Tibetan criteria—is critical in certifying rights to
admission in the upper stratum of society, and the duration of a clan's residence determines its members' relative standing within the stratum. Clanship also regulates marriage, for Nyinba social strata are normally endogamous, and people prefer to marry within a circle of clans of status
comparable to their own. This particular legend incorporates one unusual
feature—the claim to noble origins—for other legends simply certify good
status. Finally, it suggests points of linkage between particular lines of descent and particular segments of the village, although this is obscured in
the abbreviated account above. The explanation is a historical one: that the
same ancestors founded both.

Nyinba origin legends commonly trace ties of kinship to Nepalis of high caste.[7] This too derives from Nyinba notions about heredity and social rank. Ancestral ties with Nepalis legitimize pretensions to higher ranking in a caste society and claims to status parity with high-caste Nepalis, for they show that Nyinba and these people are really the same. The way that Nyinba demonstrate this is rather ingenious: the legends describe how a brother of one of their ancestors joined a Nepali community, married with Nepalis, and essentially became Nepali. The effect of this is to give Nepalis Tibetan ancestry—which thus avoids compromising Nyinba claims of Tibetan origins. This is important, for Nyinba see themselves as Tibetan by heredity, and to their way of thinking, this makes them inherently suited to Tibetan behavioral forms. Such notions rationalize the maintenance of a Tibetan ethnic identity, which is a major advantage for trading in Tibet, although patently to their political disadvantage in a Hindu state. In two villages there exist variant forms of the origin legend which convey a contrary message. These legends describe the Nyinba ancestor as a high-caste Nepali who went to Tibet, violated caste rules there, became Tibetanized, and was outcasted by his kin when he returned home. Predictably, it is the younger men who favor the latter accounts. They presumably find it more to their advantage to emphasize stronger Nepali affiliations now that economic relations with Tibet have deteriorated (cf. Fürer-Haimendorf 1966:17, 1975:234) and as Nyinba have become more closely integrated into the Nepalese state.

Models of Social Structure in the Legend

The legends chart spatial organization and settlement patterns and their changes over time and depict key events in the evolution of structural relationships between village households. None, however, makes any attempt to explain either the Nyinba household system or polyandrous marriage— all primary points of discrimination between Nyinba and their Nepali neighbors and some of their Tibetan-speaking neighbors. While the absence of such details may be as significant as their presence, it offers far less to guide interpretation. The natural inference is that these features of social life are so unremarkable and unquestioned that they need no explaining—or that they are so deeply embedded culturally and socially that none would suffice.

[7] Exceptions to this are the clans of lamas, which claim ties only to priestly clans in Tibet; two families which claim full Nepali orgins; and the half-dozen families which claim to have migrated from other nearby Tibetan-speaking communities, and whose legends reiterate that fact.

Spatial structure and social structure are equally concerns of the legends. Thus, one of the most elaborate episodes in the Todpa legend—the re-creation of the village after its near demise—centers around the dual rebuilding of society. We hear first about the reconstruction of religious edifices, which stand as symbols of a prosperous village, and later about the massive reorganization of a village system that was dismantled when nearly all its membership was lost. As with every other legend, the Todpa one attributes present-day village structure to the effects of successive household partitions over time. Partitions between brothers, as we shall see, leave their impress on, as they create, the framework for future village structure, just as marriages contracted centuries ago are held to have established patterns for alliance and kinship alignments in the present day.

Todpa's legend begins with the common theme of three brothers in search of a homeland. The brothers settle in different areas of Humla district and the Karnali Zone. One founds the Nyinba village and is joined later by another brother. One of the two has three sons; the sons partition, and each establishes a village settlement. When the village virtually dies out, the lone survivor and refounder has three sons as well; again the three partition, and each establishes a section within a single village. But Todpa has only two sections today. The themes of founding by one and then by two men and the emphasis on three sons who marry separately reflects the tension between bipartite and tripartite models of village structure. In the legends of other Nyinba villages, tripartite and quadripartite models of structure are similarly contraposed. We find such conceptual divisions reproduced in diverse spheres of Tibetan cultural and social life. Thus there are the triads stressed in models of household and family: marriage, for example, ideally involves tripartite polyandry. Triads also are significant in religious symbolism, while in systems of clanship and social ranking, dual divisions and fourfold schemata seem to prevail (see Allen 1978; Paul 1982:46, 117–18).

The structure of the legend also reveals the tension between themes of unitary versus heterogeneous foundings. Most legends depict a single founding, which supports notions of common origins in "hearth" and "land" for village households and which Nyinba cite in exhortations for village unity today. There also are a few more esoteric legends, known mostly to elders, that describe past patterns of migration and attempt to account for the complex patterning of clan memberships in present-day villages. That the former are more common is quite predictable, given the stance of ethnic closure, the dislike of immigration, and the general prejudice toward immigrants. Nyinba prefer to portray their society as established by a limited number of village foundings in the distant past and its membership as descended from a very few ancestors who arrived in these valleys long ago.

A third theme involves the oscillation between village expansion and subdivision into separate settlements, and then village contraction and re-unification into an undivided village again. Today the former occurs when hamlets are established near outlying lands. Such hamlets seem to have existed—if episodically—for a very long time; not only legends but also the ruins on the edges of cultivated areas attest to this. The movement be-tween village-focused and hamlet-dispersed modes of settlement seems to be based, in short, on the relative balance of economic and political advan-tages and disadvantages in nucleation versus dispersion. Village growth and the expansion of landholdings into distant areas, for example, make dispersed residence advantageous from a practical point of view. At the same time, political stability is necessary to make living in small, isolated hamlets feasible. As the legends portray it, declines in population—which are often linked to political upheavals—bring households back to a single large village again.

Thus far I have mentioned only ancestors, but ancestresses figure in these legends as well. In some, husbands and wives are described as immi-grating together, which in essence makes them village co-founders. In other legends, the ancestor arrives alone, and the focus shifts to his subse-quent marriage and how it marks his acceptance within the Nyinba com-munity. Ancestors receive more attention in legends, undoubtedly because of their importance for clanship. It is all the more striking then that an-cestresses become the focus of attention at rituals, where their blessings are sought for agricultural success and village prosperity. Thus in legend and in ritual we find the major contributions that women make to home and com-munity recognized. In mundane life, by contrast, polyandry, virilocality, and patrifilial succession produce households organized around men, in which women's contributions are relatively devalued.

Finally, the legend refers to the existence of slaves. In this as in all other legends of its kind, slaves are portrayed from the master's perspective. In the Todpa case, these presumptions are taken to an extreme: the slaves are portrayed as so committed to their masters that they freely choose to raise the founding clan's lone survivor. This adds a mythic cast to a partial real-ity. For slaves in the past and freedmen in the present have expressed a commitment no less than their material contributions to the Nyinba com-munity. During slavery, they apparently chose not to escape, despite ample opportunities to do so. After being freed in 1926 by national decree, most freedmen chose to stay on in their prior villages. The disabilities which slaves suffered and which are perpetuated in social inequities today are ra-

tionalized by notions of inferiority by kinship and descent; they are inten-
sified by traditional domestic practices which continue to handicap freedmen and hinder their efforts to attain social and economic parity with their
former masters.

Perceptions of Village Growth and Decline

As Nyinba see it, the predominant concerns at the time of their ancestors'
settlement were whether or not the land was fertile and the site advantageous and whether their descendants would proliferate (*'phel-ba*) there.
The ancestors are believed to have sought portents to test for these matters
and to secure divine approval and divine guarantees of future success. In
some legends, the migrant is led to his future village home by an animal
consecrated to the god; in others, he arrives on his own and then immediately plants a special herb or grain and checks its growth. This symbol-
izes, as it magically ensures, future community growth.

Nyinba reconstruct the marriages and domestic arrangements of these
first settlers in ways that express a folk theory about social practices and
their implications for population. We know that polyandry is the rule at
present, yet the legends always portray the first settlers and their sons as
marrying separately and partitioning. How the first settlers—who are supposed to have come from polyandrous Tibet—actually married is a moot
point. What is significant is the notion that they would have married monogamously. People say that polyandry prevents the dispersion of household wealth and the fragmentation of land and that it avoids the proliferation of households, thus restricting village growth. They also suggest that
household partition was less problematic in the past, when much land stood
unclaimed and when it was necessary to expand village numbers and enhance village political strength. As if to make this point doubly clear, the
Todpa legend states that after the village's decline the refounder's sons
again married monogamously, seemingly in order to recreate and thereby
repopulate the village.

There are other elements in the Todpa legend that reflect concerns with
village growth. The repopulation of Todpa was not only accomplished on a
mundane level, through separate marriages and the production of heirs, but
was also secured through the performance of meritorious deeds. The
ancestor-refounder and his wife are said to have sponsored religious buildings and religious ceremonies expressly to ensure both the proliferation and
prosperity of their descendants.

In the Todpa legend, we see pulses of growth and decline. The village
initially grew so large as to subdivide into three parts; then political set-

backs and other problems decimated the population, which slowly returned to a viable size. Other villages' legends recount equally radical changes. The two protovillages that subsequently joined and formed Nyimatang reportedly included as many households as the present-day village and held a dominant position in the countryside. Now neither exists, and only one household of their lineal descendants remains. Nyinba tend to see this not as the product of random demographic fluctuations, but as the manifestation of forces beyond their control: political discord, divine retribution for villagers' evil deeds, and other, inexplicable supernatural interventions. In Nyimatang, conflicts with Kalyal rulers are held to have prompted massive emigrations. Barkhang is said to have suffered from a murderous demon (*btsan*). The demon was subdued by a Tibetan lama, and the village eventually was able to recover from its losses.

One of the conclusions to be drawn from this is that Nyinba today consider population decline to have been a major threat during the early development of their community. This concern must have seemed very real in the none-too-distant past. There were two epidemics of smallpox in recent decades and a previous epidemic of another disease so severe that people were left dead in their homes or lying on the roadside because there was no one to bury them. Smallpox has been eradicated, but epidemics of other diseases still recur in Humla. I witnessed an outbreak of measles and a typhus epidemic in 1974 and another measles epidemic in 1983. The measles epidemics, the first particularly, were responsible for the deaths of many Nyinba children and scores of children in neighboring Humla communities. While only one Nyinba man died of typhus, it is said to have had serious effects in neighboring Nepali villages. There is little concern in the legends with excessive population growth, although it is seen as a problem at the present time. Nyinba have only to look to neighboring Nepali villages, many of which have grown so far beyond the capacity of local resources that their people live in hunger three out of four seasons of the year. They point to these villages to illustrate the dangers of repeated household partitions and unchecked expansion. People recognize that their community is facing such problems as well and that, like everyone in Humla, they have been forced into more-marginal lands and less-profitable economic ventures.

These are some of the cultural themes and orientations that the legends express and that frame Nyinba understandings of the world they have created. There are several points to be made. First, Nyinba see their ancestors as having been vulnerable to various external forces beyond their control, as they themselves are today. Second, notions about heredity and social rank have supported the establishment of demographic boundaries and are

associated with a distinct Nyinba ethnic identity. Third, population growth
and loss are preoccupations which Nyinba see as influencing the actions
that villagers take. As we shall see, reflexive understandings of this kind
inform reactions to fellow villagers' partitions, just as they influence individual decisions to remain in polyandry or not—both decisions being subject to complex assessments drawn from diverse domains of social life.

Part 2
Kinship and Community

3
Descent, Kinship, and Alliance

For Nyinba, kinship involves commonalities in origins and common identity. This perception of common identity serves as a powerful rationale for mutual commitments in families and households and supports the solidarity men realize in polyandrous marriages. Ideas about kinship also provide the primary rationale for community closure and the idiom in which it is expressed. For this reason I begin with a discussion of cultural conceptualizations of kinship and how they validate the conduct of relationships within the community; I then turn to an observer's analysis of their role in social structure. The two perspectives merge in the end, bringing us to the Nyinba view of their community as a community of kin or, more precisely, two separate circles of relatives within a single politically and economically unified community. These two circles include the dominant landholders and a minority of freedmen, former slaves, and their descendants. Within each circle, people are differentiated by descent, kinship, and affinal ties; the same ties unite them against the world.

At the core of Nyinba kinship concepts is *ru* (*rus*), which refers to kinship through men; ru is materially manifested in the physical substance bone and is passed on in the medium of sperm from father to child. Ru provides the conceptual basis for a system of clanship. It is clan memberships which distinguish Nyinba from outsiders and determine social ranking within the community, political prerogatives, marital choice, ritual participation, and in the past, rights to property as well. Only household membership has more influence on an individual's life, and as we shall see, clan, household, and village memberships are interrelated. While clanship separates Nyinba into ranked categories, matrilateral kinship—conceived as ru transformed into blood when it passes through women—and affinal ties create links across those clans, unifying the community and providing a way to integrate those few immigrants that find their way into it.

Ru: Bone and Clanship

One can say that Nyinba "recognize" patrilineal descent, but such a statement has little meaning. Perhaps more than any other concept, descent has suffered from careless usage, and imprecisions in description and analysis bear much responsibility for the long-standing controversies about descent and its role in social structure. Even the limited Tibetan literature includes debates about descent recognition. Some writers argue that Tibetans have patrilineal descent; others say they had patrilineal descent, but it is only marginally relevant to their modern social system; still others describe a situation of patrifiliation, that is, special emphasis on father-son links; and some find no more than bilateral kinship.[1] Nor does recourse to Tibetan sources provide much help, for all relevant kinship concepts are described in terms of the same idiom: ru.

For Nyinba, descent and kinship are genealogical matters which are grounded in theories of hereditary transmissions. Ru, which literally means "bone," passes in pure form from father to child through the medium of sperm. It links people to their male ancestors of the past, back to the ancestor who first settled in the Nyinba valleys, and beyond that, to his ancestors in Tibet. The effects are not only skeletal. Seen as the template of the body, ru influences all physical and mental attributes—which makes men the primary source of their children's character, skills, and physical appearance. Women have the same bone as their fathers and brothers but can only pass it indirectly to their children through the medium of blood, which has lesser effects. In certain ways, Nyinba ideas about substance transmissions resemble European folk theories of heredity—encapsulated in physical substance, yet influencing all manner of human attributes. The differences are that the European model stresses the bilaterality of kinship, while the Nyinba model supports a system of descent.

Descent is conceptualized as a line of males over time, similar to the analyst's notion of a descent construct (Scheffler 1966–67; Keesing 1975). The terms Nyinba use translate literally as "the mark of descent," (*brgyud-*

[1] Among those writing on the subject are Prince Peter (1963:423), Róna-Tas (1955), Stein (1972:94), and Tucci (1955:204). Aziz (1978) provides a brief critical discussion of this literature. Bogoslovskij (1972), presenting an orthodox Marxist interpretation, suggests that state centralization in Tibet prompted transitions from a society based on clans to one based on class divisions. This view is consistent with reports that descent is of greater importance at the fringes of Tibetan civilization and outside the jurisdiction of the Tibetan state.

rtags) and "succession in bone," or "bone descent" (*rus-brgyud*).[2] Bone is perceived as the locus of clanspeople's commonalities, so that the line of people from past to present, and those in the present day sharing the same heredity in bone, are called "one bone" (*rus gchig-pa*) people, or "bone ones" (*rus-pa*).

This concept of hereditary bone has significance beyond clanship. It refers also to a wider category of people, a ranked category that forms a stratum of society—and such hereditary social strata seem to be characteristic of Tibetan societies (Allen 1978). The Nyinba emphasize one fundamental social cleavage: this is the division between masters (*bdag-po*)— full citizens and landholders—and "inferiors" (*g.yog-po*), or the freedmen who once were their slaves. While hereditary lamas, or Tibetan Buddhist priests (*sngags-pa*), are regarded as technically forming a third stratum, they are treated as identical to citizen-landholders in most contexts.

Thus ru has multiple references and means more than descent, clan, or any unidimensional analyst's term, although each of these terms sums up levels of its meaning. This provides another example of our lack of equivalents for segmentary concepts, which place people in sets of nesting categories of greater and lesser inclusiveness. Analyst's etic terms have focused upon the specific categories rather than the concepts or systems linking them. The most inclusive level here is stratum specific; one of the criteria of ranking is quality of bone. Strata accordingly are referred to as ru, although they also can be distinguished by the term *rig* (*rigs*), "races," or "ranks" (see Jäschke 1972:527–28). Strata then are internally composed of clans. Clans, in turn, are subdivided into lineages or "clan sections" (*rus-tsho*), a term also used for village sections, with which they are linked. Lastly, households may be spoken of as segments of the lineage.[3] We have no single term to describe all these meanings.

In their dealings with Hindus, Nyinba speak of ru as synonymous with the system of *jat,* or caste. There certainly are parallels between the traditional Tibetan system, which divided the social world into aristocrats, priests, commoners, and outcastes (Allen 1978; Aziz 1978:52–57), and the fourfold Indian *varna* system. There also are major differences in ide-

---

[2]Levine (1981b) details the levels of meaning of *ru* and its various synonyms (e.g., *rus-brgyud, rigs-brgyud,* etc.).

[3]My uses of clan and lineage follow the standard definitions. The former is the more inclusive unit; an apical ancestor is identified, but links to that ancestor are more a matter of faith than proof. Elders attempt to construct full genealogies for lineages, although many such accounts are marred by gaps and inconsistencies. In genealogies, households are depicted as lineage segments, and people describe the demise of a particular household as a demise of that ru, but this idea has no other practical significance.

ology and practice. Tibetan rulers, for example, traditionally held ascendancy over priests (although in recent centuries Tibetan rulers also were priests), and Tibetan ideas about purity and pollution are markedly different from those held by Hindus.[4] This becomes clearer when we look more closely at Nyinba notions of social inequality.

Clanship in Social Structure

In Nyinba clanship, systems of descent and social ranking intersect, a fact made particularly clear in the course of cultural analyses of kinship concepts.[5] However, ideas about kinship do not stand alone. They have their reference point and are refracted in social relations. Thus Nyinba descent also has the decided effect of placing people within a closed, intricately graded social world and of warranting their placement. This has major consequences for social relations. The intersections operative between ranking and kinship can be demonstrated with a few succinct illustrations. The clearest examples are the competitive use of clan names, constraints upon sociality encoded in ideas about the mixing of substances, and the use of clanship to certify political qualifications.

Clan names provide a simple code and way of marking relative social position. They are all the more effective in this because they do so on two levels simultaneously. First, the name immediately marks stratum affiliation. Freedmen traditionally were denied individual clan names, so all are identified by the name of their stratum. Second, the name indicates relative ranking within the (upper) stratum. Rank is established by two criteria: time of settlement (with the descendants of early settlers being ranked above more recent arrivals) and presumed status within the community of origin (ordinarily either in Tibet or a Tibetan-speaking group within Nepal). Many of the preoccupations displayed in origin legends derive from concerns with establishing duration of settlement and the legitimacy of claims to high status.

Names therefore become the currency of status rivalry, with the name itself acquiring a prestige value. The most desirable names suggest aristocratic Tibetan origins or, alternatively, high-caste Nepali affiliations. These names are not fixed, and some have changed over the last several decades

---

[4] A fuller discussion follows in chapter 4.

[5] Explorations of the cultural features of kinship systems owe much to the work of Schneider (1968) (and see Carter [1974] and Inden and Nicholas [1977] on kinship concepts in South Asia).

in response to a clan's altered social position or to changing fashions in prestige.

Prestige appears to be the primary motivation in the selection of alternate names of Nepali origin. All indications are that clanspeople choose a name by its caste associations—and then turn around and use the name to buttress claims to high status. I have seen Nyinba clans abandon Chetri clan names for ones in use by higher-caste Thakuris, ostensibly for precisely this reason.[6] Young people more often give the Nepali name, which accords with their greater concerns about securing social acceptance from the politically dominant Nepalis. Elders tend to give the Tibetan name, which is more traditional and presumably has greater meaning to them. Both tend to use the Nepali name in dealing with officials. It also is mostly elders who hold knowledge about the community-wide clan system. Younger people know only their ranking relative to close kin, neighbors, and friends.

Solidarity between clanspeople, however, is expressed less in terms of shared rank—although clanspeople may stand together in its defence—than in terms of common kinship. While clanship is a type of kin relationship that is based on common ancestry and lasts indefinitely, it gains meaning, is understood, and has to be continually invoked through the use of kinship analogies and kinship idioms. Thus clansmen and -women address and refer to each other by the terms for parents, children, grandparents, grandchildren, or siblings, according to generation—and conduct their relationships roughly after patterns established with their own parents, siblings, and so on.

It is through kinship analogies too that people explain how and why clanship regulates marriage and sexual relations. Like close kin, they say, persons of common descent may neither wed nor engage in sexual relations. That is incest, both a crime and a sin.[7] In theory, heavy jural and

---

[6] Elders and young people alike argue that the Nepali clan name is a "translation" of the Tibetan one. They justify such translations by reference to history or status considerations. For example, they may refer to origin legends which depict individuals of Nyinba clans settling among high-caste Nepalis—and see this as legitimating their right to that caste title. Also found are arguments about status equivalence. Pal clan members argue that their forebears were rulers in Tibet and they are thus entitled to call themselves Thakuri, the caste of Nepal's rulers.

[7] Barkhang village's major clan contains three intermarrying lineages. Some people take this as proof of disparate clan origins and suggest that these lineages were amalgamated to reinforce village unity. Whatever the reasons, this is quite legal. Nepali law permits marriage and sexual relations between agnates whose common ancestry lies more than seven generations past (Regmi 1976:6). This also is in accord with Tibetan marital prohibitions (see Prince Peter 1963:423).

mystical sanctions apply against incest: expulsion from the community in traditional law, severe penalties in Nepalese law, and the belief that the couple's health will suffer, that their bones will weaken or break, and that any children they produce will be sickly and die. In practical terms, the threat of these sanctions has not been entirely effective, and incestuous liaisons continue to occur. Most common has been incest among people related naturally, that is, sexual relations with a relative who was born out of wedlock or between descendants of that illegitimate person and members of his or her natural clan. When paternity is not legally acknowledged, formal legal sanctions are impossible to apply. Less common is incest between distant clanspeople. There also have been two cases of incest within families in the past few decades: one between father-in-law and daughter-in-law, the other between father and daughter. In none of these cases was there any intervention, despite the shock and disgust that people openly expressed. This may be due to the general patterns of noninterference in others' private sexual affairs. Notwithstanding this reluctance to intervene, incestuous couples—like others who offend local morality—have faced gossip and very strong social disapproval.

Incest rules are related to a larger set of ideas about the mixing of substances, which derive, in turn, from ideas about shared bone and the physical similarity that entails. The closest, or inner, circle of clanspeople may not mix sexually, but may "mix mouths," that is, share eating utensils that would mix their mouth secretions (*zhul*). Those more distantly related, including cross-cousins, may not "eat together," which means that they should not share cups and plates, but may engage in sexual relations and marriage. (Those that marry may do both.) Outside this circle, both commensality and sexual relations are proscribed. These are among the ways that discrimination is expressed against newer immigrants. Upper-stratum individuals rationalize this by beliefs that outsiders are different—and inferior—in ru. Commensality provides a trenchant index of this, and the phrase "similar mouth" is as likely to be used as "similar bone" to refer to Nyinba of equivalent social standing.

Ultimately clanship serves as a mark of Nyinba-ness, and membership in a reputable Nyinba clan is a necessary prerequisite for civic entitlements, specifically, rights to full citizenship in the society. As in many tribal and peasant societies, citizenship is defined differently within the local group than it is by the modern nation-state. Nyinba extend rights of full civic participation in local contexts only to taxpaying landholders who belong to established clans. They explain this by saying that both tax paying and high clan position are necessary proofs of social responsibility, the logic being that only those individuals who own land and whose clans are long resident have proved their responsibility and have the proven heredity for it. By similar reasoning, new clans are unknown quantities; their members are unpredictable and cannot be trusted. While having questionable maternal antecedents can compromise a person's political effectiveness, it cannot disqualify civic participation, because of the lesser weight placed on heredity through women. Finally, notions of hereditary suitability underlie restrictions on political involvements by freedmen. The reasoning again is circular and particularly insidious, for the proof of freedmen's unsuitability is their history of powerlessness.

Full rights and prerogatives vis-à-vis the state now theoretically extend to Nepalese of all castes and classes. All Nepalis can own land, vote in government elections, seek legal redress, and hold office. Nonetheless, Nyinba without proper clan credentials still do not participate fully in affairs of the village panchayat, the local administrative unit sponsored by the national government. That freedmen never served as panchayat council members until the massive elections of 1976 can be attributed to the extension of local criteria of civic entitlement by descent to the national political arena. Even though the clan has no direct political relevance—it does not act as a unit in political, legal, or economic affairs—it substantiates rights to civic status by establishing a key parameter of an individual's social identity which spills over into higher-level political fields.

I have described Nyinba clanship as a suprakinship institution which finds its source and rationale in kinship, which is understood largely in kinship terms, and which has only limited economic and political significance. This presents major contrasts with descent systems described in the literature and notably with the classic African systems. Much has been made of the failure of so-called African models to clarify features of descent elsewhere. Despite this, the classic African cases continue to provide our clearest exemplars, ones against which new cases perennially are tested. Some of the features that figure prominently in models developed to account for them have proved more helpful in cross-cultural comparisons and in clarifying features of new systems, and this is true for the Nyinba case as well.

One of the more fundamental assumptions has been that descent entails corporate groups which are actualized through their functions—economic, religious, or political. The reliance on functions as definitive features of groups or associations is in itself problematic. Fortes and Evans-Pritchard, in their introduction to *African Political Systems,* preferred to speak of a coordination between lineage structures and political systems and to analyze how existing lineages serve as primary political associations, most notably in the type of society characterized as acephalous (Fortes and Evans-

Pritchard 1940:6–7; see also Fortes 1953:26; 1969:294). For Nyinba, descent does not generate any effective corporate groups and has no direct economic and little religious significance. Nevertheless, it has politico-jural resonance. Individuals have no political status except as validated by and in terms of their clan membership.

Greater problems have arisen from early tendencies to reify clanship and from presumptions that clanship necessarily involves groups built around persons with common descent (Holy 1979; Strathern 1973). That this presumption has been so difficult to set aside may be attributed to its deep roots in the history of the discipline. It extends as far back as Rivers (1924) and was perpetuated through Radcliffe-Brown (1929). It also owes much to earlier analytical tendencies to envision social structure in the form of groups through which societies function, rather than the more abstract principles and norms that shape and are shaped by social behavior. Frameworks of analysis may have changed, but the weight of long-established definitions has been hard to break—as we can see in the persistence of this issue. Fortes, who wrote more, and more authoritatively, than any anthropologist of his generation on the subject, came to distinguish between descent as a principle of social identification and as a principle for the formation of political and/or economic groups constituted by descent credentials (see Barnes 1971:239; Fortes 1969:287). Yet his concern always returned to how descent supports corporate-group formation (1959:211).[8]

Ethnographic work in the sixties and seventies showed that this was not always the case. One response was the refinement of analytical terminology to reflect this fact and better serve cross-cultural comparisons. Added were terms such as descent constructs (chains of genealogical linkage that connect people with their ancestors) and descent categories (modes of categorizing people by descent linkages, with no implication of common action), as opposed to descent groups (Scheffler 1966:543–44). However, these are analyst's distinctions, which do not always effectively capture the concepts people use or the complex arrangements and alignments of social life. The Nyinba provide a particularly instructive case in this regard. If they were to be categorized, one would call them a society with descent

---

[8] Compare Fortes's minimal definition: "Descent can be defined as a genealogical connexion recognized between a person and any of his ancestors or ancestresses. It is established by tracing a pedigree" (Fortes 1959:207) with: "Since descent confers attributes of status relating to a person's place in the external social structure it is bound to operate by placing persons in categories or groups. . . . Empirically, descent groups are constituted by the fact that all the members of a group in a given society have the same form of pedigree and all their pedigrees converge in a single common ancestor or group of ancestors. Theoretically, they are necessarily corporate groups, even if the corporate possession is as immaterial as an exclusive common name or an exclusive cult" (Fortes 1959:208).

constructs and descent categories, but no descent groups. Yet descent is not kept strictly separate from the major social groupings that do exist: households, village sections, and villages. Instead, the two sets of memberships—in households, sections, and villages, and in clans—intersect and are seen as interrelated. One way to interpret this is to say that the linkage at the level of the cultural model reflects existing coordinate relations—and thereupon further influences social practice.

Descent and Territory

Nyinba clans do not assemble for any purpose, nor do they engage in any collective activities. Corporate territorial—or politically and spatially bounded—groups such as villages depend not on clanship, but on membership or affiliation in constituent landholding households. Yet there is considerable overlap between the composition of specific villages and clans. One reason for this is the practice of patrifilial inheritance, which means that succession to households ordinarily passes on lines that parallel descent. This coordination between lines of inheritance, succession, and descent has further consequences. For one thing, earlier-settling clans are likely to have expanded most and to be represented in a larger number of village households than are the clans of later settlers. Their greater numerical representation reinforces the members' sense of greater proprietary rights in those villages and seems to further support village exclusivity, in the same way that the presence of a unique set of Nyinba clans reinforces the sense of exclusivity and closure against the world.

The overlap between clan and village memberships also provides a rich field for people's own discussions and analyses of social structure. In many such discussions, the concern lies with explaining apparent "exceptions": cases where early settler and founder clans do not predominate or where actual village composition is quite mixed. Nyinba tend to explain these exceptions by reference to specific, historical events, such as periodic admissions of immigrants and occasional succession by daughters and daughters' husbands in households without sons. I find these exceptions to be more the outcome of regular reformative processes within social structure, an issue I shall raise again. What is important here is that the overlap exists, has social repercussions, and produces its own cultural momentum, influencing the idioms in which clanship and village structure are discussed and contextualized.

Associations between descent and territorial units are expressed, and become quite tangible, in the use of identical names for parallel segmentary levels of village and clan, in restrictions placed upon the inheritance of sacred offices, and in notions about the jurisdictions of local gods. Regarding the first, we find that in three villages out of four the village's name also is used to describe its major, first settler's clan. Nyimatang is the exception to this, because it is an amalgam of formerly separate villages, each with its own founding clan. There the former villages now act as village sections and each is linked with the clan of its founder, so that section and clan names coincide. Among the other villages, readers should be most familiar with Todpa, which illustrates these identifications well. Todpa's founding clan, Pal, is described as *the* Todpa clan. People are as likely to say, "My clan is Todpa," as to say, "My clan is Pal."

Similar identifications are expressed in the practice of using the same term for village sections and lineages. *Rutsho,* which literally means "clan subdivision," may be used for both. This is considered an "old," that is, traditional, term, and younger people are more apt to use the Nepali loan-word *patti,* which describes the localized descent units found in caste Nepali villages in Humla. These villages are spatially divided into different patti, and patti members own adjacent plots of farmland. Many Nyinba see the two terms as synonymous, although others do not. One man suggested that patti signifies more what people think of as the *sa* dimension of village structure. Sa, a term I shall discuss again, means land, space, and territory. Rutsho conversely tends more to evoke notions of commonalities in clan-ship.[9] Yet Nyinba also note that their villages can and do include members of disparate lineages and that membership in a descent category does not entail membership in a territorial group, or the reverse.

Descent, however, is entailed in the inheritance of ritual offices, specifi-cally that of *dangri,* or priest to the god which possesses the local spirit medium. This office passes in a line of both unbroken patrilineal descent and continuous household succession. Dangris who serve clan gods and their mediums, moreover, must belong to the clan which that god repre-sents. The office also commonly falls to clans and households of village section founders. In all instances, pure heredity is crucial and is given reli-gious sanction.[10] As the brother of one current dangri priest recounts:

> For generations our ancestors have held the offices both of dangri
> priest and *tsobo,* which commemorates section founding. Five

[9] Rutsho also is used to describe branch lineages dispersed among different villages. There is a third term given for sections: *yul,* which means village. This may recall past conditions of possibly greater autonomy and greater territorial dispersion of village sections; it too suggests notions of localization.

[10] Similarly, the preferred Tibetan Buddhist lama is a man of true lama (*sngags-pa*) hered-ity. Such a man is thought to be more effective, although there are respected lamas who gained their expertise by training alone.

generations ago my ancestor and his older brother decided to partition the household. Normally both offices would go to the eldest. But their father objected and on his deathbed willed that both go to my ancestor, because the eldest was illegitimate, the son of his wife's lover. There was much quarrelling over this. The elder brother bribed local leaders and thus got to be tsobo. But dangri had to go to my ancestor; to do otherwise would have been opposed by the god.

Finally there are local deities. These are conceptualized as holding a kind of jurisdiction and guardianship over certain groups or categories of people, which involves protecting them against supernatural and naturally caused disasters. In return for this, people must worship the deity periodically and must maintain a suitable shrine. The relationships are particularistic, so that the deities guard and are worshipped by clans or households or villages, and different clans, households, and villages have their own special gods.

Household gods (pho-lha), for example, are expected to safeguard the property and members of the households that worship them.[11] Nyinba say that relationships with these gods have a long history, that they were first established by the ancestor who founded each household line, and that they were perpetuated by partitioners from, as well as successors to, that household. Successive household partitions have given the same gods to numbers of households within a section or village, and this is formally recognized by observances of annual village-wide ceremonies.

Village gods (*yul-lha, gzhi-bdag,* and *sde-brgyad*) are thought native to village soils and are worshipped by every villager—rich and poor, citizen-landholder and freedman alike—at every calendrical agricultural rite. In return, the god safeguards community welfare. Village gods are thought to be particularly sympathetic to their freedmen constituents for two reasons. Freedmen are said to be autochthons and certainly are the most disadvantaged group in the community, thus both the most deserving and the most needful of protection.

Clan gods (*rus-lha*) hold responsibility for the welfare of clan members. Practices of worship vary greatly among the different clans and tend to vary

---

[11] Nyinba also speak of the traditional Tibetan house god (called *mkhar-gyi rtse-bla, khang-ba'i gnas lha,* or simply *khyim-lha*) who migrates through the house during the month and seems to be concerned principally with its physical integrity. It should be noted that pholha refers not only to a household god, but also to the god staying on a man's right shoulder (*pho-lha dgra-lha dkar-bo*). It has been suggested in the literature that the pholha is a clan god (see Macdonald 1980), but Nyinba informants argue that patterns of succession to pholha worship make it a sa, or land, god associated with landed households.

with the clan's size and local status. The smaller, newly established, and therefore lower-status clans invariably have the smallest shrines and the most perfunctory annual rites. The gods of hereditary lama clans are worshipped daily in the village temple and only by members of the specific clan. Large clans other than those of village founders seem to have the largest and most elaborate festivals, which the entire community attends. This suggests their strong position within the Nyinba community. Paradoxically, the founder clans themselves do not hold clan ceremonies. Instead they sponsor collective worship of their ancestors (*a-'bi* and *mes-mes*)—the reputed village founders.

Ancestor worship undeniably conflicts with Buddhist doctrines of reincarnation. Lay people see no problem in this, and lamas rationalize ancestor worship as a folk practice and a survival from pre-Buddhist, or Bon, religion. Nyinba go so far as to impute mystical powers similar to those of minor deities and far greater beneficence to the ancestor and ancestress. Thus they celebrate them and at the major autumn harvest festival seek their advice for the year. In this festival, the more important figure is the ancestress, "Grandmother Goddess of Prosperity and Agricultural Wealth." Almost every villager attends this festival; there is no distinction made between the lineal descendants of the ancestor and other village residents. This suggests that the ancestors' role in village founding and their significance to the entire village population hold precedence over the fact of their founding a local clan.[12]

Thus there are four types of divine beings of peculiarly Nyinba significance. Two, household gods and village gods, are described as guarding groups formed around sa, "land," "space," or "territory." That is, they are concerned with corporate groups that exercise claims over land. Ru gods have jurisdiction over descent categories, and clans with substantial populations are honored by collective worship. Ancestors belong to both villages and clans, but only those that founded villages are worshipped—and in their village-founding capacity. This is a divine order whose relationship to the social order stands unobscured. In both orders, the role of descent is given lesser significance. Clanship authorizes a certain kind of participation in the Nyinba community: it labels people, regulates their marriages, and supports the sense of proprietary rights in a certain Nyinba village. However, the actual clan to which an individual belongs is ulti-

[12]Todpa provides one exception to this. During an additional celebratory rite, members of clans other than Pal act in the roles of (Nepali) untouchables, that is, outsiders and inferiors. While this and other elements of the ritual suggest Nepali Hindu influence, this does not negate the fact that Todpa villagers find it important to express the social precedence of founding clans.

mately of little importance, so long as it has been granted status parity in the community.

I have said that Nyinba explain the incomplete overlap between clanship and village membership historically. In fact, there are parallels between Nyinba folk theories and the arguments of early anthropologists. We have seen how Nyinba phrase their accounts in the legends. One or more brothers are described as founding a certain village; their immediate descendants partition and so create the framework for village sections. Circumstances then bring about increasing clan diversity within villages. New immigrants settle and are given vacant properties or marry women of households without male heirs, thus adding new clans to the village. People do not see this as a problem, since clan membership has limited influence over group affairs. However, they do see this as the cause of divergence from an imagined ideal past, when clan and group membership neatly corresponded.

For the Nyinba case then, long and tortuous debates about the primacy of descent or territorial principles, about whether one is an epiphenomenon of the other, are largely irrelevant. That they are shown to be irrelevant is partly an artifact of the method of analysis used here, which begins with people's own models rather than taking the analyst's categories as the starting point and trying to fit the data to them. It is an artifact too of the Nyinba sociocultural system, where principles of descent and political or territorial memberships are distinguished clearly. While there are points of crossover and conceptual identification, they are limited. I have been able to review them here in the space of a few pages, and they pertain largely to the spheres of naming and ritual and cosmology. These are enough to remind individuals that diverse aspects of social life are not wholly separate: that clanship and household intersect at some points and that the intersection has tangible significance. If the source for it is understood in historical terms, that is the case with many Nyinba understandings of their society today.

Categories of Kinship

In speaking of kin generally, Nyinba use the term *nyenpun* (*gnyen-spun*), which literally means "affines-siblings," and individuals use this term to describe their own relatives and personal kindreds. The system of kinship terminology is illustrated in figure 3.1, which also shows how terms are applied under circumstances of polyandrous marriage. Nyenpun may also be used to specify a narrower range of kin: the relatives within a person's own generation. In this case, they are further differentiated as either "sib-

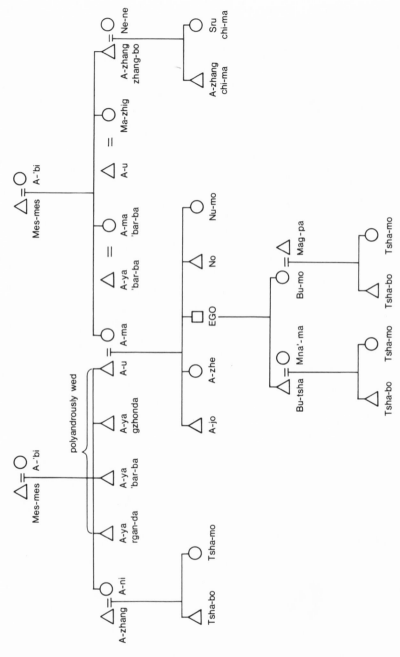

Figure 3.1 Nyinba Kin Classifications: Terms of Reference

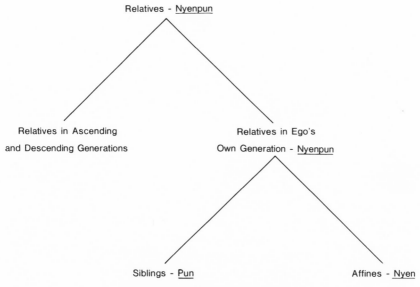

Figure 3.2 Categories of Relationship

lings" or "affines." These form the basic categories of Nyinba kin relationships (fig. 3.2).

Cross-generational relationships are described through the linkage of reciprocal kin terms. For example, there is a term for the relationship of mother's brother and sister's child (*zhang-tshan*), one for the relationship of father and child (*pha-ba*), one for mother and child (*mā*), and one for mother-in-law and daughter-in-law (*mna'-sgyug*). Finally, Nyinba distinguish between different types of kinship which can be traced from parents and their siblings. This they term the "four roads of kinship": via the father, the mother, the father's sister, and the mother's brother. These roads again yield kin who are differentiated as siblings or affines to one another (fig. 3.3).

Nyen thus includes cross-cousins and relatives through cross-sex links who are marital partners par excellence; it also is used to describe other marriageable individuals.[13] *Pun*, by contrast, includes siblings plus paral-

[13] Cross-cousin marriage commonly is found in the small-scale Tibetan-speaking societies of Nepal (e.g., Dolpo [Jest 1975:259]; Helambu Sherpa [Goldstein 1975a]; Langtang [Hall 1978]; Lo Mantang and Baragaon [Schuler 1978]) as well as among many Tibeto-Burman-speaking groups. However it is anathema to nomads and agriculturalists alike in Tibet. The reasons for this difference merit further consideration.

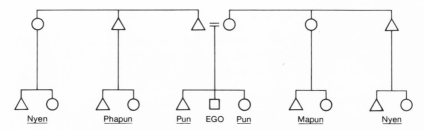

Figure 3.3   Relationships Created through Parents and Their Siblings

lel cousins or relatives through parallel sex links. These in turn fall into patrilateral and matrilateral subcategories: *phapun* and *mapun*. The former, literally "fathers' siblings," or "siblings through fathers," comprises agnates and distant relatives such as FFBSS and FFBSD (S = son). More distant agnates, those five or more generations from the common ancestor, are termed "clan siblings" (*rus-pa'i spun*). The term pun without any modifier refers to the children of one father or of polyandrous co-husbands resident in the same household. Nyinba categories of relationship thereby differentiate genealogically close and distant kin and distinguish kinship from clanship.

Affine is not an entirely adequate translation for nyen. In its colloquial English meaning, the term "affine" corresponds to only a part of the Nyinba concept. It is problematic too in its association with presumptions of alliance theory, which does not really fit the situation here. For Nyinba, nyen encompasses real and classificatory cross-cousins who are proper marriage partners and the people one has properly married. If one marries a non-cross-cousin, kin terms are adjusted to those for cross-cousins. The term also is applied to households linked by marriage and to clans that, being of equal rank, can and do intermarry. Nyen thus involves a class of individual or kinship and collective or group relationships.[14] What is distinctive in the Nyinba case is that relationships between nyen are seen as generated through nonagnatic kinship, that is, relationships stemming from women.

[14] I have translated nyen as affine and pun as sibling in preference to elaborating a cross-parallel distinction, as commonly is used for describing Dravidian kinship systems. Nyinba kinship terminology (abridged in figure 3.1) incorporates Omaha skewing rules, with relatives via same- and opposite-sex sibling links being classified differently, and contains spouse-equation rules which accord with cross-cousin marriage (see Scheffler 1972). In the past, Tibeto-Burman kinship terminologies have been compared to Dravidian systems (Allen 1976), erroneously, I believe.

The Dimensions of Matrilateral Kinship

Nyinba conceptions of nondescent kinship and kinship through women are subsumed under the notion of *t'ak* (*khrag*). Ideas about t'ak, literally "blood" or "blood kinship," are more difficult to explain than those about ru, because they incorporate several dimensions or categories of relationship which we usually treat quite separately. What adds to the complexity is that these categories crosscut one another, and there are circumstances where individuals have a choice of which to emphasize.

The notion of kinship through women is grounded and given expression in the terms of general theories of substance heredity. Just as fathers transmit their bone to their offspring, women transmit their sexual substances, which form their children's blood, or t'ak.[15] The substance a mother transmits to her children, however, is not the blood she got from her own mother, but the bone that came from her father, transmuted to blood. This is not a matrilineal notion—there is no concept of a direct line through women. Rather it is a hybrid line, going from father to daughter to daughter's children. It also passes on, attenuated, to other kin for one or two generations more through successive links of filiation. The result is that all relatives who are not agnates, are not affines, and have such a tie of blood three generations past or less are t'ak. At the same time, t'ak is defined by its bone origin from a specific clan and takes that clan's name. This suggests that what is ultimately shared is the substance of clanship.

Thus we might say that the concept of t'ak has a multiplicity of meanings. We also could put it another way and say that t'ak is a single concept for which we lack a comparable analytic category. Nonetheless, there are analytic concepts which apply to certain dimensions of t'ak relationships. One is complementary filiation. This fits Nyinba notions about secondary, matrilateral links to a clan via female transmission of bone residue as blood. Like descent, complementary filiative ties are significant for individuals' social identities and influence their position within the community. T'ak also encompasses relations of matrilateral parallel siblingship. It links the children of sisters and their descendants for three generations—so long as the relationship continues through parallel sex links. This is the dimension of t'ak that may be described as blood siblingship: it parallels the siblingship of agnates and similarly precludes marriage. Finally, the chil-

---

[15] Tibetans reportedly speak of flesh (*sha*), rather than blood. While Nyinba speak both of flesh and blood when describing a mother's connection to her child, all serious discussions of heredity focus on maternal blood transmission.

dren of blood siblings of opposite sex are considered affines created by
t'ak. By this, Nyinba place the source of affinity in maternal ancestry.

T'ak thus includes a wider span of relatives than ru and a broader range
of kin types. It is ramifying rather than exclusive. It also is seen as less
important. This is reflected in ideas about blood as a substance which has
less effect on personal character than bone heredity, which cannot be
passed on directly, and which has effects that wear off after three generations. From an observer's perspective, these views are misleading, for t'ak
has great importance for Nyinba social relations. It is critical in pedigrees,
it is as imperative as ru in regulating marriage, and it creates close kinship.
Above all, it counterbalances the isolating effects of clanship and links
members of the society. That kinship through women is de-emphasized accords with the stated view that women are less important members of the
society, and relates in turn to the systems of descent, patrifilial succession
and inheritance, virilocal residence, and a household system centered
around men and their plural marriages.

Let us give closer attention to each of these dimensions of meaning. To
begin with, t'ak provides a type of secondary affiliation to a clan and recip-
rocally gives clanspeople a formally articulated tie to the children of their
women. Underlying this is the notion that ru is transmuted and its effects
transmitted in attenuated form (Levine 1981b). Thus individuals are he-
reditarily tied to their mother's clan; they have close relationships to its
members and a stake in its identity. In identifying themselves, people will
say, "I am Pal clan ru and Khyungba t'ak." [16] This is why matrifilial antecedents have direct consequences for ranking.

This I have described as complementary filiation, a concept that has
proved unfortunately problematic in application. Part of the problem arose
from the fact that Fortes, who introduced the term, never clearly defined it.
Adding to this, the term seems intrinsically ambiguous. It describes a type
of relationship which complements unilineal descent reckoning, while
grounded in ties of filiation. The result is that complementary filiation has
been used imprecisely and for different kinship phenomena. In some contexts it has been treated as a kind of matrilateral filiation given special importance in patrilineal societies, or the reverse in matrilineal ones. In other
contexts it has been regarded as a foundation for double unilineal or cog-

[16] Following is a list of Nyinba clans, given by the name in common usage and, in parentheses, the number of household heads who are known to be members of that clan: Druwa
(31), Rawal (26), Khyungba (24), Pal (18), U-Tsang (7), Dungkarra (6), Lama, or sngags-pa,
clans (5), Tombogta (4), Khangsarra (1), clans from elsewhere in northwest Nepal, e.g.,
Dolpo (7), Byansi clans (5), and recent immigrants from Tibet (2).

natic systems, as well as having other meanings (Fortes 1953:33–34; Barnes 1971:245–50; Keesing 1970; Leach 1962). Such very different modes of kinship reckoning cannot be accommodated under the same term—ties to a mother's patrilineage are quite a different phenomenon from membership in a cognatic category or a nascent matrilineal descent line. The former use seems to be commoner in the literature; it describes a distinctive type of kinship phenomenon and is applicable to Nyinba kinship, so this is the sense in which I shall use it here.

Complementary filiation links individuals to clans other than their own. Nyinba recognize such links through serial steps of matrifiliation proceeding over generations. Let us look at this phenomenon from one ego's standpoint (fig. 3.4).

In both diagrams, the individual's t'ak is D. However, this individual can also speak of having B or C t'ak, albeit in minor degree. Such a usage is inconsistent with the notion that men and women cannot transmit their blood (which would imply cognatic descent). Yet people find this socially appropriate and a way of describing ties to many different clans. This is the very essence of t'ak: nonspecific and accommodating a great range of relationships.

The second principal concept relevant to t'ak is matrilateral siblingship,

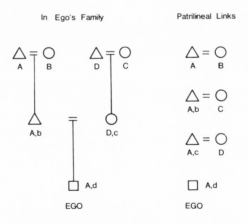

The large letter represents the ru, or
clan; the small letter t'ak, or
complementary filiation

Figure 3.4 Nyinba Complementary Filiation

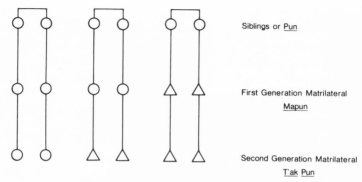

Figure 3.5   Matrilateral Siblingship or *Mapun*

the relationship between matrilateral parallel kin of the same generation. These are termed mapun or t'ak pun. Sister's children are first-generation matrisiblings; their same-sex children, male and female, perpetuate this relationship (see fig. 3.5).

Matrilateral parallel siblings are comparable to close agnates and equally are close and important relatives, although only within a limited generational span. The limitation derives from the perceived nature of blood, whose effects wane over succeeding generations. First-generation matrisiblings, who are mothers' sisters' children, invariably are close, no matter how near one another or how far from one another they live. By the second generation, the relationship is contingent on external considerations. Mapun of equivalent age, gender, or similar circumstances who live near one another may work to keep a strong relationship. Others observe the formalities—ask after one another's affairs, extend hospitality, and provide minimal aid in crises. But this is a less imperative tie of kinship. The relationship is still recognized in the third generation, but has little social significance. After this the genealogical connection may be remembered, but it does not decide the relationship. People may treat one another like pun; they also may marry, or they may ignore one another. Contrast this with the relations of distant patrisiblings who, as agnates, have the link of common clanship—thus interests in proper marriages of members, ranking, and civic prerogatives—to sustain their relationship.[17]

When people speak of their t'ak, they tend to focus on the mother's natal family or household, the source of matrisibling relations and of comple-

[17]The practice of terming distant relatives through t'ak "blood siblings" (rather than "matrisiblings"), and distant agnates "clan siblings" (rather than "patrisiblings"), highlights the distinction drawn between kinship and clanship (compare Nuer *mar* and *buth* [Evans-Pritchard [1940] 1969:193–94]).

mentary filiative ties. The representative par excellence of this household is
the mother's brother, successor to headship from the mother's father or fathers. As is often found in patrilineal societies, the mother's brother is an
indulgent and much-loved relative. His home is always open to his nieces
and nephews, and he plays a crucial part in their weddings, the most elaborate of Nyinba ceremonial events. People also have a close relationship
with their father's sister. When asked to compare the two, Nyinba sometimes describe the relationships as of equal importance; at other times they
characterize the mother's brother as more important, the warmer and closer
relative.

The children of mother's brother and father's sister are of course nyen, or
affines, to one another. Whereas one is linked by complementary filiation
to one's mother's brother's children's clan, and one's father's sister's children are linked similarly to one's own, neither share substance in common.
Another way to understand this is to see father's sister's children as having
blood from one's bone, while the bone of the mother's brother's children is
the source of one's blood. However, this is not the way the Nyinba phrase
it; what they stress is that these relatives have neither similar bone nor similar blood. Cross-cousins and classificatory cousins by cross-sex links
therefore are entitled to marry. People reason that this relationship of
affinity comes through t'ak, as it begins in kinship ties through women.

In summary, relationships through men and women both entail kinship—different varieties of kinship—made tangible through the language
of natural substance. Ru marks a narrow set of relatives and forms the basis
of the ranking system. T'ak encompasses a wider range of relatives, but of
limited genealogical span. It includes what we would describe as matrilateral kin and patrilateral kin who are not agnates and influences ranking via complementary filiation to clans. While people identify bone as the
source of stratum ranking, they also cite the impact of blood heredity, and
in practice status is assessed on effectively bilateral grounds. We can see
this in anomalous cases such as mixed-stratum unions—whose offspring
belong to neither stratum. In the natural idiom through which kinship is
conceptualized, bone is the principal substance, transmitted through men,
and the basis for what we term descent. Transmitted through women, bone
becomes blood, a secondary and evanescent substance. Blood relatives of
opposite sex produce children who are nyen, potential marital partners of
equivalent status, and if they marry, the process of bone to blood to affinity
begins again among their descendants.

Thus the model of Nyinba kinship specifies cyclical processes. Kinship
evolves lineally through the distinct types of kin that Nyinba recognize and
repeats itself over generations. It exists, not in permanently fixed catego-

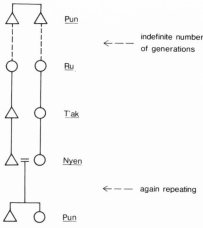

Figure 3.6 Lineal Cycles of Kinship

ries, but in movement through a closed circle over time, as is appropriate to a closed community (see fig. 3.6).

Inasmuch as t'ak derives from bone, one might conclude that Nyinba place the origin of all classes of kin relationships in bone, or male-transmitted substance. At the same time, their notions about kinship and affinity affirm—if implicitly—that women play a significant role in the kinship universe. This is an issue difficult to resolve. Nyinba say that kin relationships through men are primary, more important, and longer lasting, while kinship through women is shallower and derived. Nyinba cultural models generally downplay the significance of women's contributions—to their households and children's heredity alike.

Descent and Affinity

In many societies where the structural concomitants of clanship are few, relations of alliance play a more significant role. Among Nyinba, cross-cousin marriages occur, especially among the wealthiest households, and people describe regularized alliances between certain clans and villages which occurred in the past and commemorate these in origin legends. These facts, however, no more mean that Nyinba have an alliance system than the entailments of ru mean they have a descent system. The images of intergroup alliance—like those of villages populated by a single clan—refer to a reconstructed past. Marriages at present involve pragmatically oriented decisions and are gauged by possibilities for mutual economic and political aid and enhancements of social standing. Wealthy and high-ranking households prefer to take spouses from a rather limited circle of economic and status equals—who tend to be closely related—while immigrants use marriage to raise themselves into a new and more exalted circle of kin and affines.

Here the practice of marrying cross-cousins is seen as neither a right nor an obligation, but can be a desirable option in certain circumstances. Cross-cousin marriages are not distinguished—Nyinba categorize all people they marry as nyen, whether they are real mother's brother's or father's sister's children, more distant relatives known by the same kinship terms (*tsha-bo, tsha-mo, a-zhang chi-ma,* and *sru chi-ma*), or more distantly related persons who are then reclassified as cross-cousins. While there is no consistently expressed preference for one type of cross-cousin over another, all marriages repeated over generations that I could document involved matrilateral cross-cousins.[18]

The advantages to a cross-cousin marriage are that husbands and wives are already well acquainted and the in-marrying spouse joins a household of relatives instead of strangers. Such marriages are repeated only when the alliance has proven satisfactory in the previous generation and when other prerequisites for a desirable union are met, that is, when the boy(s) and girl are matched in age, matched astrologically, and when they appear to be compatible.

Marriage, as I have said, is confined ordinarily within the boundaries of the stratum, and Nyinba define strata as endogamous groups. This raises questions of whether marriage regulations create, or are a product of, bounded strata, and whether structural priority lies with the alliances that circumscribe them or the descent units that compose them. Such questions become meaningless when tested against cultural models of kinship. Here ru defines bone and mouth—thus clan affiliation and marital possibilities. Ru, which encapsulates both, is the prior fact. It relates agnates, is the source of t'ak, and eventually produces nyen, the offspring of male and female kin, themselves close enough to be ideal sexual partners, yet different enough not to "break the bone" in incest. This produces a lineally recycling system of kinship, in which descent and affinity are two sides of the same coin and which, as we shall see, can serve as alternative paradigms for substantiating bonds within the community.

---

[18] It is possible that I missed marriages where wives move in alternating directions. I should note that Schuler (1978:142) and Vinding (1979–80:327) also note inconsistent formulations of cross-cousin preferences in other Tibetan and Tibeto-Burman-speaking groups.

Community Integration and the Incorporation of Immigrants

Nyinba see themselves as a community closed to outsiders. They are a distinctive ethnic group, with a unique Tibetan dialect and customs which mark them off from other, neighboring groups. Endogamy is the norm and exceptions to it are rare, as are instances of migration. Yet the community was formed by immigrants, occasional immigrants still join it, and occasionally people still leave. Although migration is disapproved of, there is a way to deal with emigrants and new arrivals: to forget the former and integrate the latter. Incorporating immigrants is a very slow process, spanning generations—necessarily so, because it requires making kin and affines of them.

The first decision made about new immigrants is their placement within strata. Among the handful of people who have settled in Nyinba villages over the past few generations, most have been ranked in the upper stratum. All of these were initially treated as inferior to members of established or old clans within that stratum, but as superior to slaves-freedmen. In the present and in the world of legends, new arrivals are treated rudely, and the rationale for the discrimination is twofold: different culture and different substance.

To become accepted, immigrants must become like other Nyinba. They and their children may learn the culture, but they can achieve a place in the Nyinba kinship universe only through intermarriage and Nyinba substance inheritance. Immigrant men and their sons and grandsons have found it easier to intermarry, partly because hypogamous marriage is acceptable and partly because there are periodically more marriageable women than places for them, due to polyandry.[19]

Immigrant men may pass on questionable clan status, but marriage to women of good clans provides their children the gift of good t'ak—relatives of accepted pedigree, complementary filiation in a better-ranked clan, and respectable maternal heredity. This makes it easier for those children to marry, and if they marry well, their children gain an even-better position. Eventually, after careful marriages of four or five generations, immigrant clans are effectively transformed into Nyinba ones. People explain this as the outcome of the cumulative effects of good blood over generations. Although technically the bone remains the same, it is also seen as somewhat altered and improved. This is why members of newer clans prefer to stress their affinal ties, while members of old, established clans draw attention to their exclusiveness and the purity of their descent lines.

---

[19] Hypogamy is given symbolic expression in wedding ceremonies, which place wife givers in a superior position, a fact Nyinba themselves observe.

Daughters of immigrants may find it harder to marry, but the legacy of their heredity is more easily overlooked and sooner forgotten. Their children—of good clan and new blood—are less stigmatized, and only the more punctilious and rank-conscious Nyinba avoid commensality and intermarriage with them. By the third generation, immigrant blood is of little concern to anyone. In this way, intermarriage transforms immigrants into Nyinba citizens by equipping them with proper substance and pedigrees, as it gives them kin and affines in the community.

Blood transmitted through women may have less value, but it has this significance: it crosscuts descent categories and, like the marriage of its bearers, integrates the society.[20] It gives people an interest in clans other than their own. Moreover, it provides new immigrants a way of developing ties to other clans. This is expressed in the idiom of substance and justifies their emerging place within the community. Thus blood, like bone, features in Nyinba perceptions of themselves as a unified community.

The Nyinba community has never been self-governing and lacks effective political institutions to support its unity. What holds people together and reinforces their isolationism are a sense of ethnic commonality, shared standards for behavior, and common religious institutions. The fact that Nyinba dislike taking newcomers into their community could be explained by pressures on local resources. However, they also discourage emigration, which would alleviate those same pressures. These are two sides of a general pattern and clearly are cultural matters, grounded in perceptions of shared substance, common kinship, and long-standing patterns of marriage within strata. The ways in which these endogamous strata are linked now can be explored.

[20]The intermediary social position of women for the Tibeto-Burman-speaking Tamang is elegantly conveyed by March (1983). What she describes as "linear continuity" may be reflected in the tendency of Nyinba men to provide genealogies consisting of generations of lineal ancestors, while women give broader genealogies showing the links between living kin and affines.

4
Dependence, Domesticity, and the Legacy of Slavery

Nyinba form a stratified community. Ranking pervades concepts of descent, and the most fundamental division of all is between *dagpo* and *yogpo,* that is, "masters" and their former "slaves" and "inferiors." The dagpo are socially and numerically dominant, comprising approximately 87 percent of the population. Although the slaves were freed over half a century ago, they and their descendants remain subordinate and dependent upon their former owners. Slavery was more than an economic relationship, and dependence today is more than an economic matter; it interacts with kinship, political, and religious systems and reacts upon the system of gender inequality as well.

Dagpo, whom I will call citizen-landholders, and yogpo, or simply freedmen, are separate groups, yet mutually dependent upon one another. Their separation is expressed symbolically and has the decided consequence of perpetuating differential access to privilege. Citizen-landholders rationalize this in the context of ideas about ru heredity—that the two groups are racially distinctive and the freedmen are inferior—and also infuse slavery with historical salience through the legends that they tell. Freedmen do not deny the importance of ru, but use other ideas about heredity to advocate a higher position for themselves. Regardless of their disabilities, slaves in the past and freedmen today seem no less committed to the community than masters and citizen-landholders. Both have contributed to the making of Nyinba culture and social structure. Both are a part of it, and this held and holds slaves and their descendants to it, despite the disadvantages the former have suffered and have little hope of removing at present.

The interdependence of masters and slaves found its most elaborate expression in, and was based upon, interlocking systems of domestic organization and domestic economy. Briefly stated, slaves traditionally formed households which were monogamous and organized around women and which supported the patrifocal polyandrous households of their masters. Nonetheless, they abandoned these traditional domestic forms soon after they were freed and replaced them with those of the dominant society. Freedmen almost immediately began arranging virilocal marriages in place of uxorilocal ones, and they began marrying polyandrously as soon as they became economically independent and could afford to do so.

Premises of the Ranking System

Nyinba justify inequality by their theories of hereditary attributes, which are given tangible expression in the concepts of bone and blood, and distinctive features of their system of inequality follow from that fact. Bone (rus) is passed on through males; it is the basis for conceptualizations of clanship and provides the idiom in which commonalities within, and differences between, the strata are understood. Women pass on blood (khrag) to their children, a concept which encapsulates notions of bilateral kinship and has implications for ranking as well. Nyinba hold that the sources of physical characteristics, appearance, aptitudes, character, and even morality are predominantly bone in its pure form and to lesser degree bone transmuted in women's blood. These ideas justify the separation between strata in three major ways: in sexual contact and marriage, commensality, and the division of labor. It is these ideas which provide continuing support for discrimination against freedmen today.

Citizen-landholders hold that sexual relations and marriage are proper only between similar sorts of people—similar, that is, by rank or stratum (although not between kin or clanspeople whose relationship is so close that sexual relationships would break their bone). Sex with slaves or their freedmen descendants is seen as particularly objectionable, because they are "impure" (*btsog-pa*). This is permanent impurity; it is an inherent quality and can be transferred in sexual relations. What this means is that any citizen-landholder who marries a person of the lower stratum or any citizen-landholder woman who as much as has sexual relations with a freedman, becomes polluted as well and falls to his level. Similar ideas support proscriptions against commensality. As we have seen, the concepts of mouth and bone are used synonymously in describing shared heredity and similarity of substance. Like sex, oral contact with freedmen involves the transfer of physical substances, but its effects are uniform and can pollute citizen-landholder men and women equally.[1]

[1] Men are not censured for occasional sexual relations with freedwomen. The explanations given are that they are affected less by contact with sexual substances during intercourse and

Inherent, hereditary impurity also makes slaves and freedmen more suited to despised and polluting work. Nyinba society is not occupationally differentiated, so this has had only narrow effects upon the division of labor. What happened is that slaves were allocated the household's unpleasant and polluting agricultural and domestic chores and had to perform defiling and demeaning roles at public ceremonies. This continues today—dependent freedmen still are assigned the worst chores, serve other community members at feasts, and perform ritually dangerous and polluting tasks, although putatively less frequently than in the past. One key difference between past and present is that there is little citizen-landholders can do now when a freedman refuses to meet a specific demand. In addition, freedmen's equal rights in law have obliged citizen-landholders to limit displays of discrimination. For one example, no one today dares call any freedman *yogpo,* "inferior," to his or her face. And even though Nyinba of the citizen-landholder stratum have not stopped regarding contact with freedmen with distaste, they try to conceal this within the forms of local etiquette.

These conceptions of ranking are not unique to the Nyinba. In Tibet, inequality was structured on similar lines. Tibetan society was divided into four ranked strata: priests, aristocrats, commoners, and outcastes (Aziz 1978:52–57), with the position of Nyinba slaves and freedmen closest to that of outcastes. Both were set apart by inferiority and hereditary impurity. Outcastes, however, seem to have suffered an even greater stigma than freedmen. One possible reason for this is their full-time specializations in despised occupations: they were butchers, leather workers, scavengers, carriers of corpses, and so on, all occupations deemed sinful in Buddhism.[2] Their treatment also suggests that they were seen as more polluted than Nyinba slaves and freedmen. They were required to live separately (Bell 1928:137–38, 290; Landon 1905:210–13), and other Tibetans reportedly regarded them with revulsion (Aziz 1978:58). The sole advantage that outcastes held was that they were free. Thus their circumstances can be contrasted with household slavery in Tibet, which seems to have been defined primarily in economic terms (Strong 1960:147–62).

A major source of difference between Tibetan and Nyinba systems lies in their scale. In Tibet, hierarchical ranking crosscut large population aggregates, whereas ranking systems of the small, endogamous Tibetan-

---

do not run the risk of impregnation by a person of lower rank. Proscriptions against oral contact concern the sharing of eating utensils. However, citizen-landholders may eat food cooked by slaves or freedman and drink water carried by them. Their touch, unlike that of Hindu untouchables, is not polluting.

[2] The performance of similarly defiling occupations characterized outcastes in Buddhist Japan and Korea (Passin 1955).

speaking communities in Nepal are idiosyncratic and vary from one valley to the next. While these systems may be internally hegemonic and dominate social relationships within a society, they are externally irrelevant. Thus Tibetan speakers in Nepal may cite internal ranking systems and refer to notions of hereditary ranking in supporting claims of superiority over members of neighboring communities (see Fürer-Haimendorf 1975:270), but such claims have no value outside their own closed societies. Their only effect is to reinforce tendencies to local endogamy, because of the notion that marriage with inferior outsiders would lower an individual's status and produce children of inferior heredity. Tibetan speakers in Nepal also consider wealth in their evaluation of an individual's or community's standing. However, this is another type of ranking entirely and one more open to change. By contrast, hierarchy based on ru heredity is held to fix character indelibly and to be immutable over time.

Tibetan-speaking populations in Nepal also live within a larger, Hindu caste system. Because they are beef eaters who disregard core Hindu prohibitions, they are ranked rather low, and most people interact often enough with Hindu Nepalis to understand the system and their position within it. There are enough similarities—the fourfold ranking system in Tibet and the fourfold varna system, the view of inequality as intrinsic and inherited—for Tibetan speakers to move easily between the two systems. The similarities lead to questions of whether Tibetan models of inequality might have derived from or be linked to Hindu ones. Upon closer comparison, however, the differences appear so marked as to outweigh any superficial similarities. To begin with, behavioral forms differ: the Tibetan system requires no separation during eating or from ordinary physical contact, occupational specialization is limited, and the upper Tibetan strata are not separated by strict rules of endogamy (Aziz 1974:23–24). Second, the concept of pollution differs fundamentally. For Tibetans, pollution (*grib*) can be incurred in diverse ways: through illness—leprosy particularly—angry states of mind, murder, and slaughter of animals, as well as through menstruation, childbirth, and contact with death. People suffering pollution may become nauseated, or develop sores on their bodies, headaches, goiter, or confused states of mind. Moreover, pollution angers the gods.[3] Perhaps the greatest difference between the two systems is that Tibetan-speaking communities in Nepal invariably grant highest rank to the lineages of their first settlers.[4]

---

[3] Compare Ortner (1973) on concepts of purity among the culturally Tibetan Sherpa of northeastern Nepal, and contrast Dumont (1970) on India.

[4] Thus for the people of nearby Dolpo, the distinction between the upper two strata rests unambiguously on time of settlement. As the ethnographer Jest observes: "Nous n'avons pas affaire ici à un système rigide de castes avec son déterminisme, mais à une forme souple qui

There is textual evidence that a uniquely Tibetan hierarchical system has existed for centuries. We find similar systems among the Tibeto-Burman tribal groups of Nepal's middle hills as well (Allen 1978), and apparently all of them are based on concepts of bone heredity (Levine 1981b). In Nepal these systems coexist with the system of caste; Nyinba themselves see points of similarity between the two and use the language of caste to describe their own ranked strata. But the logic of hierarchy, the ranking of individuals, and the rules regarding relationships between members of different ranks unquestionably derive from the Tibetan system (Höfer 1979:145–46). These differences and the differing concepts of pollution may be among the reasons that Nepali Hindus pay no heed to the Tibetan ranking system. Instead they accord all populations of Tibetan origin and Tibetan language an identical caste position, above untouchables and below Hindu high castes and Hinduized non-beef-eating tribal groups.

Nyinba hierarchical distinctions, relevant to Hindus or not, are concealed from them and all outsiders. One reason is that Nyinba prefer presenting a united front to the outside world. Also, I suspect, upper-stratum members fear admitting that they interdine and live in close contact with a set of people they define as inferior. This would undermine attempts to improve the group's status in the eyes of Hindus. We have seen that individuals are concerned with their caste position and how this is manifested in the use of Nepali clan names and claims of common ancestry with Nepalis. To outsiders then, the Nyinba are a homogeneous and unified community, except to neighbors who know them well and Tibetan speakers conversant with ru distinctions. Within the community, the freedman stratum is unambiguously inferior; outside, they simply are Nyinba, and together, the two strata form a single community and, to Nepali Hindu eyes, a single caste.

The Present Views the Past

Slavery ended in 1926. This means that reconstructions of it must rely upon existing written materials and whatever oral historical accounts can be obtained. The problem is that both sources are limited. There are few citizen-landholders alive today who were young adults before slavery ended, and the last such former slave died in 1979. Added to this, former slaves never were comfortable discussing conditions of their servitude with me, although they were more than willing to describe their struggles after

doit s'adapter continuellement à l'arrivée de nouveaux venus que la société locale est obligée d'accepter. On observe d'une part une défense des privilèges de la strate la plus élevée et une réelle souplesse dans l'élaboration des règles concernant les autres strates" (1975:253).

emancipation. There is just one major document on Nepali slavery, Prime
Minister Chandra Shumshere Rana's national appeal for its abolition (1925),
and a few other descriptive texts (summarized in Caplan 1980; Höfer
1979: 124–31). The lack of such documents, however, may pose less of a
problem than one might imagine. First, Nyinba seem to have created a
slavery system that was unique in Nepal. Moreover, it is Nyinba understandings about slavery in the past that form the basis for their evaluations
of it and that inform relations between citizen-landholders and freedmen
today.

Characteristically, Nyinba offer a legend to explain the existence and
origins of slavery. Within its brief compass, the legend (abbreviated here)
describes how a group of people came to be enslaved, reaffirms their status
as an ethnically different population, and justifies their inferior status:

> When the ancestors of the present-day citizen-landholders arrived
> in the Nyinba valleys, they found a small occupied settlement near
> what was to become Barkhang village. The original residents wel-
> comed them and shared the land, but the citizen-landholders were
> greedy. So they tricked ancestors of the slaves-freedmen by advis-
> ing them to plant parched grains for a better harvest. As planned,
> the crops failed, and the ancestors of the slaves had to sell their
> lands for food. Now landless, they moved northeast to an area up
> the Dozam River. But the altitude was too high and nothing would
> grow. In despair and facing starvation, they sang:
>> To the north is Tibet
>> To the south Nepalis
>> All that grows here are low shrubs, for staffs
>> And nettles instead of real grass[5]
> Then the citizen-landholders were able to persuade them to return
> as their slaves.

While the legend may speak eloquently to Nyinba sensibilities, it is far
more likely that their slaves were purchased. There was a market for slaves
in Nepal; the slaves consisted largely of Tibetan, Tibeto-Burman, and
Nepali speakers who sold themselves into slavery out of impoverishment,
were sold as children, or were punished by enslavement for criminal of-
fenses (see Caplan 1980: 172–73; Höfer 1979: 124–27). Nyinba choose to
believe that the slaves initially formed a distinct population resident in the
Nyinba valleys, one with its own distinctive culture. This meant that the

---

[5] This is recalled in the texts of wedding songs traditionally performed by citizen-landholders
and now used by freedmen as well.

slaves belonged in the Nyinba region; yet because they were different, ignorant, credulous, and basically inferior, they rightfully came under the control of citizen-landholder ancestors. This quasi-historical, quasi-mythical charter and the beliefs about ru heredity justify a hierarchy involving slavery which had economic, politico-jural, ritual, and domestic consequences, and which has a continuing impact on social relationships today.

Slavery and the Domestic Economy

The Nyinba offer a classic case of a closed "Asian" system of slavery (Watson 1980:9–10). As in other such systems, slaves formed a distinct ethnic group. They were separated by kinship from their masters and were never allowed to become full and equal participants in the society, even when manumitted. Watson (1980), following Goody (1971), has explained this exclusivity in terms of land scarcity, which also influenced the prevalence of slave ownership and the uses to which slaves were put. In the Nyinba case, limited land for agriculture certainly affected slavery by limiting the need for slave labor. Not every household owned slaves; it seems that considerably less than half did so at the time of emancipation, and some of those households had only part shares in slaves. Slaves substituted for or supplemented their masters' labor in the wealthier households and reportedly were needed most when there was a shortage of female household workers, as happened when polyandry was rigorously observed. The outcome was a system of slavery small in scale and domestic in nature.

In Nyinba slavery, practical utility and prestige mixed; slaves formed a reliable supplementary labor force, but were an expensive way of obtaining that labor. Slave adults and capable adolescents worked for their masters three days out of four for eleven months of the year. They were employed primarily in agriculture: weeding and fertilizing the soil, plowing, and sowing grain. Slave men helped with herding and trading, but they were not permitted to trade independently, since they could not be trusted with the pack animals and quantities of grain carried far from home. Moreover, their inferior social position made it virtually impossible for them to deal effectively with Nepali or Tibetan trading partners. Slave women also washed clothing, processed grain, cooked, served meals, and made woolen cloth. Men spun wool and sewed. These tasks generally followed the sexual division of labor, in which women are responsible for the majority of agricultural tasks, except plowing and sowing, and men engage in trade.

The difference was that slave men also were used for women's work, espe-cially labor-intensive agricultural chores such as weeding. In addition, slaves served food and drink at community gatherings, relieving their mas-ters of such obligations and by this enhancing their prestige. Finally, slaves washed the clothing of the dead and disposed of dangerous ritual objects, polluting activities which citizen-landholders lacking slaves had to do for themselves.

In return, it was the masters' obligation, jointly for those who shared slaves, to maintain them. Slaves had to be provided with an independent domestic establishment: a small house, housewares, and other necessities of domestic life. They also were given use rights in marginal plots of land, which in total seem to have been roughly equivalent to 15 to 20 percent of an average holding for landed households today. The masters retained title and paid assessed taxes and therefore could reclaim the lands at any time. Needless to say, such a small amount of land, which slaves could tend only in their free time, proved inadequate for family support. It was supple-mented by food doled out from the masters' stores—food which the slaves themselves had helped produce.

The bottom line of Nyinba slavery was that the slaves were the property of their masters, a form of chattel. Citizen-landholders were perfectly straightforward about this. Elders unabashedly described past transactions in slaves—the variations in price and the various modes of transfer: by sale, gift, dowry, and inheritance. Prices fluctuated, reportedly ranging upwards of eighty rupees for a healthy young man, an amount worth four yak-cow crossbreed calves or four thousand rupees, equivalent to almost four hundred dollars in 1974–75.[6] This was a large sum of money and added to the costs of maintenance; for people could keep many slaves.

Slaves ordinarily were inherited with other property, and rights in them were subdivided in household partitions. The wealthiest families might contribute a slave, preferably female, to a daughter's dowry to support the bride and work for her in her new home. Elaborate weddings today recall and symbolically reproduce this custom. A freedwoman accompanies the bride to her marital home carrying her dowry, sits beside her at the wed-ding, and anoints the groom's head with butter on her behalf. Nowadays the freedwoman returns to her own home after the celebrations are over. A slave would have been an extravagant contribution to a dowry and a rare one, just as today it is rare to contribute as much as a domestic animal or a

---

[6] In 1983, this was equivalent to over $550, because the price of large domestic animals had doubled, although the rupee had declined against the dollar. One informant claimed that as much as Rs 120 once was paid for a slave. This still is lower than prices recorded elsewhere in Nepal (Caplan 1980:176).

small plot of land.[7] Slaves also might be transferred upon their own marriages. In theory, the owner of a male slave had to release him in marriage to the slave's wife's owner, due to slave uxorilocality. Nyinba say that there was no financial exchange in such marital transfers and explain this by their distaste for "buying" and "selling" spouses—for slaves as for their own children. However, other evidence suggests that the male slave's owner continued to receive his periodic labor services after the marriage.

Although not all Nyinba owned slaves, Nyinba slavery was common and a focal institution, particularly so in comparison to the rest of Nepal. At the time of emancipation, Nepal's slaveowners numbered less than .3 percent and slaves less than 1 percent of the population. In the Karnali region, slavery was almost as rare and apparently even more small-scale: slaves were a little more than 1 percent of the population, and 2.5 percent of households were slave-owning (Rana 1925:35, 64). That the Nyinba community included such a large proportion of slave owners might be ascribed to their relatively greater wealth. Yet Nyinba are hardly among the wealthiest people in Nepal. Instead reliance on slaves owed more to the special value they had in labor-short polyandrous households.

While the Nyinba economy was not dependent upon slavery, households rich in land and poor in women relied greatly upon supplementary slave labor. It is not surprising then that slaveowners showed great resistance to emancipation initially. Yet most soon turned to wage labor, and only the wealthiest households attempted to keep their former slaves on as full-time dependent workers. Some households simply waited for their slaves to go of their own accord; others forcibly turned them out; and still others helped them become independent, finding them land from households without heirs. In the end, all slaveholding citizen-landholders abandoned a system which they say served them well and which their heirs continue to describe nostalgically. Part of the reason for this progression—initial resistance, followed by diverse responses and the eventual withdrawal from reliance on slavery—can be found in changing conditions in the regional and local economies.

All the indications are that the need for full-time workers had declined by the time of emancipation. As we shall see, Nyinba had lost control of many of their best lands by the early twentieth century. These were the low-lying lands that could be double cropped, and they were taken over by Nepalis who lived in villages located below Nyinba ones. These villages

[7]Unlike in northern India, dowries impose only minor costs for parents. For all but the wealthiest households, they include little more than dishes, pots, pans, and agricultural tools. Wealthy women also may receive domestic animals, lifelong use rights in a plot of land, or, in the past, a dowry slave.

had expanded greatly; they desperately needed land themselves, and they used every possible means of obtaining nearby Nyinba fields. The Nyinba response was to expand up the hillside, into more marginal land, and to increase their involvements in the salt trade. Slave labor was useful for the first, but not for the second, since salt trading demands responsibility, resourcefulness, and independent decision making incompatible with slave status. And at the same time, a substitute for slave labor became available in the increasing number of nearly landless Nepali villagers living just an hour or two away. Thus slavery probably had become less necessary and relatively more expensive at the time it was abolished.

More than practical concerns had to have been involved, or Nyinba would have sold or freed their slaves voluntarily. The demise of slavery awaited a decree imposed and enforced by the central government, which also provided recompense according to the value of each slave freed. Despite this, Nyinba slaveowners resisted the change for a while. Eventually all but the wealthiest—who had the greatest use for a full-time dependent labor force and could afford the costs entailed best—switched to casual labor. In part, the recalcitrance displayed by rich and poor slaveowners alike can be explained by the way in which the economics of slavery was infused by its prestige value. This recalcitrance and the upheavals which followed emancipation also attest to slavery's cultural and social-structural centrality and to the fact that the social hierarchy formed around slavery was integral to political, religious, and in particular, kinship and household systems.

Kinship and Domesticity

Marriage and domestic organization provided the cornerstone for the arrangements of Nyinba slavery and remain central features of freedman dependency at present. It is ideas about kinship too that provide the primary idiom for discussing cultural, social, and natural differences between citizen-landholder and freedman and continue to have the greatest influence upon their interpersonal relationships today. At base, Nyinba themselves appear to understand slavery in terms far more of kinship than of economic oppositions.

There are four principal ways in which kinship defined the identity of slaves and separated them from the dominant majority. First was ru, or bone heredity, which placed slaves in the lower stratum and made them ineligible to claim clan identities. Second was the different organization of slave households, which made them the mirror image and complement of their masters' households. Added to this were other features of domestic

organization deemed crude, unstable, or simply dysfunctional by the dominant majority. Finally, slaves lacked effective kin relationships in the community. Slave obligations to their masters superseded those to their kin and
affines, which strengthened ties between the former at the expense of ties
within the slave stratum.

Ideas about ru lay at the source of slave subordination. And the fact is
that citizen-landholders and freedmen alike operate from similar notions
about heredity and rank. We have seen how immigrant men attempt to improve the heredity and status of their offspring by marriage into prestigious
clans. Freedmen who have acquired property have done exactly the same
thing, marrying citizen-landholder women unable to make better matches.
One day I heard a former slave go so far as to assert publicly that his children's and grandchildren's marriages with the upper stratum would bring
their descendants to the level of citizen-landholders within a few generations. Citizen-landholders were outraged by this statement and rejected
it—citing the primacy of descent and its immutability.

The salient fact about slave households is that they were monogamous,
uxorilocal, and small in size, whereas those of citizen-landholders are and
long have been polyandrous, virilocal, large, and multigenerational. This
is a contrast people of both strata make, and they project this view in their
reconstructions of household genealogies. Slaves occupied what were
known as "small houses" (*khang-chung*), located behind the master's
"great house" (*grong-chen*). The names are apt. I have seen a number of
slave houses standing today (mostly occupied by poor freedmen), and they
consist of two small rooms and a small barn. Relatively speaking, they are
less than one-quarter the size of citizen-landholder homes. And one may
assume that the homes still standing today were the better ones.

The households themselves formed around a woman and her husband
and children, that is, they comprised a small nuclear family. Necessarily
the arrangements for this were made by the slaveowners, who decided to
keep slave women at home and bring them husbands from other slave
households. Nonetheless citizen-landholders believe that this domestic
"female focality" and the greater attention to kinship through women associated with it were traditional practices of yogpo prior to their enslavement.
This view derives from Nyinba folk evolutionary theories, which hold that
uxorilocality and matrilineality are more primitive—and maladaptive for
the groups who practice them. The difference in domestic systems had two
consequences: it reinforced discontinuities between the two categories of
people, and it supported citizen-landholder polyandry.

It is easy to visualize how female-centered households served as a prop
for the patrifocality of the masters. The masters were polyandrous, which,

logic would tell us, involves more married men than women. Added to this, the citizen-landholder population overall includes more men than women. Here we can speak only of the present day, although it is possible that the same practices which produce a high sex ratio at present also were operative in the past.

At present, there are 118 men for every 100 women among citizen-landholders and 116 men for every 100 women in the population as a whole. This is considerably higher than the sex ratios of 95 to 102 recorded for most national populations. Nepal has a sex ratio somewhat higher than average, 105, and Humla has a sex ratio higher still, at 109 (Nepal 1984: 11–13). Although one can expect to find random fluctuations in births and deaths producing variable sex ratios in such small populations as that of Nyinba, more than random events are involved here. Nyinba express strong son preference, and this seems to be associated with the better treatment of sons, which in turn seems to explain their better chances of survival. The sources of this preference lie in virilocality and male inheritance—which make sons the support of their parents in old age—and in polyandry, which limits marital opportunities for women. Disapproval of leaving daughters unmarried and constraints upon out-marriage present another drawback to having daughters.

Nyinba citizen-landholders say that their preference for sons has an effect on child care. Mothers, for example, are said to breast-feed daughters less, although this is difficult to document, and to be more apt to leave them alone when they go off to work. It also is said—and this I repeatedly observed—that mothers give their female children foods of poorer quality: the less-preferred grains and less meat and milk. Whatever the complex of factors involved, the effects are indisputable: female infant and child mortality is much higher among citizen-landholders and more than reverses the biological advantage girls hold at birth. As table 4.1 shows, freedmen show quite the opposite pattern. This would be consistent with their differing domestic traditions, although the small number of cases makes it impossible to treat the data as anything but suggestive.[8]

While the high sex ratio may have its own logic, it also creates its own contradictions. It becomes problematic because it occurs in a society where agriculture is important and where women are responsible for the bulk of the agricultural work. In the past, slavery was used to supplement an inadequate household labor force, a function now fulfilled by casual laborers,

---

[8] The total rates of infant and child mortality given in figure 4.1 were not atypical for mountain regions of Nepal during the 1960s, prior to the introduction of public health programs (Gubhaju 1985:37). Humla still has not benefited from a substantial improvement in health services. I should add that deliberate infanticide—the outright killing of an infant—is rare and occurs primarily in cases of illegitimacy.

Table 4.1 Infant and Child Mortality Among Citizen-Landholders and Freedmen

	Infant Mortality[a]		Child Mortality[b]	
	Deaths per Thousand Births	Births (N)	Deaths per Thousand Births	Births (N)
Males				
Citizen-				
Landholders	186.8	182	98.5	132
Freedmen	300.0	20	176.5	17
Females				
Citizen-				
Landholders	245.4	163	111.1	126
Freedmen	157.9	19	76.9	13
Total				
Citizen-				
Landholders	214.5	345	104.7	258
Freedmen	230.8	39	133.3	30

[a] For children born between 1965 and 1982.
[b] For children born between 1965 and 1977.

occasional servants, and rarely freedmen maintained in small households as full-time workers. The fit between the two systems was so close that it seems as though the slavery system was developed precisely to meet the needs of a polyandrous society. Slave households were organized around the women lacking in the master homes, and slaves of both sexes performed the work of women. They served food, carried wood and water, walked behind their masters carrying loads of grain, and weeded the fields.

The organization of households around women and the use of slaves in women's work had further effects which were reproduced and ramified throughout the sociocultural system. On one level, female focality made slave women more important to their masters in a practical sense. Slave women also were the central figures in their homes and had more stable domestic lives. At another level, these facts made women the symbolically dominant gender. Finally, slaves as a class of people came to be symbolically associated with women, just as citizen-landholders are associated with men, who are dominant and predominate amongst them. For example, slaves of both sexes (as is true of freedmen today) were seated in marginal spots otherwise reserved for women. Like citizen-landholder women, slaves were economically dependent on male citizen-landholders and were denied full participation in politico-jural affairs. Slaves would take food from their master's plates, as wives take food from their husbands' plates, while the reverse never would occur. And even the small plots of land used by slave households were called by a term which also means dowry land. Thus Nyinba compounded ideas about social and gen-

der inequality, so that in a symbolic sense masters constituted the male segment and slaves the female segment of society in both systems.

However this did not imply the reverse; it did not mean that citizen-
landholder women were regarded as like slaves. Nor did anyone think that
slave men were like women in any commonplace sense. Instead the situation was one of parallels drawn between two subsystems of inequality and
between persons in those subsystems.[9] In this way, the unequal relationship
between master and slave comes to be identified with the dominance of
men over women, and disabilities of women with those of slaves. At the
same time slave women were seen as less disadvantaged vis-à-vis their men
than citizen-landholder women were to their men, because of their domestic situation, uxorilocal residence in particular, and in terms of their symbolic dominance.

That slave men and women alike were placed in conditions of economic
and political dependence and lived in households organized around women
may have affected their interpersonal relationships. However, more than
half a century after emancipation it is impossible to discover the precise
effects this had. Similarly, it is unclear whether slave women's greater importance to the masters gave them greater influence with them. All we
know is that slave women did not have to worry about being forced, penni-
less, from their marital homes by discontented husbands, as can happen to
citizen-landholder women in divorce. While this is a considerable advantage, it did not give them more esteem in society or make them better liked.
In fact, slave women seem to have been distrusted and were thought to be
more envious of citizen-landholder wealth and prerogatives than their men-
folk were. I say this because they were more commonly identified as
witches and possessors of the evil eye and because envy is thought to be
directed at those to whom one is close and who are more fortunate than
oneself (see Levine 1982a).

Slave domestic arrangements, however suited to slaveowner needs, also
contravened certain values of the dominant society. Nyinba argue that this
contravention was responsible for domestic instability, frequent divorce,
family breakups, and the like among slaves and the freedmen who persisted in these practices. They also say that because slave men married out
of their natal households, they "forgot" their ancestry. The notion here is
that stable household residence supports the retention of genealogical
knowledge and the remembrance of patrilineal ancestry—and this applies
to citizen-landholder men who marry uxorilocally as well. Failure to re-

[9] Correlatively, Ortner (1981:360) argues that systems of prestige and ranking virtually always seem to have powerful interactions with the gender system, but that prestige "encompasses" gender, in that it has the greater consequences for social life.

member descent and to take proper account of kinship ties also is blamed for the high incidence of "incestuous" marriages among freedmen today, although common sense would place responsibility more upon the small number of marital partners available within the largely endogamous freedman stratum than on ignorance or immorality. Finally, citizen-landholders say that uxorilocality, or the continual replacement of sons by outsider males, angered house gods.[10] When such a god is displeased, everything can and will go wrong. Here the supposed consequences were continued impoverishment and decline in numbers. All these arguments may be circular, but they are based on assumptions firmly held.

It is true that slaves maintain only the shallowest of genealogies and the narrowest of kin networks.[11] Of course slaves could do little for their kin either tangibly or intangibly in matters of prestige. They lacked economic resources to help one another and the freedom and the legal right to support kinsmen or kinswomen in times of trouble. They even lacked control over where they and their children lived and over their own and their children's affinal relationships. These simple rights were superseded by the interests of their masters.

In place of strong relations with kin, slaves developed special relationships with the master family. These were conducted in an amalgam of kinship and hierarchical distinctions. For example, slaves addressed their masters as "lord" and "lady" (*jo* and *jo-gzhon*), although members of one citizen-landholder clan also use the term "lord" to address their fathers. Masters referred to slaves as "sons" and "daughters" and addressed them by name, which marks their junior social position, although they also addressed slaves much older than themselves with consanguineal kin terms. The exclusive use of consanguineal terms is deliberate. Affinal terms would be tantamount to suggesting that stratum intermarriage had occurred, and such terms were not used until recently, when citizen-landholders found themselves with actual freedmen affines. Sanctions against intermarriage were never enough to prevent illicit liaisons between citizen-landholder men and slave women, and a number of freedmen today are the products of such unions. If sexual relationships between slave men and citizen-landholder women occurred, they were better hidden—because the punishment would have been extremely severe (Höfer 1979:80).

Slaves served the needs of their masters: their domestic lives were molded to support their masters' households, and their own ties with kin

---

[10] Specifically the *mkhar-gyi rtse-bla* (see chapter 3, note 11).

[11] Freedman can trace their genealogies back no further than three or four generations, while citizen-landholders list six, seven, or even nine generations and can trace kinship links to an accordingly greater number of lineal and collateral relatives.

were superseded by fundamentally inegalitarian relationships assimilated to kinship idioms. At the same time they were blamed for these practices. Slave domestic organization was considered dysfunctional, their lack of strong kin ties was another shortcoming, and their very heredity was used to justify their subordinate position (see Levine 1980a:208). Externally viewed, the slaves were exploited by their masters. At the same time, they were not without some control over their lives and not without influence upon the sociocultural system. This was achieved indirectly, through influence upon politics and most powerfully in religion.

Politics, Law, and Ritual

Legally slaves are property, and as such they have no independent identity in public life. They lack the protections and the rights of full civic status in the society (see Kopytoff 1982:219–21). For Nyinba slaves this meant exclusion from local councils and the inability to defend themselves in courts or to seek redress from those who had injured them. Nyinba simply say that the slaves had no *'ang* (*dbang*), or power, no say in decisions that affected their lives, in either formal or informal contexts.

Nonetheless slaves were not wholly subject to their masters; they had several means of self-protection. Nyinba do not trust any legal system; this applies both to the justice dispensed by their own elders and the formal legal system—all are seen as corruptible. People argue that justice can be found only with the gods, and they hold that local gods intervene actively in local affairs to rectify human-made injustices. Divine justice is especially important for the powerless, and the most powerless of Nyinba were slaves. In addition, gods were thought to be especially solicitous of the slaves, out of pity and also because of their special status as autochthons. Slaves, in consequence, were able to use the god's shrine as a refuge. If ill-treated, they would visit there, appeal for aid, and even seek sanctuary. The sanction was that the god would judge the case and visit retribution upon a master who had been unjust. Nyinba can cite a number of cases where this is thought to have occurred. One of the most celebrated involves a household whose members continue to be afflicted with mysterious illnesses, attributed to their wrongful accusation and punishment of a slave for stealing and selling sheep during a trading trip. Another household has seen every one of its men die when they reached adulthood, because, it is said, their forebears engaged in the slave trade for profit.

The institution of spirit mediumship also worked to protect slaves. Mediums are divinely chosen, and people think that gods often chose slaves as their mediums as a mark of their concern. The fact that the humanly appointed offices of lama and nun were closed to slaves gave this even greater significance. Mediumship has provided slaves, and still provides poor and powerless freedmen, a way to influence public opinion through the pronouncements they make while possessed. The idea that mediums sum up community consensus is not simply an observer's interpretation. Nyinba say that the medium does not always manage to summon the god into his body and when he does not, he speaks what he wishes or what people expect to hear.

Ideas about divine justice and mediumship provide some of the strongest examples of slave and freedman inputs into a shared culture and social structure. That is to say, slaves were not entirely at the mercy of a system created by their masters; they had an impact upon it. Slaves certainly must have promoted these practices, and some of the sources of these ideas certainly must have come from them as well. The extraordinary commitment of slaves and freedmen to Nyinba culture undoubtedly owes much to the creative role they played and which continues to make Nyinba culture meaningful to them.

Escape, Emigration, and Nyinba Identity

Despite the hardships slaves suffered and the disadvantages freedmen continue to face at present, surprisingly few have left the community. Of course slaves were not free to leave, but in the rest of Nepal escapes were common. Nepali law provided few penalties for escapes, especially prior to emancipation, when government sympathies had turned against slavery. From 1910 on, slaves who remained outside Nepal for three years could buy their freedom; after ten years they were freed automatically. Certain areas the government wanted colonized were exempt from any obligation to return slaves to their owners (Caplan 1980:173; Rana 1925:32, 43). Nonetheless Nyinba slaves do not seem to have left.[12] The only event that comes close to an escape is when a mistreated slave ran away from his master, but he went no farther than to seek sanctuary in the next Nyinba village.

There are cases of freedmen who permanently left in the upheaval following emancipation, although the number is impossible to determine. Several more young freedmen left in what they described to me as a spirit of youthful adventure, but they soon returned. The jobs they found in Nepalese and Indian border towns were menial, the work was hard, and they were lonely, unable to function well in a different language, and un-

---

[12]Rana suggests that slaves aided in their escape by Indian labor recruiters met with very harsh treatment abroad (1925:31). Nyinba slaves may or may not have known of this, but they probably had other apprehensions about escape to India or Tibet which may have been used to rationalize remaining at home.

comfortable with the climate and diet. A few freedmen tried to create a
new community several days' walk away and began the laborious tasks of
clearing fields and building homes there, but they experienced a series
of misfortunes. They too returned home, to found the freedman hamlet
Madangkogpo. A few of the poorest freedmen left their villages in 1982
following a series of famines. But they left their homes intact and did not
sell their fields, which suggests that they too hope to return.

Clearly the slaves and freedmen felt that they had no better alternatives
elsewhere; but the perceived lack of better alternatives is due in part to the
strength of their Nyinba identity and involvement in the community. Slaves
were Nyinba, ethnically and culturally. They spoke the same Tibetan dialect as their masters, worshipped the same deities, and assigned similar
meanings to their experiences. Slave commitments to their owners were
strong as well. As individuals, they spent long hours together, the households of slave and master were joined for many purposes, and their relationships were assimilated to idioms of kinship. All this served the purposes of the masters more than those of the slaves—or so it seems to an
outside observer. However we must remember that these slaves were not
culturally and socially passive, but contributed to the community and its
culture. Instead of leaving after emancipation, most stayed on and tried to
better their lot economically by clearing new fields and gaining title to vacant, heirless estates and by building their own village on vacant lands near
at hand.[13]

We can contrast the position of slaves with that of other peoples living
amidst the Nyinba. Three villages have included Nepali ironsmiths—an
untouchable caste—for generations. The ironsmiths do not lay claim to
Nyinba identity, and most do not bother to learn Tibetan. They dress differently, worship different gods, and maintain their strongest relationships
with caste fellows in other villages. For Nyinba, they are economically
useful, but socially irrelevant. The fact that Nyinba slaves were, and freedmen are, members, albeit lower-ranking, in a small, closed, culturally and
socially unique ethnic group also contributes to their continuing commitment to the group today.

Emancipation: Economy, Politics, and Polyandry

Most freedmen stayed on, and all who did so continued to live in or retain
affiliation in the villages where they were slaves. This, however, did not

[13] The sort of bonds between masters and slaves which I have described here were foreign to
Nepali systems of slavery, despite the comparable economic arrangements. While individual
slaves may have developed close interpersonal ties with their masters, they did not do so with
their masters' group (see Caplan 1980:179–80).

mean that they were content to continue under conditions of dependency. Many among them quickly set out to become economically self-sufficient, and some of the most profound changes between slavery and freedom have been in the economic sphere. Freedmen who were successful promptly severed relationships with their masters. At the same time, they began forging their own marital alliances, strengthened their commitments to kin, and transformed their domestic arrangements. Changes in the political system continue to prove recalcitrant, and freedmen have not acquired the rights of full citizens, nor have any been able to establish a strong position in local politics. As we have seen, this is justified by their heredity and their presumed unfitness for holding office and exercising power.

Not all freedmen have managed to become self-sufficient. The critical period seems to have been the first two or three decades following emancipation. Those who established themselves at that time are now self-supporting, while those who failed to do so still depend on work for their former masters. The most fortunate were the few freedmen families who acquired landholdings belonging to heirless citizen-landholders. They were able to move—virtually overnight—from landlessness and poverty to a citizen-landholder standard of wealth.[14] During this period freedmen with energy, enterprise, and enough family workers also managed to clear large tracts of uncultivated land and develop properties of their own. A few freedmen chose to remain with their masters in support-for-service arrangements modeled after those of slavery. It is they who put the least efforts into opening up new fields and who today are the poorest of freedmen.

What we find is that changes in the household economy seem to have permitted or provided the impetus for other, domestic changes. In effect, freedmen adopted a citizen-landholder style of life as soon as they could afford to do so, and more than anything else, this has meant a citizen-landholder style of marriage and domestic organization.

I have described slave monogamy and shown how slave households were centered around nuclear families with women at the core. Once they obtained property, however, freedmen began to abandon these sorts of domestic arrangements for the large, polyandrous, extended families they associated with citizen-landholders. This seems to have been a matter both of styles of household management and prestige. The Nyinba household economy supports, as it is supported by, large, male-centered households, and large landholders need a large labor force. Freedmen who came into substantial properties also tended to acquire herds and pack animals at the

---

[14]Freedman acquisitions of property occurred five times during the period 1930 to 1945. These freedmen were aided by powerful citizen-landholders who were promised a portion of the property and future political support. However, once they had settled in, these freedmen failed to keep their promises of support.

same time (while those who developed their own properties tried to acquire herds and pack animals when they could afford to do so, to improve their standard of living). As Nyinba see it, the only way to juggle the multiple economic involvements of agriculture, herding, and trade is through polyandry and the economic specialization of brothers. This nevertheless cannot explain why the poorer freedmen abandoned traditions of uxorilocal marriage. Clearly cultural preferences were involved in these decisions for change.

The five freedmen families that acquired landed estates also began a policy of intermarriage with the upper stratum. This has been easier for wealthier freedmen, because they can offer more to the occasional citizen-landholder woman who finds it difficult to marry, because of the limited marital opportunities for women in a polyandrous society.[15] Freedmen are quite open about their reasons for seeking such marriages: the promise of good blood to improve their children's heredity. This may be the eventual outcome, but there have been other effects in the meantime—and one of them has been to widen the social gap between landed estate holders and other freedmen. The landed freedmen are upwardly mobile in other ways as well, and it is they who strive most to model their lives after those of their former masters and to associate with them on as equal a basis as possible.

The majority of the freedmen, known as small householders (*khang-chā*) after the name given the households they formed during slavery, live very different sorts of lives from those of the freedmen in landed estates. Their circumstances, however, vary widely, according to the degree of economic self-sufficiency they have achieved. The poorest have essentially been left behind in circumstances resembling those of slavery, and they live—for all practical purposes as well as in name—in small households like those of their slave forebears. Some even live in the very houses their parents and grandparents occupied. These houses are owned by their former masters, upon whom they remain dependent economically.

The initial decision these freedmen made to stay with their masters proved to be a major miscalculation, for ending dependency becomes more difficult with each passing year. This is because most of the better lands have been taken, and only the steepest, rockiest, least-favored land is left. Also, poor households tend to have smaller memberships and are most vulnerable to partition and losses of household members to migration. This

---

[15] Despite the high sex ratio, it still is difficult for women to find husbands, although the degree of difficulty varies from year to year. Thus there are six cases of wealthy freedman boys who have managed to marry citizen-landholder girls who either were from poor families or had been involved in scandalous affairs. There also are three cases of poor citizen-landholder men marrying freedwomen from good homes.

creates a vicious circle, for it means that these households lack the labor force necessary to open up new lands, which offers the only way out of their poverty. With each passing year, hopes of economic improvement recede. The end result is that freedmen who have remained dependent have also remained monogamous and in small nuclear-family units, and they continue to meet the needs of their employers for female labor. All that has been altered is their patterns of postmarital residence. Although they occasionally marry uxorilocally, most marriages are virilocal, with the deciding factor being which of the spouses has more property or a better economic situation. Despite the soundness of this reasoning, citizen-landholders disapprove; they say it is something they never would consider, although they are unlikely to ever find themselves in comparable circumstances.

Certain freedmen rejected dependency at an early date. They left their former masters and started up on their own, bringing available wastelands under cultivation. This required enterprise and hard work and involved years of hardship. A small group tried first to settle an area south of the Nyinba valleys and failed. In the 1950s they were granted access to an unoccupied, forested valley between, and belonging to, the villages of Barkhang and Trangshod. The hamlet the freedmen created, Madangkogpo, is at a relatively low altitude, approximately 9,500 feet. Its lands are rich, and there is adequate irrigation, although the northern and shaded location limits productivity. This move has provided more than land, for it has given these freedmen greater personal and political autonomy than held by those who stayed within the populous major villages. Madangkogpo freedmen who had an adequate work force and were able to sustain high levels of work did remarkably well. Two of them have attained a standard of living almost equal to that of citizen-landholders within a single generation. The initial group later was joined by several dependent freedmen from Barkhang and Trangshod. Although still largely landless, these people say they prefer living in Madangkogpo, simply because residence apart gives them more independence—reduced interactions with former masters and thus greater control over their own lives. Still, a separate hamlet does not mean separate political status, for its membership is subject to decisions made by the larger village to which it belongs.

In Madangkogpo, contrasts between the domestic circumstances of rich and poor freedmen become particularly clear. The better-off households are large and extended, and their more recent marriages have been polyandrous. The poorer households are small, and their marriages remain monogamous. The general associations between domestic forms and wealth are reproduced throughout the freedman population, as table 4.2 shows. Here we see that landed freedmen follow domestic forms identical to those of citizen-landholders. Quite different arrangements prevail among small

Table 4.2 Citizen-Landholder and Freedman Household Structure, 1983

Household Type	Mean Number of Husbands at Marriage	Percentage of Uxorilocal Unions in Head's Generation	Mean Household Size	Total Number of Households
Citizen-Landholder	2.2	0.6	7.7	107
Landed Freedman	2.2	0.0	8.4	9
Small Household	1.1	21.0	4.8	19

householders. I have collapsed all small householders into one category, because to have done otherwise would have required subdividing the group into three or more subtypes with correspondingly fewer representatives in each. Thus we find polyandrous and large households among the wealthier freedmen in this group, but the majority of households remain small, monogamous, and only occasionally uxorilocal.

Thus freedmen who were able to do so moved from supporting the polyandry of their masters to forming their own large, extended, and polyandrous households. This, I have said, must be understood in terms of the multiple advantages attributed to marriages and households of this type. Given the existing sexual division of labor, there is no better way of managing a complex domestic economy. And it is to be expected that freedmen who found themselves with large parcels of newly acquired land would model themselves after the only system they knew. At the same time, large polyandrous households convey an image of strength and success that must have been particularly appealing to recently emancipated slaves—just as appealing as the chance to lay claim to one of the core Nyinba kinship values: solidarity between brothers. By contrast, the principal advantage associated with the shift from uxorilocality to virilocality among poorer freedmen seems to have been largely a negative one: avoiding the disapproval of the dominant majority—who paradoxically blamed the slaves for a practice the majority had perpetuated.

Politics, I have said, is another matter. In Nyinba villages, most offices and other political prerogatives are assigned to households and not to individuals. Some of these were assumed by the freedmen who moved into heirless citizen-landholder households. Others, however, were not, and the distinction made is particularly telling about criteria for eligibility in the Nyinba political system.

Briefly stated, freedmen were permitted to exercise rights and obliga-

Houses and fields of Todpa and Barkhang villages. Fields of a Nepali-speaking village can be seen in the distance (top right).

Todpa village looking westward. Members of the large house in the center of the picture are in the process of partition and have constructed separate front doors.

Top right: A temple household (*gompa*). This house is unusually small, because it was constructed initially for solitary meditation.

Bottom right: Reling, a shrine and Buddhist temple maintained jointly by Nyinba villagers and the neighboring community of Tsang.

Plowing and sowing
winter wheat.

Traveling to northern
Humla in spring.

Work for a four-year-old girl: carrying mud for house construction.

By fourteen, a boy is expected
to spend his spare time
spinning wool.

A lunch break in the fields—buckwheat pancakes with just-picked apricots and chilies.

The author threshing buckwheat in the fields, 1983.

Members of a Nyinba temple household at their front door.

Guests in ceremonial procession to a wedding.

Villagers take up willow staffs at the outset of wedding festivities. Together they challenge the groom's party and delay them in a nightlong contest of songs.

The man who leads the bride to the groom's home. He wears a traditional embroidered robe with conch-shell rosaries, an amulet, arrows, and brass mirrors.

Dancing following a wedding.

A Nyinba woman in all her finery.

A woman's ceremonial headdress. It is made of silver embellished with gold on a leather frame and decorated with large turquoises, corals, and seed pearls.

A former *thalu*; at seventy-seven years of age,
he is the most-senior elder in Todpa.

A village lama.

Trangshod celebrates its Mani festival in the middle of winter.

tions that were critical for household participation in local village organization and rights and obligations associated with the national political system—such as tax paying. This is hardly surprising, and the consequence was that landed freedmen continued to pay the taxes owed on their properties and to undertake rotating offices associated with the work of village maintenance, such as planning for collective rituals. They also fulfilled obligations of *trongbat,* which is a mutual-aid association of households with common origins. Yet they continue to be barred from direct participation in local decision making—exactly the sorts of activities I have linked with the concept of full citizenship and which are associated with descent credentials.

Thus membership in a property-owning household has given these freedmen the right to work alongside citizen-landholders in matters of village maintenance and the wealth necessary to do so. It also has ensured them higher social standing and greater prestige than other freedmen have. However, it has not given them politico-jural equality, in the sense of being able to stand alongside citizen-landholders and chart the future course of their villages. Even to this day, landholding freedmen have not often run for high offices in the elective panchayat council, nor are they known to participate actively in local meetings. Not until 1976 did any freedman obtain a seat on the local council—at the same time as untouchables were admitted and when its membership expanded sevenfold due to redistricting and reorganization. While landed freedmen are far more likely than others to attend ceremonial functions, they still are seated in places signaling low ranking—inside the room, but next to citizen-landholder youths. By national law, freedmen are the political equals of citizen-landholders. But equality locally, in a small community distant from government centers, is another matter.

That freedmen remain second-class citizens must be explained in terms of ideas about *ru* ranking. Heredity continues to matter so much because it is believed to lie at the root of individual character and therefore to affect political aptitudes. Stigmatized heredity also is the reason for continuing citizen-landholder objections to intermarriage (although censure of such marriages has failed to prevent them entirely). Thus in the position of landholding freedmen we find equality with regard to household statuses together with inferiority in descent-cum-stratum ascription. These combine as the critical determinants of politico-jural status in the Nyinba community.[16]

---

[16] As we shall see, descent must be seconded by household membership for rights to full status. Take the case of a Nyinba man who married a freedwoman and joined her household shortly after emancipation. His descendants are classed with freedmen and effectively lack

There are several facts to remember here. First, past circumstances of slavery are recapitulated in a persisting system of economic, political, and kinship inequality and continue to have a major impact upon the life circumstances of freedmen. Second, slavery and the inequality associated with it are very deeply embedded in Nyinba culture and social structure. Third, masters and slaves were part of, and held complementary positions within, a single sociocultural system. Some of their interdependence lingers on, although the freedmen able to afford to do so are eagerly pursuing assimilation into the upper stratum. Finally, there is the slaves' and freedmen's remarkable commitment to Nyinba society—despite the disadvantages they suffered and still suffer within it. The only explanation to be found lies in the strength of their ethnic and cultural identity. Slaves and freedmen have had no other identity translatable to the wider society and they seemingly found and find life more meaningful within the Nyinba world. This can account for the relative infrequency of emigration and slave-freedman preferences for community endogamy, which in turn reinforce the more general pattern of community closure.

If the chapter began with cultural models of descent and hierarchy, it has ended with an emphasis on marriage, household, and social structure. The system of slavery provides our first glimpse into the consequences of marital arrangements in Nyinba society. Citizen-landholder polyandry, which maximizes the number of household males and minimizes the number of household females, seemingly determined the shape the slavery system took. The fact that polyandry is highly valued, that it serves as an index to social standing, and that it also supports a certain system of domestic economy probably led freedmen to adopt it as soon as they could afford to do so. The responses of freedmen who obtained vacant estates provides as well our first glimpse into the significance of households in Nyinba social structure. Landed households are named, corporate, and stable, and exist in perpetuity. Membership within them is based on succession, rather than on descent or kinship, which is why they were open to freedmen, as they have been open to the steady stream of immigrants who have populated the Nyinba community—without reversing the obstacles to immigration that ideas about ru impose.

---

these rights, despite their highly ranked clan. By contrast, the children of citizen-landholder men and freedwomen raised in landed households stand in an intermediate position: they are considered neither dagpo nor yogpo, but "mixed" (Tib. *shag-tsa*).

Part 3

Domestic Processes
and the Paradox of Partition

5

The Trongba Household in Village Structure

Nyinba households are the key units of village social structure. They are corporate and exercise political, legal, economic, and ritual prerogatives in the wider society. Virtually all collective action is organized through households, and of special significance here, villages regulate their size through restrictions on household formation and through constraints upon their partition. This effectively blocks opportunities for immigrants to set up housekeeping in Nyinba villages, provides additional support for community closure, and goes hand in hand with descent exclusivity and normative endogamy. In consequence, household membership canalizes individual action within the village, and individuals derive a pivotal social status from their households—one approached in significance only by the statuses conferred through descent and stratum memberships. Individuals, as well, consider it desirable to avoid partition and maintain a unified household with resources undivided from one generation to the next. The avoidance of partition, of course, means polyandry, which gives Nyinba households their unique form and mode of functioning.

We have seen the cultural supports for community closure and some of its social consequences, including endogamy and constraints on migration. Closure also has an economically practical dimension. Agricultural and grazing lands are limited, and more important, Nyinba perceive these as resources that cannot be shared any further. Yet these facts—that the society has closed itself off and has so little land to share—are not the products solely of sociocultural dynamics or economic concerns, in isolation or interaction. Nyinba do not live alone in Humla; they have a history of interrelations with neighboring peoples, and Humla's political environment in particular has played a major role in shaping both the ways Nyinba view the world outside their community and the community's physical boundaries.

Humla was ruled by a set of related families of Thakuri caste for hundreds of years, and their descendants have continued to dominate Humla politics. The rulers pursued policies that exacerbated the problems of local environmental limitations, while they reinforced sociocultural insularities. Specifically, they consistently took Humla's best agricultural and grazing land for themselves and, as their populations grew, encroached upon lands used by Tibetan and other lower-caste peoples.[1] They also undermined, in an apparently deliberate way, existing institutions of local leadership among their subjects. One result was that Nyinba and other peoples like them came to place greater weight upon vertical ties to their rulers and the later successors to their power and less upon horizontal ties of solidarity within their own group and with ethnically similar groups. Another result was that Nyinba households gained a strength and significance commensurate with the weakening of village-level political institutions. It is impossible to reconstruct these processes with any precision, but there is no disputing the consequences today: that Nyinba households exercise multiple functions commonly falling to more purely political institutions in other societies.

The Legacy of External Rule

Insularity and ethnic differentiation among Tibetan-speaking communities of Humla are marked (Fürer-Haimendorf 1975:269–71). Each group has its own dialect, unique cultural patterns, normative endogamy, and an associated status system in which descent credentials have only local value. Insularity cannot be attributed to geography, for ethnic boundaries exist independently of features of Humla's difficult terrain. Many villages are separated from others of their ethnic group by major rivers and high mountain passes, yet this does not prevent the maintenance of social relationships. At the same time, they live near villages of other groups with which they have little contact. Nyimatang, for example, is closer to Tsang than other Nyinba villages are, but this has not caused Nyimatang villagers to adopt Tsang customs, marry Tsang men or women, or even maintain more sociable relationships with Tsang individuals than other Nyinba do. The

[1] The Humla caste hierarchy includes, from highest- to lowest-ranking groups: Brahmans, Kalyal (Shahi) and other (Singh) Thakuri, Chetris of diverse clans (held to be descended from the legendary Khasa of the past), Byansi (who claim mixed Chetri, Darchula Byansi, and Tibetan origins), beef-eating Tibetan speakers—or "Bhotia" like the Nyinba—and below them the occupational castes, with ironsmiths (Kami) seemingly most numerous in Humla, followed by tailors (Damai) and a very few shoemakers (Sarki), all scattered in villages of other castes or groups. Clearly there are few Brahmans although there are no census counts by caste group. Nyinba seemingly "accept" the caste system, in the sense of operating in accordance with its rules, without accepting Hindu ideas that dictate their (low) position within it.

way in which ethnic boundaries are drawn cannot be traced to any natural facts of geography; instead it owes much to facts of past rule and the division of subject peoples among their Thakuri lords.

Humla was ruled by Kalyal Thakuri for a period which lasted approximately four hundred years, ending only with the annexation of Humla by the Nepalese state in 1789. "Kalyal" refers to a dynasty within the Thakuri caste and also the confederacy of petty chieftains that they formed, which initially was based in five villages of Humla and the Karnali Zone. After their defeat by Nepali forces, Kalyal heirs rose to power again and established themselves as local representatives of the national government, a role in which they continue today. During their reign, they enriched themselves by imposing heavy taxes on their subjects; afterwards, their heirs managed to continue extracting tribute from former subjects and continued to well into the twentieth century. This undoubtedly contributed to the impoverishment of Humla—now one of the poorest districts in the country. Taxes were assessed as shares of the harvest; when they were not paid, the rulers seized villager's cattle or other prized possessions and did so with impunity. It is likely that the Tibetan groups were preyed on most, because they were culturally different, persisted in social practices offensive to Hindus, and were wealthier as well, although all lower-ranking castes probably suffered.[2]

Even more damaging than excessive taxation has been the legacy of Kalyal's division of subject peoples and deliberate suppression of effective political institutions. This can be traced in part to their own political disunity. First, there was no paramount Kalyal chief, and each chief or lord in the confederacy had rights over separate villages. This meant that different Tibetan (and other subject) communities were controlled by different Kalyal lords, who did not necessarily come from the Kalyal seat nearest to them. Thus the lords ruled independently of one another, there were no grounds or occasions for common action among the separately ruled groups, and more likely there were impediments to it.

A second factor leading to disunity was the rulers' mode of inheritance. They passed on rights over serfs and land, not by primogeniture or any unitary form of succession, but by partible inheritance.[3] The result was that

[2]Postconquest documents refer to Kalyal as Asya, lords of the land, and record various complaints against them. In 1846, for example, we find a request for a year-round garrison to control the "lawless activities" of Humla Kalyal (Regmi Research 1971:66), and in 1843, an order to restrain fraudulent, forcible collection of funds from the "common people" and to cease making claims on their property (Regmi Research 1971:213–14).

[3]This and other descriptions of the Kalyal period come from oral historical sources, checked whenever possible against written documents. For example, Nyinba assertions that Kalyal practiced partible inheritance is corroborated by accounts of identical practices among other petty chieftains of preconquest Nepal (see Stiller 1973:34–35, 47–48).

as the ruling group expanded, its holdings were subdivided repeatedly among an increasingly larger pool of royal claimants. For Kalyal subjects, this meant continual divisions in their obligations and political loyalties. Over time, villages themselves came to be divided among different lords. Barkhang, for example, initially was held by one lord, later was apportioned among two, and had been divided into three by the time of the conquest of Humla and its incorporation into the Nepalese state. This meant that taxes went to three different lords and that intravillage disputes had to be referred to the mediation of different men living days' journeys apart. If the present is any index of political action in the past, disputes among subjects were magnified by the power struggles of their leaders.

Even after the conquest of Humla by Nepal, Kalyal continued in their dominance of former subjects. This was tacitly supported by the central government, which made accommodation with them and found them best suited to the new administrative positions it created. Humla was not a district the government had much interest in and they ruled it lightly. This gave leading Kalyal even more scope for their traditional management of Humla politics, and they remained well into this century the de facto rulers of Humla. They continued as local mediators and lawgivers—a role that extended to disputes over land. Nyinba and other Tibetan speakers in Humla claim that the lords frequently seized desirable lands for their own use and favored fellow villagers and kin in land disputes. Nyinba claim too that Kalyal generally showed preference to the higher castes, but that they sometimes could counter this with valuable gifts and bribes. These conflicts over land were a chronic problem, for Nyinba villages are situated in heavily populated valleys at the edge of the Hindu-Buddhist contact zone. They are near two Kalyal villages and share common boundaries with two Chetri villages and a third, Thakuri village. It certainly is credible that they came out the worst in struggles over grazing lands, and there is other evidence to support their claims of a progressive loss of lower-altitude agricultural lands to the Chetri and Thakuri villages beneath them.[4]

Until recently, the central government's involvements in Humla focused primarily on tax collection. The government reportedly assembled the first tax rolls directly after conquering the area. This was followed by a revised tax roll early in the nineteenth century, a third in 1852, the major one—upon which the current taxation scheme is based—in 1868, and an update and revision of this in 1889. In order to manage the tax collection program

[4]This may have been a general problem for Tibetan villages throughout the Karnali Zone. As Bishop states: "Thakuri, Chhetri and Brahmin castes. . . . gradually extended their holdings as they pushed the Bhotias of Tibetan extraction to higher, less agriculturally productive terrain along the high northern border reaches of Humla and Mugu, or confined them to isolated enclaves farther south" (1978:537).

and for other practical purposes, the government appointed one or more local headmen (Nep. *mukhiyā;* Tib. *rged-po*) in each village. The institution of headmanship, however, promptly fell under, and was manipulated by, Humla's Kalyal power structure. To begin with the office reportedly went to richer men who were friends of influential Kalyal leaders. After they were appointed, these headmen continued to maintain their relationships with their Kalyal patrons and to support their policies. The fact of the matter is that it was dangerous to do otherwise. Nyinba legends recount the murders of local leaders who acted against powerful Kalyal men. Even in recent times, Kalyal men have managed successful economic reprisals against headmen who disobeyed them.

Alliances with Kalyal patrons also could be quite profitable. Although headmen were assured a stable income in the exercise of their legitimate functions, they could realize even greater profits through extralegal maneuvering. The opportunities for profit, moreover, tended to increase with the degree of extralegality. The most regular source of income was the lawful commission for tax collection (Caplan [1975:15] suggests this was worth 2.5 percent of the taxes handled). Slightly less legitimate were the proceeds of taxes on unregistered land, that is, land put into production after the last tax assessment of 1889. It was not until 1976 that the government compelled registration and received the taxes on such lands. Taxes are paid in cash; in the past they were quite heavy, and headmen could benefit enormously from their commissions and the taxes they pocketed. Total taxes, however, have risen only marginally since 1868; inflation has eroded the value of the rupee and thus the value of cash taxes. By the time the system of collectors' commissions ended and all lands were registered, tax collections were worth little.

Another right was to reallocate vacant properties. Headmen could reallocate these properties to themselves or choose among competing claimants, which meant an opportunity to favor political supporters, gather new supporters, or simply enrich themselves by demanding bribes. The five freedmen who acquired vacant properties did so by bribing headmen and promising their continuing political allegiance—promises which we have seen were promptly broken. In addition, headmen were entitled to judge minor civil cases and to keep whatever fines they imposed. Cases concerned with family law, such as disputes over divorce and inheritance, were a particularly lucrative source of income, from both the legal fines and the extraordinary illegal bribes people recall having paid to sway headmen's decisions. If headmen had the backing of powerful Kalyal patrons, they had more power themselves to act extralegally, to decide cases to their benefit, and also to protect their supporters' interests. This was the situation throughout Humla, and Humla people of all ethnic groups and castes describe the power structure of the more-and-less-recent past as a hierarchy of greater and lesser *thalu* (Nep. *thrālu*)—a term that means power broker, or big man, and conveys a sense of the virtually despotic exploitation that such men engaged in and which had such devastating effects upon Humla villages.

At the top of the hierarchy were Kalyal thalu, men who had pushed themselves into high positions and who had supporters in their own villages, other Kalyal villages, and villages of former subjects. There were only two or three such big thalu per generation; their names still are remembered, and they are the subject of narrative tales that elders recite. They worked through minor thalu in other villages, most effective among whom were headmen. Nyinba headmen, for example, ordinarily supported Kalyal demands for their traditional share of the harvest, because, as I have said, to do otherwise was dangerous and would rule out Kalyal support at times of major disputes. The fact that Nyinba villages included two or three headmen—who often had allegiance to different Kalyal patrons—was a force for divisiveness, just as were the allegiances which villages held to different feudal lords in the past.

Ultimately this meant that headmen—the major political figures in Nyinba and other Humla villages—were appointed without regard for community interests and community welfare. Their power was enforced by a distant and disinterested central government and sustained by the hated Kalyal thalu who effectively ran Humla. Their first obligations were to Kalyal, and they continued on by Kalyal approval, irrespective of the support of their own people and often to their own villagers' disadvantage. For the past two hundred years, the political system in Humla was based upon chains of patron-client relationships that had their origins in a feudal past. This perpetuated the divisions between and within villages that originated in the past and also explains Nyinba distrust of government, the distrust of justice at official hands, and the lack of effective traditional institutions of leadership.

If the central government now has become an effective presence in Humla, it has done little to counterbalance persisting local inequities. In 1962 the government instituted a system of elective councils (*panchāyat*), which are supposed to encourage collective decision making. However there was nothing to prevent already powerful men from gaining control over the councils. Ordinary Nyinba may be elected to minor offices and may take a role in the council decisions, but when major disputes or large sums of money are involved, Kalyal thalu invariably intervene. In response to this, village factions align themselves with one or another of the prominent Kalyal men who have won recognition in national politics. However, there are some advantages to the present system: offices are elective, and elections have provided an efficient means of dispensing with leaders who have proven insensitive to the needs of their constituents.

The government has made no attempt to reverse the long-standing political fragmentation of the Nyinba community or other communities like it in Humla. While it has given the village a recognized position as a distinct unit with important administrative tasks (most notably tax collecting), it never has recognized Nyinba as a separate political entity. I do not know if this is because of a general policy of downplaying ethnic and tribal distinctions, is the result of high-caste Hindu maneuvering aimed at weakening Nyinba and other Tibetan-speaking groups' unity, or is the outcome of uninformed attempts to draw up balanced districts. In any event, the four Nyinba villages were subdivided from the outset and were assigned to two different panchayats, each joined with, and dominated by, a large high-caste Hindu village. In 1976, a change in rules permitted Barkhang, Todpa, and Nyimatang to form their own panchayat council, which now is run in greater accord with Nyinba traditions. Trangshod, nonetheless, elected to remain with Simikot, the district capital, allegedly because of the difficult road separating it from the other villages (and which stops no one from attending winter weddings), more probably to take advantage of economic opportunities in the capital. Thus when they finally had the chance, Nyinba chose not to unify. Apparently they saw no advantage in formal political unity. Certainly their history has offered no experience of its possible benefits.

In what ways then do Nyinba form a coherent society and from what do they derive their unity? More particularly, how is it that villages are able to achieve stability over time in the presence of divided loyalties and of an illegitimate and corrupt system of clients using ties to Kalyal patrons for individual, personal ends? And how is concerted community action carried out in the absence of effective leadership? One of the explanations is to be found in the strong corporate households that play a key role in internal village organization. These households hold certain interests in common and must coordinate certain activities to achieve goals important to all. However, for Nyinba the rationale for village unity is to be found in a theory and model of common household origins and in a common line of village succession converging in one or more recognized ancestors and village founders. This is the model which people present when called upon to give an account of their community, and it is one congruent with many realities of Nyinba village life. At the same time, it stands in contradiction to other realities, such as clientage and the thalu system—which are regarded as immoral and are muted in formal folk explanations of social structure.

Nyinba Village Organization

Nyinba villages are important, as might be plain in the very name given the community: Four Villages of the Sunny Valley. Despite the forces for disunity and their virtual impotence in external political affairs, village households are able to act jointly in numerous internal matters. To take some more conspicuous examples, they regularly cooperate in the sponsorship of collective rituals, in regulation of access to common land, and in control over rights to village residence and membership. This makes villages closed corporate units, able to reject immigrants and disallow moves from one village to another.[5] If village households have a collective interest in discouraging gains and losses in membership, it is because village functioning is predicated upon maintaining a roughly stable household membership and a stable allocation of communal responsibilities.

Some of the most significant collective village activities are ritual ones. People see these as necessary, for reasons we would consider mystical, but they consider pragmatic, to propitiate local deities who can safeguard the crops and ensure the success of trading ventures. These rituals require considerable planning: people have to be appointed to collect household levies of grain and make arrangements for the feast and ritual performance. Villagers are punctilious both in meeting these responsibilities and attending the events. Whereas public politics constitute an arena mostly for powerful, wealthy men, collective rituals involve all villagers regardless of wealth, age, and gender. In addition, these events are quite meaningful. For individuals, the experience of collective village unity may be conveyed primarily in such rituals and the celebrations following, and these enactments of unity may provide a counterbalance, however slight, to the forces for disunity in this society.[6]

Village control over land derives from very different interests and has to be managed in ways very different from the regular staging of rituals. Each

[5] Such moves have occurred only three times in the past several generations, each time due to exceptional circumstances. In one case a poor household that had lost most of its lands to the adjacent Nepali village of They reclaimed forest land near Nyimatang. It eventually moved to Nyimatang and rebuilt its home there, but still is not treated as a full village member. The second case involved a profligate couple who mismanaged one estate in Barkhang and later were invited to assume the estate of a childless couple in Todpa. The third case, mentioned in chapter 4, occurred well over sixty years ago and involved a slave who left a cruel master for sanctuary in another village, where he settled and later succeeded to a vacant estate. All three households have been plagued by misfortune, all attributed to divine displeasure for the moves.

[6] These rites are comparable to those reported by Fürer-Haimendorf for the Sherpa (1964: chap. 6, and especially pp. 185–86). By contrast, the Sherpa rituals Ortner has analyzed in detail mostly reinforce individualism and social atomism (1978: 161–62, 167).

village holds residual rights in certain sectors of land in the Nyinba valleys, and member households hold rights of ownership over specific pieces of improved farmland within that territory. Unimproved lands, forests, and pasturelands are collectively held. Claims to these areas rest upon tradition (and are the outcome of earlier land disputes), even though all forests, pastures, and uncultivated lands actually were nationalized in 1961. The convention is that all landed, or taxpaying, households have absolutely equal rights in such land. Thus when forests or pasturelands are converted to agricultural use, each household is entitled to an equal share—a fact of significance for understanding patterns of partition.

Village households also synchronize productive activities that make use of land. The entire village moves as a group from one pasture area to the next, so all will have fair and equal access to grazing. Households coordinate dates of plowing, harvesting, and movements of the herds onto harvested land to feed off the stubble. From one perspective, such coordination is demanded by the fact that individual household plots are small and interspersed among other villagers' lands and by the need to ensure fair access to limited pasturage and to prevent overgrazing. From another view, coordination of village action permits the use of common pasturage and the dispersal of a household's fields across the village's territories. In response to this, village households join together in hiring an outsider, typically an impoverished high-caste Nepali, to patrol the fields and assess fines against owners of animals which stray and destroy crops. The fines are determined at a semiannual gathering which takes the form of a feast—which the past year's fines have subsidized.

In the past, villages came to collective decisions solely on nonproblematic public concerns; this function has been transferred to the institution of the panchayat council today. These councils continue to deal with comparatively trivial matters on which a consensus is likely to be reached. Some recent examples include how to distribute the burden of ceremonial food assessments fairly—that is, in a way consonant with villagers' differing abilities to pay—how to respond to a government demand for porters during the height of the agricultural season, settlement of a paternity case in which three men were implicated (the child was to inherit its mother's estate, so property was not at issue), and settlement of an engagement broken shortly before a planned wedding (and which might have involved thalu in the past). Local thalu, by contrast, were called upon to arrange transfer of a tiny vacant property to a non-Nyinba man who was married to a Nyinba woman. This had created much controversy locally, widening a pre-existing factional split in which Kalyal thalu already were involved.

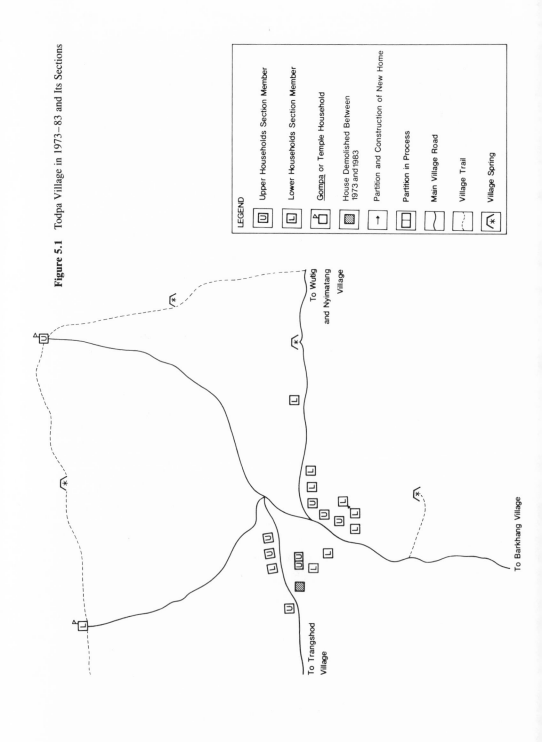

Figure 5.1 Todpa Village in 1973–83 and Its Sections

LEGEND

Upper Households Section Member

Lower Households Section Member

<u>Gompa</u> or Temple Household

House Demolished Between
1973 and 1983

Partition and Construction of New Home

Partition in Process

Main Village Road

Village Trail

Village Spring

To Wudig
and Nyimatang
Village

To Barkhang Village

To Trangshod
Village

Villages and Village Sections

Each village is divided into two to four sections. The origins of these sections are referred to the first partition from a village-founding household (Nep. *nai;* Tib. *gtso-bo*) or to the household of a later immigrant to a previously founded village. These sections play a relatively limited role in village organization, but they do have major conceptual significance and serve as "structural markers," defining key points in the village's evolution over time. Section is my equivalent for the Nyinba terms *rutsho* (Tib. *rustsho*), *yul* (Tib. *yul*), and the Nepali loanword *patti*. The first literally means "clan subdivision," the second "village," and the third describes localized lineage segments in Nepali villages. Village sections are not coterminous with descent categories, and this is important to keep in mind. Rather they are composed of households with a common partition history. To reiterate, the model of village structure takes as its center point the founding households. The first partition from these creates households that in effect found village sections. Later immigrants may join the village and in so doing found their own sections. It is from these households—through a series of branch partitions—that all present-day households within a section and village are said to derive.

Today, village sections are relevant primarily in the ritual sphere. Section members, for example, are seated together at rituals, and the seating places are rotated from one event to the next, with the explicit aim of expressing section equality. Sections take on complementary roles at weddings, and their members jointly host one another at New Year's celebrations. In some villages, each section has its own lama and dangri priests, while in others these ritual experts minister to members of any and all sections. In the past, Nyinba villages seemingly sought to match their section systems against government administrative structures by allocating a headman to each section. The village of Barkhang, for one, added a third headman to represent its third section in dealings with the government. The fact that headmen exercised major political functions in the past suggests that sections were more important at that time. While that role may be limited today, Nyinba still try to keep their sections roughly balanced in size, and villages have reorganized section systems to compensate for excessive gains and losses in membership or unequal rates of partition.

Section names often have a territorial referent. "Lower Households Section" and "Upper Households Section," for example, are common names, although sections are incompletely localized units. When households partition, they try to build their new homes alongside one another. People cite several reasons for this, among them the facts that brothers expect aid and mutual support from one another and that villages impose certain joint obligations on newly partitioned households in their capacity as trongbat. However, when adjacent house sites are unavailable or the partition was especially acrimonious, brothers may locate farther apart. Later, when the once-new houses fall into disrepair and have to be rebuilt, there will be less reason for living near one another. The kin relationship will be more distant, due to the generations elapsed since partition, and there will be fewer mutual obligations. Thus time takes households with common origins farther and farther apart. We might say that contiguity is common in sections, due to certain structural factors, and varies with spatial exigencies and personal considerations, but is neither imperative nor the product of any structural principles. Figure 5.1, which maps Todpa village, illustrates these sorts of residential moves and their end result: the lack of fit between house placement and section memberships in the village.

The Trongba Household

Nyinba ideas about households follow a Tibetan model, more specifically a model derived from Tibetan peasant household systems. In Tibet, there were several categories of peasant serfs, and each formed a distinctive type of household consonant with its special political and economic circumstances. The most prominent were the wealthy "taxpayer" trongba, who had hereditary rights in extensive landholdings, with correspondingly large tax obligations to the government. These serfs managed their own peasant village and could be described as full citizens within the village. Their households were large and polyandrous, and they avoided partition in order to pass their estates undivided from one generation to the next.

Beneath them in the local status hierarchy were "small smoke" or "small household" serfs. This included individuals who held lifelong, but noninheritable, rights in small plots of land in exchange for their labor and also mobile serfs who engaged in wage labor on a contractual basis. Both types of small household serfs supported themselves as individuals and were taxed as individuals. Thus, Goldstein argues, there was no need or advantage for them to maintain large households, unlike the taxpayer serfs who needed a large work force to manage their extraordinary tax obligations. Also there was less to keep brothers together and less reason to avoid partition, inasmuch as there was no property to conserve intact from one generation to the next. This, he suggests, led to their tendency to marry monogamously and to live in small nuclear families. (Goldstein 1971a, 1971b). The Nyinba also recognize a corporate, landholding household known as trongba and noncorporate dependent "small households" of landless freedmen. In addition to these, there are "adjunct households" established primarily for divorced women, which were found in Tibet as well.

Trongba have both politico-jural and domestic dimensions—they undertake political, economic, and religious obligations and at the same time encapsulate families. All such obligations fall upon households as groups, not upon individuals, just as offices and valuable material possessions are considered the property of the household as a whole, not any individual member. Because trongba also include families, ideas about kinship reinforce their solidarity. Individuals' expressions of loyalty to their households thus can be seen as deriving partly from the status that household membership confers upon them in the larger society and partly from the fact that the household is their home, the locus of their family life. And the fact of the matter is there is no other group individuals could be loyal to and no way they may disengage themselves from the larger household of which they are members.

Both trongba and khangchung, or small households, are households in the sense of being co-resident groups of people who cooperate in production and consumption. However the trongba is corporate and exercises politico-jural prerogatives disallowed for other households. This special status is marked in a number of ways: by a name that confers a certain distinction, by a pedigree tracing household members' links to a village-founding household, by special shrines to one or more household gods, and by the form of the house itself, distinguished by certain architectural features. The final feature of trongba status—the prerequisite for its effective functioning and ability to meet local and national tax obligations—is the estate in productive property, especially land.

To begin with, the distinctive name is important. It conveys the household's unique identity and reflects its reputation and standing in the community. The names of the most prominent Nyinba households, for example, are known throughout Humla. After partition, the wealthy and prominent households tend to adopt or be given a new name almost immediately, whereas the poorer, more marginal ones may go for years without a name. No one bothers naming them, because they may not survive. Appositely, the poorer Humla Tibetan communities—whose members marry monogamously as often as polyandrously, partition frequently, and follow a small-household model in the way they organize and speak about their households—do without household names entirely. For the Nyinba, trongba permanence, continuity, and a name go hand in hand.

The name chosen conveys distinctive household characteristics, such as spatial location in the village, the traditional office it holds, the exploits of a famous ancestor, and the like. For example, Chimigpa, "Spring Ones," is a household near the village spring, and Dangri holds the traditional office of dangri priest. *Gompa,* hereditary lamas' households with attached Buddhist temples, tend to have religiously significant names. Names also are rather conservative, so there are "Upper Houses," for example, which were once located above, but now are in the center of, a village. People are known and referred to by their household's name followed by their personal name, or more politely, a kinship term. Thus one would speak of Gongma'i *ani,* my paternal aunt of Gongma household. The names of households that die out are swiftly "forgotten," as the households lose their corporate identity and their property is merged with that of their heirs.

Trongba must also have pedigrees to link them to a recognized founder household. Most householders cannot recite the entire list of succession, and to do so is unnecessary. What they must know is their household's point of partition from a section-founder household or, minimally adequate, from a well-known household whose own succession from the section founder is unquestioned. Beyond that, the matter is referred to elders who are knowledgeable about how the present-day village evolved from one or more founder households and can identify main and branch households (and also the rare household which is unrelated to a founder). In partition, the elder brother is seen as falling heir to the founder household, younger brothers as creating new, branch households. The former is described as the inner (*nang-ma*) one, the latter the outer (*phyi-ma*) one. This reflects where they first make their separate homes: the elder brother's family takes the former hearth room, while the younger cooks on the outer hearth near the stairway. Being an inner trongba is of little consequence except in the case of successors to actual founder households.[7]

Another characteristic feature of trongba is the shrine to pholha household gods. The shrine is as simple as a bundle of arrows, one added every New Year, atop a box containing grain, salt, and old coins. When partitioners move into a new house, they take a single arrow from the inner house, "plant" it, and build their own shrine around it. A count of the arrows therefore should establish a household's age. However, touching the shrine is considered dangerous, and outsiders are not even permitted to look upon it. I, for one, saw such shrines only a few times in my several

[7] *Tso,* or tsobo (*gtso-bo*), the term I translate as main or founder household, appears in the literature as headman, chief, and clan deity (Carrasco 1959:50; Jäschke [1881] 1972:434; and Kihara 1957:203, respectively). The founder household's contemporary head is honored with special beer at collective rituals. People state that tso households exercised functions of leadership in former times, but were unable to provide substantive information about this, and the subject figures in no legend I know.

years' stay in Nyinba villages, and this was a special honor, to mark my closeness to the family concerned. The gods themselves are envisaged both in animal and human form, although the shape they take seems to matter less than their willingness to protect the household and safeguard its prosperity. The objects used for the shrine mix acknowledged symbols of prosperity (salt, grain, and coins) and symbols of male continuity (specifically, arrows). At marriage, the hand of the bride is literally tied to the shrine of her husband's home, and the thread is left on the arrows. Non-trongba lack such gods; gompa—lama's households—enshrine recognized Tibetan Buddhist deities in their place.

Gompa differ in several other ways. They stand outside village lines of succession, having pretensions instead to descent from great Tibetan lamas. They are spatially separated from the village (figure 5.1), ideally located above it and in a "pure" place. Some of their land derives from donations in return for their religious services to the village. Nominally another type of household, they are the status equals of trongba, intermarry with trongba, and organize their domestic lives on identical lines, which is why I have treated the two together in all contexts but that of religion.

Trongba households occupy a large and imposing structure described as the "great house" (grong-chen), unquestionably among the finest examples of domestic architecture in western Nepal. All conform to a standard plan (figure 5.2). All contain an inner, windowless room where the household shrine and food stores are kept, a main cooking and living room, a south-facing room where meat is stored and a junior couple may sleep, and an outer corridor-cum-hearth, all this above a maze of barns for various domestic animals and below a set of roof storage rooms. Recent years have seen some changes made in house construction. There have been a few improvements, most notably glass windows and true stairs in place of notched tree trunks, both introduced in the late 1970s. At the same time, the quality of wood used in flooring and panelling has declined, because of the loss of local forests and resulting hardwood shortages. However, the numbers and types of rooms and their placement have stayed the same for over one hundred years, as tours through old houses confirm. There are some cases of trongba in wretched quarters, households impoverished from poor economic management or unwise partitions, but these save and hope to rebuild a proper house.

Houses are also private space. While neighbors and non-Nyinba feel free to congregate on one another's roofs or the yards that encircle a home, they never enter a house uninvited.

The estate in land and other forms of productive property have major material and conceptual importance. They support households' ability to

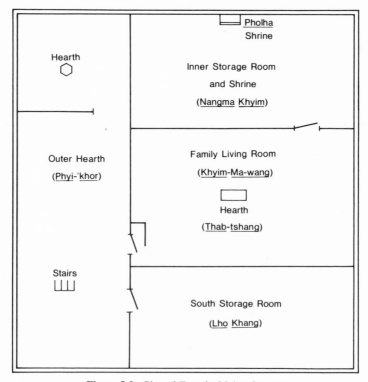

Figure 5.2 Plan of *Trongba* Living Quarters

meet such community obligations as the expenses of festival sponsorship
and the discharge of temporary offices; they provide the resources to pay
taxes and also the ability to maintain the style of life that citizen-landholder
Nyinba value so highly. In fact, all property of value is owned by trongba,
not only land and domestic animals, but also buildings and their furnish-
ings, pots and pans, tools, religious artifacts, and precious jewelry. Individuals have rights over nothing but the clothing on their backs, the bed-
ding they use at night, and simple jewelry. The other items they wear and
use are household owned and cannot be alienated except by household decision. This does not apply to cash profits from trade, which traders re-
invest at their discretion, and the dowry property of newly married women,
stored separately until there is assurance that the marriage will last. If a
household loses its land it loses its trongba status, although until the members die, there is hope of regaining that property, in effect, reincorporat-

ing.[8] Among the most prestigious trongba are those holding "old lands," that is, those that have retained the choicest fields in large, undivided plots across generations. To do so requires maintaining the trongba intact, without partitioning, which depends upon the observance of polyandry.

Trongba also have special obligations within the village. I have mentioned the contributions of grain required for staging village ceremonies; there also are a number of rotating offices that only trongba hold and that are essential for the success of those ceremonies. The most demanding office is aptly named "worker." The worker is responsible for a vast range of collective village activities: he plans certain of the calendrical rituals, organizes people in the protection of crops against animal depredations, coordinates village planting and harvesting schedules, and hosts visiting officials. However burdensome the office may be, the term lasts only a year, comes but once in several decades, and involves few special expenditures. There are a few other offices concerned with the coordination of one or another annual ceremony, but these are relatively undemanding. Gompa are exempted entirely from these responsibilities; instead their members are obliged to officiate in the Buddhist segments of village rituals.

Certain trongba and all gompa hold hereditary offices, including headman, dangri, and lama. The power of the headman may have waned in recent decades, but ritual officiants still are very important to the community. Dangri, or priests to village spirit mediums, are essential for local ritual performances involving mediumistic trances and prophecies. Their role is taken so seriously that when one elderly dangri priest died in 1982 and his modern, educated son refused to assume his functions, the village fined him, and kin and friends exerted so much pressure that he acquiesced after a few months. Later he declared that he had been much moved by the investiture ceremony and was glad he had reconsidered. Lamas officiate at Tibetan Buddhist rituals designed to secure community welfare. This and their education make them leading figures in the community and give them the authority to act as mediators in local disputes.

Nyinba models of village structure are based upon the concept of unitary origins. That is, all village households are thought to have derived from one or more recognized founders' households, by a series of (rare) parti-

---

[8] Movable property is not so important in maintaining trongba status. Domestic animals and material goods enhance the household's standard of living, but are impermanent, unlike land. They can be sold and easily acquired again and they are given away in daughters' dowries. The idea of the household as holder of an estate of movable and immovable property is summed up in the term *dudtshang*, literally "smoke habitation." Other Humla Tibetans use only this term, and never trongba, for their less-permanent, less-well-endowed households.

tions over generations. Nyinba tend to speak of this as a common source in hearth and describe village households as "split from a single hearth" (*thap-ka gchig nas phye-phye-wa*). The original, founding households stand at the core, with the later households branching out from them. This is the charter for a certain equality among trongba. Although households may hold differing rank, according to their members' stratum and descent, and may be differentiated by their wealth and political prominence, these differences are deliberately muted in the conduct of most day-to-day affairs. All trongba households have the same obligations to the village and all participate in equal measure in collective calendric ceremonies, weddings, and funerals. All pursue a similar style of life, with similarly constructed houses, similar clothes, and the same domestic items. The rich obviously have better-quality homes and a greater quantity of goods, but these are differences in degree and not marked gulfs in status. Poor households, furthermore, take pains to provide hospitality as fine as that of their wealthy neighbors, and all serve identical foods. Predictably Nyinba find it shameful to work for, or take loans from, fellow villagers, so shameful that neither employers nor workers nor borrowers nor lenders ever mention such occurences publicly. It is also inexcusable to openly cite relative clan rankings, and no one ever calls a man thalu to his face. Differences are privately expressed and are manifested mostly in quiet ways, such as in patterns of commensality and marital choices.[9]

Trongba and their Dependencies

Most Nyinba households are trongba, 158 out of the 183 households extant in 1983. Because they alone have full rights in the village, other households must be linked to particular trongba in order to stay on. The form this linkage takes ordinarily involves a pervasive dependency, so much so that the subsidiary household is no more than a part-household, largely encompassed by the dominant trongba. Non-trongba are of two types: the small households of slaves and freedmen and the adjunct households of divorced trongba members who have relinquished full rights to the estate.[10] These

[9]Thalu provide an exception to the norm of concealing inequities. Thalu, of course, cannot avoid operating openly and, moreover, enhance their power by its enactment. One must remember, however, that these thalu are political middlemen; they arise in response to external political conditions and they represent a system considered exploitative and illegitimate.

[10]There also are the homes of landless Nepalis who work for Nyinba, mostly of low, but some of high, caste. All consider themselves temporary residents in Nyinba villages and members of their original village, voting, being counted in censuses, and joining festivals only in the latter.

households have no independent economic, political, or ritual standing and derive their sources of economic support and of political and ritual articulation through their ties to a particular trongba. They are decisively separate only in the matter of family affairs.

Roughly two-third of freedmen still live in the small households associated with slave times and identified with the Tibetan households of similar name. These are distinguished from trongba in ways both symbolically significant and materially marked. First, the houses they live in are physically small, regardless of their wealth, and built on a different plan. Second, they lack shrines to household gods. None can cite a line of ancestry, either of descent or household relevance, and none has yet affected a household name. No matter how much property they own or how much land they have reclaimed, they cannot be considered estate-holding households (*dudtshang*, see n. 8). This is one of the reasons these households were not encouraged to register their lands and did not pay taxes officially until the mid 1970s. They are, moreover, obliged neither to meet community-wide obligations nor to undertake rotating offices and provide grain for collective rituals. Nonetheless, households which remain dependent upon their former masters still meet traditional obligations of serving food and undertaking mystically dangerous roles at those rituals. By contrast, freedmen who succeeded to vacant estates assumed all the prerogatives of trongba when they took over their properties.

The small household had no independent identity, nor does it today. Rather it merged with the trongba, or great household, in the conduct of certain domestic and all intravillage and extravillage affairs. The two acted as a unit economically, politically, and in religion, with the great household leading and the small household taking a subordinate position. In slavery, the two worked as one, with small householders taking on the least desirable tasks. This earned them most requisites of life, food, clothing, and the like, from great household stores. Today economic arrangements are contractual and vary according to the small household's degree of dependency. Labor obligations and payments have to be negotiated and periodically renegotiated. In all political affairs, the great household represented its slaves, and even today no small householder can stand alone in village councils. In the past, the small household was under the protection of trongba gods, but this seems to have lapsed today, with small households neither worshipping these gods nor expecting benefits from them. Nonetheless, freedmen still are permitted to come into contact with their great house's pholha, something no outsider can do. In these matters, the trongba must be seen as a dual household, incorporating unequal domestic units distinguished as great and small households.

The two households, however, clearly acted independently in the conduct of other internal domestic and all family affairs. The small household
kept a separate larder and separate kitchen for use during the slack season
and for the times they did their own work. Both today and in the past, dependent households had rights of usufruct in small plots of land. They
farmed these in their free time and this presumably added to their sense of
separateness. Finally, although small-household women helped care for
their masters' children, they still raised their own children apart.

Adjunct households (*zur-ba,* literally "side one") are rare—there are
only seven in all four villages today. These are created under one special
circumstance: to accommodate divorced trongba members who have produced children and heirs. Divorce is relatively unproblematic before children are born. Women unhappy in their marriages may return to their parents, although most prefer to elope with another man; men have the right to
bring a second wife home. But once there are children, the situation
changes. Men now have heirs, and women now have claims to lifelong
support. The practice of accommodating divorced people in adjunct households is a peculiarly Tibetan solution to problems of meeting the needs of
brothers who have lost rights to partition and of dislodging unhappy or un-
wanted wives. Fortunately, it is a practice that does not conflict with
Nepalese law.

Most adjunct households are centered around a woman and her children.
Most live in great poverty. This is to be expected, considering the position
of divorcees. Women have no leverage in the negotiations at the time of
divorce, unless they have powerful kin willing to support them. It is exceptional for a divorcee to end up with much land or many household goods
beyond those from her dowry, and most get no homes beyond a dark, dank
room in an unused barn. The contrast with an adjunct man is marked. Se-
ceding brothers tend to get decent plots of land and separate houses; sometimes they get the vacant small houses once occupied by the family's
slaves. As a result, adjunct households set up for men are better able to
support themselves and consequently tend to be more stable and longer
lasting.

From this one might assume that male-centered adjunct households
would be more common. However, they are not, because men have less
reason to leave their households and families. Men experiencing problems
with a polyandrous wife can gain the support of their brothers and other
household members to pressure her toward a better relationship. If this
fails, they have the option of leaving their children with their brothers and
going off to marry an heiress or widow. However, women who do not get
along with their husbands or whose husbands are tired of them have few
ways of pressuring them; they are unlikely to abandon their children and

find it very hard to remarry. This explains why there were eight adjunct women and only one adjunct man in 1974. In 1983 that man was still adjunct, but three of the households of adjunct women had dissolved (two women had remarried and one had died), while yet another woman had separated and formed a new adjunct household. There is one other case of an adjunct household formed for a man in recent years. This household persisted three full decades and ended only with the man's death in the late 1960s.

It is not only in resources, but also in prestige that adjunct women are disadvantaged. Unmarried women are invariably suspected of trying to entrap others' husbands; they also lack the expertise to defend themselves in major disputes. Adjunct men can call upon their brothers for aid, and as they usually have remarried, are no threat to local morality. For a man, the major advantages to adjunct living are freedom from trongba responsibilities and a new marriage. For a woman they are freedom from a miserable marriage and independence. Obviously only a small minority of men and women find the advantages to outweigh the relative poverty and lowered status entailed by severance from their trongba.

Finally, adjunct households are totally dependent, economically, politically, and ritually, on the trongba of which they are no longer full members and over whose decisions they have no authority. The trongba owns all the property the adjunct household uses and pays the taxes on the land. The trongba is the official representative of the adjunct household in all local politico-jural affairs. It subsidizes the adjunct household's participation at ceremonies and is responsible for its life crisis rituals, principal among which are funerals. In this the adjunct is similar to the small household, but its members are under no service obligation and are the status equals of trongba members in descent.

In theory, the trongba can incorporate any number of dependent or part households. In practice, dependent small and adjunct households are rare (tables 5.1 and 5.2). The incidence of dependency, moreover, has been decreasing over time. This is because trongba occasionally partition, while small and adjunct households have stayed constant or have had their numbers decline. In the past, small slave households were in demand and could be established anew by trongba or at least divided among them when they partitioned. Nowadays the trend is to wage labor, few can support dependent households, and many existing small households are moribund. There are differences even between 1974 and 1983, and I have used the earlier data for this reason. Even though dependent households were somewhat more common in the mid 1970s, they were unusual—and a mark of unusual wealth. As we can see in the tables, the vast majority of trongba stand alone: 82.9 percent in 1974, and 84.2 percent by 1983. Nonetheless,

Table 5.1   Estates and Dependent Households in Nyinba Villages, 1974

Village	Trongba and Gompa	Small Households	Adjunct Households	Total Households
Barkhang	43	7 (4)[a]	3	53
Todpa	25	2 (2)	—	27
Trangshod	48	6 (4)	2	57
Nyimatang	31	4 (4)	3	38
Total	147	19 (14)	9	175[b]

[a] The numbers of households which still remain largely dependent on former masters are in parentheses.
[b] By 1983, the total number of trongba had risen to 158 (1 of which had begun processes of partition), small households remained at 19, and adjunct households had declined to 7.

Table 5.2   Distribution of Single and Multiple Households in Nyinba Villages, 1974

Village	Trongba or Gompa Alone	Trongba with Adjunct Households	Trongba with Small Households	Trongba with Adjunct and Small Households[a]
Barkhang	34	2	6	1
Todpa	23	—	2	—
Trangshod	41	2	5	—
Nyimatang	24	2	3	2
Total	122	6	16	3
Percentage	82.9	4.1	10.9	2.0

[a] By 1983, only one trongba included both types of dependencies.

to Nyinba, trongba can incorporate as many households as they have to and can afford. Even a trongba held by freedmen theoretically could support a small household of other freedmen, although none do so, and the fact of close kinship would make this exceedingly awkward. The three trongba with both types of dependencies shown in table 5.2 are among the wealthiest of Nyinba households. They still need the full-time services of dependent freedmen and can afford the luxury of irresponsible marriages and divorce. In these households we can see the full potentiality of trongba as a corporation exercising politico-jural functions for its multiple member households and favoring its core of citizen-landholder, coparcener members.

Corporateness and the Nyinba Household

I have spoken of the trongba as a corporate unit, as the key constituent in Nyinba village structure, with the capacity to encapsulate dependent households. The term "corporate" has become a standard one in the anthropological vocabulary, and it has been used loosely, often to signify little more than strength of solidarity (Fortes 1969:291–92). However, when applied with precision, the term commands considerable analytical utility, and there is no clearer illustration of this than in understanding Nyinba trongba structure.

Fortes has provided the most comprehensive and closely argued summary of corporate-group theory and the most useful for understanding bases of collective action in kinship-based societies (1969:292–308). In his account, the three critical features become "universal succession" of corporate prerogatives from one generation of representatives to the next; the principle that "corporations never die" and thus that the death of individual members is immaterial to the group—ideas derived from Maine— and the notion that kinship corporations can be treated as single "juristic persons," because they can act as a unit in politico-jural affairs, although internally perpetuated through discrete individuals succeeding one another (Fortes 1969:292, 304–7).

Nyinba trongba fit all the classic definitions of corporate groups and in this are strikingly similar to other strongly corporate households described in the literature. First, they are "ideally perpetual 'right-and-duty-bearing units' in the politico-jural domain" (Fortes 1969:308). Trongba have an explicit time dimension: there are "trongba ancestors" recalled in pedigrees and a concern with future generations of successors to carry on the trongba name. We find a similar situation with the corporate Japanese household described by Nakane: "[it] is not simply a contemporary household as its English counterpart suggests, but is conceptualized in the time continuum from past to future, including not only the actual residential members but also dead members with some projection also towards those yet unborn" (Nakane 1967:2).

Not all trongba households are perpetuated. Some fail to produce acceptable successors and "die out" (*yal-ba*). This is a great tragedy for individuals and can be problematic for villages trying to sustain a stable membership in periods of population decline. This sort of predicament has prompted extralegal successions, such as occurred a generation and a half ago with freedmen assumptions of vacant estates.

Trongba also act as units in local political and jural affairs. No other social group is as effective in Nyinba society; the village certainly is not, a fact which I have attributed to the divisiveness of village politics and lack of effective indigenous institutions of leadership at the village level. Trongba themselves have an effective internal authority structure, a feature of corporate groups stressed by Weber. This is formalized in the Nyinba system of household positions, to be discussed in chapter 6. Another characteristic feature of corporate organization is that membership is restricted. In this case, recruitment is open only to heirs, their wives, and their children—who are the future successors. Finally, trongba are property-holding units. Property ownership alone cannot create trongba, however. A household cannot simply settle down in a Nyinba village, buy up land, and declare itself a trongba. This is because it lacks the appropriate pedigree, the line of succession to a recognized ancestor-founder, and an estate whose land and hearth derive from that founder. After the fact, and after many generations have elapsed, a settler may be declared a founding ancestor, which reminds us that Nyinba trongba are defined as such only by community consensus, and that the names, shrines to household gods, and so on are symbols marking a constructed reality.

None of these features of the trongba have structural priority—neither the existence of the estate in property nor its role in local politico-jural or ritual affairs. Nor, logically speaking, can a trongba exist functioning in one of these spheres but not others. Because this has been an issue of controversy in the literature, I raised it directly with several of my more reflective Nyinba informants during my second term of fieldwork. Without exception they found the question preposterous; all argued that these features were inseparable, equally definitive as I have described them. However there also was agreement that the trongba was first a collection of people and only second of political rights and obligations or material goods.[11]

The Nyinba household may be an especially good test of our notions of corporateness, because it is so strongly corporate. And this is because the entire social structure centers—in the absence of corporate descent groups and effective indigenous political and legal institutions—on the household. The state has used these households for its own organizational purposes, thus indirectly strengthening them, while having a neutral effect upon villages and undermining community integration. The consequence of all this is that the village has become little more than a supradomestic structure, similarly centered around kin and affines. To better understand what this implies, one must examine the individual household further and particularly its internal organization, which is based upon the marriage of brothers to one woman per generation.

[11] As Fortes put it: "What in the last resort constitutes the basic estate of every corporate group is its members, and its most valuable asset is the power and right vested in it by politico-jural (and usually also mystical) sanctions of disposing over them . . . (for) maintaining the corporation and, secondly, for productive and defensive ends" (1969:307).

6

Person, Family, and Household

Nyinba speak of their interests as being united with those of their families and households. Statements such as these may seem straightforward enough; resolving their meaning is another matter. Does this suggest that individuals regard their personal needs and goals as coincident with those of the larger group or, more simply, as well served by whatever brings advantage to the larger group? Clearly these interpretations oversimplify: household members often come into conflict with one another and face decisions made to their disadvantage. Should this then lead us to conclude that individuals subordinate their special interests to those of the group? This, however, seems to miss the point, and Nyinba neither phrase things in this way nor describe such dichotomies. Rather they seem to see their interests as encompassed by the household and the household as the arena in which their and others' needs must be accommodated. Understanding why individuals evaluate their circumstances in this way and precisely what this entails requires a closer look at the internal organization of and interpersonal relations within trongba households.

Central to trongba organization is a system of fixed household positions through which individuals transit over their life cycles.[1] These positions shape domestic relationships and structure public interactions as well. For one illustration, individuals' participation in traditional political contexts and traditional rituals depends upon their current status in the household— whether they are household heads or younger brothers, headwomen or ju-

---

[1] There are problems in generalizing conclusions about trongba to small and adjunct households, because they are only part households, and for the female-headed adjunct households, part families as well. When they do act by and for themselves, their internal organization is mostly equivalent to that of trongba. Where they are full families, their family life runs on lines similar to those of trongba too.

nior wives, retirees or children. Finally, trongba encapsulate families and include close kin. This means that the formal system of household roles is crosscut by personal kinship and family relationships and that these all have an impact on one another. The result is that the actions people take become the product of intersecting roles, so that ideas about kinship inform the understanding of mutual interests and the performance of household obligations, just as household positions affect the performance of kinship and family roles.

Another key fact in understanding household organization is the practice of polyandry, which is normative and occasionally found in conjunction with polygyny. This makes trongba large and compositionally unique, incorporating features of what have been described as stem- and joint-family systems. At one level, these large and often largely male households are the product of individual decisions guided by folk understandings of practical advantage—particularly the advantage found in maximizing the number of males within and across generations. At the same time, all such decisions are guided by a system of rules about household formation and recruitment and a set of general notions about how households should be structured. The result is a special type of household, one which shapes the way the domestic economy works.

Household Positions and Individual Goals

Households are the principal arena in which labor and its products are allocated in agrarian peasant societies and are also the center of people's domestic lives. In the Nyinba case, named positions such as head and headwoman provide the framework for this and a point of reference for individuals to measure their progress over the life cycle. The position a person holds also influences collective decisions and how his or her personal needs are negotiated. For this reason, the allocation of such positions becomes a major focus of conflict in Nyinba domestic life. The sources of contention are two: first, the timing of succession, and second, inequities between persons of the same sex and generation assigned to different positions. Problems of the first sort eventually resolve themselves as men and women progress through the various household positions and the family passes through its stages of development. Problems of the second sort do not. This is because brothers in polyandry and wives in polygyny hold positions of greater and lesser authority, depending upon their seniority by age or time of entry into the marriage. There are tangible disadvantages to junior status for both; this does not alter with time, and individuals who stay within the household must accommodate to this. As we shall see, their responses are modified by existing kin relationships with other household members.

There are other inequities as well, related to the value accorded different household positions. For one example, persons who are household sons have a more favored status than their sisters; for another, persons currently active economically have greater standing than the unproductive retired. The welfare of the former sorts of household members is treated as a matter of greater concern than the welfare of the latter, and in some households, the former are apt to find their needs more often met. This discrimination is based largely upon economic assessments, specifically the expectation that sons and active adults will contribute more labor to their households. Such discriminations, moreover, are regarded as justifiable and the normal state of affairs. The result is that household members perceived as deserving of less do not contest their positions. Rather they effectively accept their lower valuation by family and fellow household members and, by necessity, pursue their goals from a disadvantaged position.

1. Household Head

Headship is the core household position. It is the position to which Nyinba grant the greatest formal recognition and the one in terms of which all other household members find their rights defined. The term most often used is *khyimdag* (*khyim bdag*), literally, "master" or "owner of the house."[2] The key to this is formalism, that is, formal representation and formal authority in internal decision making. The head attends, and participates most in, local political gatherings and plays a major role in deciding the allocation of male tasks, such as which of his brothers, sons, or fathers will take the sheep to Tibet and who will stay home for the agricultural season. He has the final say over the allocation of cash and collective trading and herding profits, and he coordinates the male sphere of the household economy with the female sphere, which is under the headwoman. However, styles of household management vary markedly, and an ineffectual person who is head may actually have little input into decisions and simply voice the decisions made by others.[3]

Although headship is so important, marks of it are relatively subtle. There is no special term of address, and people are described as khyimdag only when dealing with outsiders or in formal political contexts. Nonetheless, there are certain reminders. For one thing, the head has first rights to

[2] Another term in use is *trong-bai a-pha*, or father of the household (compare Goldstein 1978a:209).

[3] Compare Acharya and Bennett (1981) on household decision making in Nepal.

occupy the seat directly beneath the main beam and pillar in the hearth room. For another, he holds a certain precedence in marriage, as we shall see. Furthermore, his right to the final say in household decisions offers the possibility for control over matters that concern him as an individual. Some men take advantage of this, but most give the welfare of siblings and others high priority. The paradox is that the head's authority and power are very real, yet only obliquely acknowledged and exercised in subtle ways. This is another manifestation of hierarchy obscured by expressions of egalitarianism that is a key theme in Nyinba life, which we found with clan distinctions and which also undermines effective leadership in Nyinba villages today.

Headship ordinarily is held by only one man at a time, regardless of the number of competent adults in the household. It passes from father to eldest son, or from father-in-law to an in-marrying son-in-law, or *magpa* (*mag-pa*), upon the former's death or final retirement.[4] Only if the next generation is too young will the headship pass to the head's younger brother. Once assumed it is never withdrawn, with the exception of cases of patent incompetence. Headship is transferred slowly and usually smoothly, the father gradually relegating more responsibilities to his successor, until he has surrendered them all. This marks his retirement, which most men will not accept before their sixties. There is no ceremony marking any point in the transfer; succession is a process, not a discrete event.

This does not apply in the case of magpa, which provides our first illustration of conflicts over household succession and of how kinship and family relationships affect the discharge of household responsibilities. If these transferrals of headship are not always smooth, it is because relationships between parents-in-law and magpa are not always amicable. If they are not amicable, it is because, as Nyinba see it, the magpa is an outsider, not a son. Ironically, parents-in-law distrust magpa for the very reasons that brought them to their home: that they have "renounced" their own parents and brothers (*pha-sa gtong-ba*) for what are perceived as personal and economic advantages. Correlatively, the magpa is said to resent being under a father-in-law's, instead of a father's, authority. Nonetheless, men become magpa when their marriages are unsatisfactory or when their households

[4]The magpa becomes the head of his wife's natal household and manages its estate, thus fulfilling obligations that otherwise would pass to a son. Father-in-law and son-in-law nowadays validate this relationship via a legal document, and Nyinba claim that legally speaking the magpa becomes equivalent to an adopted son in Nepali law. Nyinba do not see this as adoption in a kinship sense, in that the magpa is never regarded as a son or equivalent to one. Rather they see this as a substitution of persons for household purposes, or adoption in a household sense (cf. Aziz 1978:172).

are poor, and they say they put up with the short-term disadvantages for eventual independence and headship in their own homes. Such marriages, however, are rare; they numbered fewer than 7 percent of all unions in 1983. Accordingly, when Nyinba speak in general terms of head-successor relationships, they refer to the more common and more amicable relationships found between men who also are fathers and sons.

The ordinary processes of succession apply only when the requirement for competency in household management is met. Incompetence, irresponsibility, or repeated failure to meet ordinary expectations can lose a man his position, delay his achieving it, or lead to unusual compromises in the distribution of tasks related to headship. As the following cases show, headship also requires the consent of those led, brothers and wives alike.

> Chobel and his two younger brothers decided to remarry after their wife died and they agreed upon a very young woman. She developed strong relationships with the younger two men, but never grew close to Chobel. A short time after this marriage began, Chobel was caught stealing a religious object from a Humla temple and sentenced to one year in prison. When he returned, the wife refused to acknowledge his resumption of the headship. This and his loss of face in the community for the theft contributed to a loss of authority in the household. His brothers replaced him and assumed headship jointly.

> Dawa is a landholding freedman in his early thirties. His father was about to retire and had transferred many of the head's responsibilities to him. But then Dawa got his neighbor's daughter pregnant (they were citizen-landholders), and the neighbor brought legal action against him. His father had to organize supporters in his behalf. This strengthened the father's authority both locally and in the home and led him to resume the full exercise of headship.

> Nyima's wife died when he was in his forties and the eldest of their four sons was nearing twenty. To avoid the risk of producing another set of children who would compete for control of the estate and fearing problems commonly found between grown sons, their wives, and a stepmother, he decided not to remarry. However Nyima could not act effectively as head without a wife to coordinate the female sphere of household activities, and behavioral norms ruled out working closely with a daughter-in-law. The son, furthermore, was mature and hard working. The result was that the son married and the transferral of headship was accelerated, so that Nyima retired decades before he otherwise would have.

These accounts show the critical role that wives play in validating headship. This is partly a matter of expedience. Headman and headwoman must be able to work together because their roles are so closely connected. Each relies on the other to coordinate male and female spheres of domestic activities, and this is most easily achieved when they are married. Fathers-in-law and daughters-in-law are hampered by the respect and formality that ordinarily characterize their relationship—except where they are closely related, as in cross-cousin marriages. A wife's influence, however, can extend further than this. For one thing, she can determine whether the eldest brother succeeds to headship, as is customary, and whether it stays with him. This is due to her role as headwoman and the headwoman's general power in the home.

2. Headwoman

The position of headwoman does not exactly parallel that of the household head, because of the very different circumstances women and men face in systems of virilocal residence and fraternal polyandry. All the men are close relatives, either fathers and sons or brothers, except in the relatively rare cases of uxorilocal magpa marriage. The women ordinarily are unrelated, which leads them to treat their interests separately. They tend to ally themselves most closely with core male household members, rather than with other household women. This exacerbates competition over limited household resources and, because of the considerable advantages involved, fuels major conflicts over succession to headwomanship.

The conflict of interests between household women has two further sources. First, women's primary moral obligations are to their separate sets of children. Second, women's rights in the trongba are never as secure as mens' and remains less secure throughout their lives. They enter households as outsiders and remain in them only if they can win the acceptance of their parents-in-law and the affection of their husbands. This depends in large part on their work contributions and on bearing sons who can assure their support in old age. Because household prerogatives derive wholly from relationships to household males, there is little incentive for women to forge alliances with one another. There is one major exception to this: uxorilocal marriage, where the women are related as mother and daughter. Nyinba also observe that aunts and nieces in cross-cousin marriages tend to have more harmonious relationships. And, as we shall see, problems similarly are minimized when co-wives are sisters. There also are some mothers-in-law and daughters-in-law who simply get along well together, manage to share responsibility, and pass on headwomanship without conflict, but they are in the minority. What this suggests is that Nyinba view kinship in households, like kinship in any transaction, as the most reliable basis for trust.

People often remark on this. They also note that struggles for power between mothers-in-law and daughters-in-law are inevitably self-defeating. The mother-in-law, for one, can make excessive demands, assign her daughter-in-law all the heavy labor, and so on, and try to delay the loss of her own position. However, when the daughter-in-law finally becomes headwoman, she can be equally difficult and make her mother-in-law's retirement miserable by withholding food and pushing her parents-in-law out of the warm hearth room where the rest of the family sleeps. This has happened often enough, and there are enough cautionary tales to provide fair warning to everyone. Nonetheless the same struggles for ascendancy and the same tragedies of interpersonal discord between mothers-in-law and daughters-in-law are repeated generation after generation. These are problems that eventually end with the deaths of the parents-in-law. By contrast, conflicts between co-wives may be even more serious, and they have no resolution, lasting the women's entire lives.

While the position of headwoman is normally held by the senior wife of the head, there are exceptions to this. For example, the head's mother may manage to hold on to her position after her husband's death or retirement. Such a crossover in generations is possible because mother and son are used to cooperating in household affairs. Father and daughter in uxorilocal marriages probably could manage the household together too, although I have never seen this happen. Other exceptions may be traced to household politics and issues of competency. A few years ago, a senior wife who was barren and had managed to alienate all of her husbands lost headwomanship to her junior co-wife. Other barren senior wives have led households, so this was not the issue. Rather it was the woman's inability to work cooperatively with key household personnel. Poor management and declining health are reasons a number of mothers-in-law have been forced to retire early.

The headwoman's duties involve supervising and assigning tasks related to women's work. This includes weeding, washing clothes, storing agricultural produce, and deciding what can safely be sold versus what is needed in the home. Like the head, the headwoman sits in a special place above the hearth, with the head to her right, her eldest daughter or junior wife to her left, and children and retired in-laws—dependents, that is—opposite and below her. She cooks there, with household members surrounding her, and this facilitates her domination over mealtime conversations. Since she serves the meals as well, she can regulate the portions to reward her allies with better or more food. People joke about this; they also see it as an abuse of prerogatives, one that may give rise to quarreling and if continued may lead to serious problems.

The position of headwoman is marked even less than that of head and is given no official governmental recognition. However, and this is a key and quite a predictable exception, headwomen are honored at weddings.

3. Junior Coparceners

In most Nyinba households, there is more than one "brother" in a given generation. That is, there is more than one male pun, a term that describes all the siblings born from a single marriage. Since all pun marry polyandrously and sometimes jointly marry more than one wife, their children can have widely varying parentage. From a structural standpoint, these siblings are no different from brothers and sisters whose parents are the same. Internally their relationships may differ, and there are ways in which kinship counts. As we shall see, brothers describe fraternal solidarity as dependent on the closeness of their kin ties.

The eldest brother normally becomes the head; the others are junior to him and are expected to acquiesce to his leadership. It is a fair summation of relations between brothers to say that they are shaped both by the ideal of cooperation and implicit, if limited, hierarchy. This does not mean that younger brothers are effectively powerless in household affairs. Rather their position is of rights and responsibilities attenuated, but similar to those of the head. Thus a younger brother may be described as khyimdag, "master of the house," but the eldest is distinguished as the "real" household head.

This unequal distribution of authority ordinarily creates few problems. From childhood, eldest sons are instructed by their parents to look after younger brothers and place their welfare on a level with their own. Later, their joining in a common marriage that produces a common set of children can—if the marriage is successful—bring them even closer. In my years with the Nyinba I never heard anyone complain of an eldest brother letting his interests dominate, although I did hear of several younger brothers described as self-centered. Some elder brothers were considered unfair in repeatedly sending one brother on winter salt-trading journeys, but major inequities invariably were blamed on the headwoman for favoring one brother or another and influencing the head's decisions accordingly. Who really is at fault in such cases is another issue, but Nyinba, men and women alike, more often blame a wife than a brother.

Thus the division of responsibilities in the trongba demands very different behaviors from older and younger brothers, and Nyinba parents raise their sons differently, ostensibly to prepare them for this. From childhood, the eldest is encouraged to be serious, to take on responsibilities, and to lead his younger siblings, and the younger ones are encouraged to rely on him. This applies to play, to their earliest work efforts, and to their earliest interactions with fellow villagers.

Although relations between brothers are ordinarily cooperative, the ultimate sanction that younger brothers hold is the right to demand partition. That right is guaranteed by Nepali law, which follows Hindu legal traditions. It gives brothers an equal interest in household property and the right to obtain their share upon reaching legal majority. These legal rights run counter to Tibetan traditions, in which brothers who separate from their trongba may leave with little or nothing (see Aziz 1978:144–45; Goldstein 1978a). For Nyinba, partition is a last resort, and ordinarily brothers trust first to appeals to kinship morality and second to threats of not working for the household group.

4. Co-wives

Relations between senior and junior co-wives are predictably the most conflict ridden in a household. This is because the women are the nuclei of separate families and potentially of separate households. From the outset, their interests are divided. The first wife is known as the household's "daughter-in-law" (*mna'-ma*) and the latter as the "second wife" (*chunma*), a term held to be somewhat derogatory and never used to any woman's face. Technically both are daughters-in-law, and when speaking formally or in public, the first wife will be described as the "senior" (*rgan-da*) daughter-in-law. The immediate source of tension between the two is the unequal distribution of household authority, exacerbated, when both are fertile, by their responsibility to their children. When the senior wife becomes headwoman, her control over household resources allows her to benefit her own, at the expense of co-wives', children. This rivalry and the resulting inequities are mitigated when the co-wives are sisters, trained in childhood to work together, and concerned about one another's needs and one another's children, who are their own nieces and nephews. I can cite a case to illustrate the effect of sisterhood on co-wives' relationships.

> Yogma household had three brothers who serially married three wives. The first two were sisters, and the third was unrelated. Although the first wife and older sister was headwoman, she shared her prerogatives with her sister. They alternated sitting above the '

hearth to cook, cooperated in managing household stores, and so
on. The two of them excluded the third wife from any important
decisions. Although a beautiful woman and much loved by her
principal husband, she lived a life of effective marginality in her
marital home.

Again we see how kinship and family impinge upon the conduct of
household relationships, and the consequences are nowhere more grave
than in the relationships between co-wives. Women who are unrelated have
separate kindreds, and even those who are related produce separate families. The existence of distinct families within a single household intensifies
competition over resources and weakens commitments to the welfare of the
larger group. The result may be incessant conflict, progressive deteriora-
tion in interpersonal relationships, and eventually relationships so damaged
that partition seems the only possible resolution. This serves as one of the
strongest arguments against polygynous marriage.

5. Household Children

The circumstances of children vary according to their gender and birth
positions; there is no ideology of equality of treatment for boys and girls,
or for first- and second-born children. Boys are preferred explicitly, for
reasons of trongba rules and trongba structure. Sons are needed to succeed
their fathers; they are better trusted for management of the estate and
simply the better vehicle for perpetuating the trongba and its ancestors'
names. Girls are seen as useful primarily for establishing alliances with
other households, but as contributing little directly to their natal households. Although they are acknowledged to work harder than boys as children, they are lost to other households as adults. Because of this, boys are
said to be better treated, better fed, and better clothed—more conspicu-
ously indulged. The preference is for sons and is most strongly expressed
for the eldest.
    Children of different sexes make different contributions to the household
economically. Girls are workers from an earlier age, baby-sitting for siblings, following their mothers to the spring and carrying tiny jugs of water
home, and removing stones from grain; later they pasture cattle, weed
the fields, and so on. Boys do little more than fetch things for their elders
until their mid-teens, when they begin undertaking adult labor responsibilities. Children are seen as essentially nonproductive household members,
and once they begin to be productive, they are no longer considered children, but rather adults. Unlike their Hindu neighbors, Nyinba do not see

children as necessary to families for ritual or symbolic reasons. Rather they are necessary to households and largely for political reasons. A childless couple is pitied because they lack children to care for them in old age, but pitied even more for the lack of proper successors to the estate. From a household perspective, children are valued for what they will become, for their potential role as successors and transmitters of trongba corporate continuity.

6. Retirees

Retirement occurs when the next generation fully assumes the rights and duties associated with headship or headwomanship. There are three basic factors influencing the treatment of retirees: how well they formerly discharged their household responsibilities, how productive they remain, and their kinship ties—being parents, grandparents, and so on, to other members of the household. Thus we find men who were good household heads better taken care of when they age, and competent and fair headwomen more fairly treated by their daughters-in-law. Also, men and women who have their own sons in the household tend to be better treated than those without. What retirees need most is a decent level of care when they are no longer economically productive, although many are denied this. The ideal, hardly ever met, is an early release from work so that they can devote their declining years to religion, to better prepare for their next rebirth. If poorly treated, however, the elderly have no place else to go and must make the best of a bad situation.

Competence, Conformity, and Mutual Dependence

Nyinba express great concern with work competence—it is one of the major considerations in choosing a spouse; and one of the greatest compliments that can be paid a man or woman is that he or she is skilled and hardworking. However, there always are individuals who seriously fail their households. The commonest problems, as is no doubt true anywhere in the world, are failures in performance and responsibility. The prototypical bad Nyinba household members are the persons who shirk work, those who emigrate for personal ends, and among traders those who spend their profits on themselves. Laziness and irresponsibility are major concerns here because they affect the entire household; they can also exacerbate problems in interpersonal relationships and accelerate the progress toward partition or household extinction.

The first example to consider is that of a lazy wife. The presence of such a woman in a household can be disastrous, due to predominant polyandry, the low sex ratio of women in trongba, and the heavy work responsibilities they carry. To cite a classic case:

> A Barkhang household was poverty-stricken until about two decades ago, when they inherited the estate of an heirless widow. Previously there was little work to do, but after the inheritance, wife Kardzom's laziness became even more of a problem. She always had hated agricultural work, and now there was even more to avoid. The household finally could afford imported wool for clothing, but Kardzom disliked weaving too and did it rather poorly. Her parents-in-law hadn't gotten along with her, for these reasons precisely, and when they retired, she took out years of pent-up resentment on them, limiting their food and turning them out of the main hearth room. The household head remonstrated with her, but nothing helped. Because of this, Kardzom's household wore rags and had to borrow food annually from those with less land than they. Kardzom had more free time than any woman in the village, but had few friends to spend it with, because people disapproved of her laziness.

There also is the recent case of a lama who put his personal desires first, deserted his family, and repudiated his religious obligations to his village.

> Tenzing headed a local temple household. However, as he explains it, he was dissatisfied with the lack of opportunity for further learning and spiritual advancement in Humla. So he abandoned his wife and children and moved to Tibetan refugee centers of monastic learning, including Kathmandu, which is where I met him. His wife remained in their home and raised their son, who now is married and has a child of his own. Yet for over a decade they were very poor, with a lone woman and no other adults to help with household support. Meanwhile, the village had to manage with one fewer lama. People dismiss Tenzing as a confirmed wanderer (*nas 'khor-ba*) who never will settle down.

Finally there are instances of fortunes made in trade, then lost by self-indulgent and irresponsible young men.

> Gyaltshan and Jigme are young men in their early twenties who became involved in high-risk trading ventures in Tibet. In 1982, they made almost two thousand dollars each, a small fortune by Humla standards. They set out for India and squandered their

money on restaurants, hotels catering to foreigners, and prostitutes. They arrived home without a cent to their names, much less the trade goods they were supposed to buy. Jigme had disgraced his parents some years previously by convincing members of another ethnic group to invest in a fraudulent business scheme. At that time, he used the funds to finance a year-long trip for himself and his new wife and left his father with his debts. Gyaltshan and Jigme's behavior was attributed to youthful imprudence. In older traders it would have been the subject of very serious criticism.

I have said that Nyinba stress the need for cooperation between trongba members and also for what we might consider personal self-sacrifice. However, this is not the way they see it. One day, I asked several people I knew to describe instances of sacrifices they had made for their households. The primary response was puzzlement at my question. When I cited what seemed to be examples from their own lives, people told me that they did not separate out their own and trongba interests in this way and offered explanations both moral and practical. Thus Nyinba are fond of saying that it is to everyone's advantage when all work hard, when household members share their earnings and the trongba profits in agriculture, herding, and trade. Similarly everyone benefits when household unity is maintained, because they stay members in a wealthier estate, which means a higher living standard and prestige locally.

These advantages seemingly more than outweigh ordinary daily frictions and occasional conflicts that occur within households. The major conflicts of interest, as we have seen, have structural origins and involve opposed household positions. These conflicts are irresolvable and are where the seeds of major discord and eventual partition lie. If people try to transcend these difficulties, it partly is because partition means poverty and political weakness for individuals and groups, men and women alike. Woman especially are powerless on their own; they also find themselves without property or independent sources of income. Household unity is important for men for reasons of fraternal solidarity as well. Although the rationales for cooperation may differ for adult men and women, they seem compelling for both. Although girl children and retirees experience the fewest advantages within the household, they also have the fewest options outside it. Perhaps this is why they are such compliant household members.

Commitments to the interests of kin are viewed as, and seem to be, among the strongest motivations for interpersonal household cooperation. We have seen how kinship smoothes over frictions between holders of opposed household positions, how the transfer of headship and headwomanship is more amicable when retiree and successor are parent and child or, second best, uncle and aunt and nephew and niece, how co-wives link their interests when they are sisters, and how the aged are better cared for when their own children are in charge. Thus roles related to household and kinship or family are inextricably intertwined. People recognize this and do their best to have kin in these positions. Although it is essential to distinguish kinship and family from household positions for analytical purposes (Carter 1984:45–46), in practice the moral and jural claims associated with each intersect and come to be compounded.

The Family Within

Nyinba households are made up of families, or, as anthropologists have it, groups concerned with reproduction and socialization of children, where kinship is the criterion for membership. Fully developed trongba comprise extended families, overlapping sets of consanguineally related married brothers, their wives, and offspring. Nyinba differentiate these families as *paral* (Nep. *pariwar*).

Compared to trongba, families are given little public recognition. They are rarely discussed outside the circle of close kin—excluding points of gossip—and have no role to play in the larger social structure. The family is de-emphasized as well in people's own descriptions of their domestic group structure, in which headship and headwomanship—themselves little discussed—are given more prominence than motherhood and conjugal relations. Placing the emphasis on households is not unique. As Bender remarks for the Yoruba: ". . . for many purposes they are more important behavioral units than families. For one thing, families are more transitory than households and lineages. For another, family relationships are played primarily in the context of households . . ." (1971:223). To offer a point of contrast, members of our society seem to emphasize familial ideals over household obligations—and then are dismayed by the former's fragility.

For Nyinba, household rules impinge on family behavior just as much as kinship and familial relations affect household functioning. To offer an illustration of this, many people express a preference for only one generation bearing children at a time, ordinarily the younger, newly married adults. Nyinba also make use of certain kinship terms to address and refer to household members and apply them with reference to household, not familial, roles. Thus children call their mother's co-wives "mother" (*a-ma*), regardless of any kinship connection, and address a real mother as "junior mother" (*a-ma gzhon-da*) if she is younger than her co-wife. Children of these women are regarded as "brothers and sisters," that is, pun, literally "household siblings," regardless of genealogical connection.[5] The household head is termed "eldest father" (*a-ya rgan-da*), again regardless of genealogical relationship to the child, the wives of the junior generation are known as "daughters-in-law" (mna'-ma), and an in-marrying son-in-law as magpa. These terms, prefixed by the household's name, are used both in address and to refer to people in conversation. Aziz reports a similar system for Tibet (1978:131).

Trongba ordinarily include lineally extended families, but some include laterally extended families as well, that is, brothers and their separate wives. This situation, which I term conjoint marriage, commonly serves as a prelude to partition, and arrangements in such households provide a fine illustration of why the distinction between household and family must be kept. I take for my example Yogma household, mentioned above in the discussion of sisterhood and its effects upon co-wives' relationships.

> The three Yogma brothers each found himself a different wife, the two eldest marrying sisters and the youngest marrying an unrelated woman. The three acted as more-or-less separate couples and had separate sets of children. While the sisters cooperated and helped with one another's children, the distinction between families always was clear. At one point, partition was considered, and this produced a temporary separation of activities relating to the domestic economy, including the establishment of entirely separate kitchens.

When there are multiple families in a unified household, people keep sexual relations and the responsibility for children separate, but share work and the benefits of economic endeavors. When a household verges on partition, they subdivide economic obligations as well.

Recruitment and Succession: Rules and Outcomes

Membership in households can be obtained only through one of two routes, birth or marriage; and household positions, such as head and headwoman, are achieved only through legitimate succession. No trongba can form itself simply by agglomerating diverse individuals under a single roof and

---

[5]The reason for the gloss "household sibling" should be apparent. By contrast, children who are the offspring of two brothers in separate households would be distinguished as phapun, "siblings through fathers" instead of pun (see chapter 3).

appointing them to these positions; similarly one cannot simply move into a trongba or cite kinship to trongba members to support claims for membership. It is necessary to be the in-born child or spouse of a successor to headship or his sibling coparcener. Children born outside the household do not count unless they are legitimized and then brought into it.

Because of this, it is important to recognize that residence is the outcome of rules of recruitment and succession, but does not in itself play a determining role in domestic-group formation. This remains a controversial point, and there is a long tradition in anthropology of treating residence as a prior or generative fact (see Carter 1984:77n). There is no doubt that residence is temporally prior in many societies, in that residential decisions are a necessary first step in the creation of domestic units, and stressing this may seem the best approach where residence is neolocal and group composition fluid. However to treat residence as prior is to argue from observed social relations rather than from the underlying concepts and rules implicated in individual decisions and, collectively, in the generation of social forms. To do so also conflates the circumstances of groups whose members are expected to live together and people who happen to form a group simply because they find themselves living together (Bender 1971:223). Nonetheless, ethnographic cases with which I am familiar show co-residence amplifying existing familial and household ties, or, as with marriage, finalizing such ties, but not creating social relationships where no such ties existed before.

These distinctions are particularly clear in the Nyinba case, because households are corporate and because household membership (thus co-residence) is regulated so strictly. It is strictly regulated because household membership alone provides access to scarce resources, most notably land, rights to full politico-jural status, and the opportunity for respectable marriages. Individuals alone who lack rights in an estate can be no more than servants, for whom residence is continually negotiated for labor services.

Nyinba express a number of formalized ideas about how household membership, succession, and inheritance should be managed. We can see these ideas, or "rules," as providing partial solutions and guidelines for determining who may live in, inherit from, and head trongba. Such rules do not form a fully integrated system, however. There are occasions when one comes into conflict with another, when there are no clear guidelines to be found, or when traditions are challenged by new circumstances. Such situations have led to new resolutions, which may themselves provide precedents for similar cases later on and which eventually may reshape notions about household formation (see Moore 1978). Here, for purposes of parsimony I present these rules or guidelines in abstract, simplified form.

1. Absolute rights to lifelong membership accrue to all children born to any married partners in the household. This rule is unconditional, but incompletely specific. For one thing, it provides no guidelines for dealing with illegitimate children of household members. People say that illegitimate children of male coparceners have rights equivalent to those of legitimate children and that illegitimate children of wives must seek their rights from their real fathers. But the practical result is the opposite. Household members do their best to quash the claims of men's children born outside the household. At the same time, wives may hide their illegitimate pregnancies, and their husbands may tolerate this rather than create a scandal. This of course means that the child becomes a full household member.[6]

2. Marriage is the only way to recruit outsiders as full household members. There are no exceptions to this, and this accounts for some of the unusual, characteristically Tibetan modes of marriage described in chapter 7. By the same logic, marriage is the only way to abrogate rights in one's natal home. When a son's (uxorilocal) or daughter's (virilocal) marriage fails, they may return home only on others' sufferance, and not as full trongba members (Levine 1981c).

3. Sons succeed to headship and the estate, daughters to a dowry when married or to lifelong maintenance if never wed. In present-day Nepali law, women who do not marry are coparceners with rights equal to those of their brothers. Nonetheless Nyinba reject women's rights to inheritance, because it would disperse property from the estate. Traditionally daughters had the right to lifelong maintenance, but even that had little impact— parents preferred to send daughters off into unsuitable marriages or servanthood, rather than being encumbered with a spinster daughter. This is because a daughter whose marriage fails is not her parents' responsibility and because a servant who becomes pregnant bears her shame away from her parents' home. Thus one norm is contravened by the more compelling commitment to another—that women should be married—and by the commonsensical notion that an unmarried daughter might clash with or intrude upon the prerogatives of the daughter-in-law, who is mother to the next generation and future headwoman.

4. Households without sons recruit a son-in-law, who comes to reside uxorilocally, to act as successor to the head. This is clear enough; what is left ambiguous is priority in heirship, specifically whether the daughter or the son-in-law has greater rights in the estate. The ambiguity becomes an open issue in divorce, and one of the consequences is the contradictory

---

[6]More often than not, however, such children suffer neglect and tend to die at an early age.

decisions of recent decades, some giving preference to the daughter, others to the son-in-law.[7]

5. Households without children to serve as heirs transfer their estates to the household most closely related by partition, and the two households—their remaining personnel and property—thereupon merge. This rule is ordinarily adhered to, and because of the high economic stakes, heir households are careful to defend their rights. There have in the past been cases where the rule is either contravened by unscrupulous headmen and thalu, or sidestepped in the face of complex, competing claims. The nature of such claims and the consequences of voiding the rule will be discussed in chapter 8.

Developmental Cycle: Person, Family, and Household

Fortes framed his model of the developmental cycle in terms of processes of expansion, dispersion, and dissolution, which he attributed to the inevitable progression of birth, maturation, and death in the individual life cycle. Domestic cycles similarly were envisaged as closed: "The domestic group goes through a cycle of development analogous to the growth cycle of a living organism. The group . . . go[es] through a regular sequence of changes during the cycle which culminates in the dissolution of the original unit and its replacement by one or more units of the same kind" (Fortes 1958:2).

There are four problems with this model, none seemingly uncorrectable. First, it has been criticized for using individual biological processes as a reference point, and rightfully so, because domestic groups may operate independently of the life-cycle changes of individual members. Second, it relies uncritically upon synchronic data and all too easily can gloss over progressive changes in household form, collapsing them into a single cycle.[8] Third, the presumption of cycle closure limits the model's applicability to nuclear and certain joint-family-type domestic units. This is especially apparent in the Nyinba case, where there are overlapping families in most households and where households are corporate and have a continuing existence beyond the lives of individual members. As the men in one generation of a Nyinba household wed, bring their wives home, and

---

[7] Indications are that daughters' rights traditionally superseded those of their uxorilocally resident spouses. However, Nepali law recognizes the son-in-law as heir, and attempts by sons-in-law to take advantage of this may have promoted changes in practice.

[8] Thus recommending the collection of complementary household histories (Carter 1984: 56–57; Yanagisako 1979:169). However, such histories collected for the Nyinba fail to show any changes in systems of household formation or management over the last three generations.

start having children—that is, enter upon their phase of expansion—their parents' family undergoes the phase of dispersion. Within this sort of multifamily household, two or more such phases necessarily co-occur at a single time. A final problem is that the model fails to differentiate between processes of development in families and households—and the two can be very different—much less distinguishing these from concurrent processes in individual life cycles (Laslett 1984:375n; Yanagisako 1979:169). I have found it necessary to keep the three analytically distinct—which does not preclude attention to how they interact.

Associated with these problems is the overemphasis upon familial development phases, which typically are the focus of developmental-cycle models. Nyinba give household processes prominence. Accordingly, their family developmental processes are shaped by and subordinated to those of the household, just as individual needs are negotiated in terms of household needs. We have seen this in the case of Nyima, the man who relinquished headship early and whose individual life cycle was reorganized to benefit the household. We have seen too the ideal of supporting the needs of the household over those of individual families, an ideal that is more easily met by related men than by unrelated household women. From a folk perspective, the household is the more important unit; from an analytical perspective, household obligations are given precedence in intradomestic affairs.

In societies with corporate households, domestic development necessarily follows a different logic. Here there are no cycles of expansion followed by dispersion, but rather episodic pulses of expansions and contractions of membership through birth, marriage, and death. There also are successional shifts of personnel from one generational set of positions to the next, most importantly the transfer of headship and headwomanship. This shift and other changes associated with it can have profound effects on the household economy and often mark a difficult period for households. The parents-in-law have become less productive, the daughter-in-law is burdened with young children, there is discord between the two women, and meanwhile, adult daughters are leaving for marriages elsewhere (cf. Smith 1977:134–46 on Japan). In addition to situations such as these, which are repeated every generation, there are nonrepetitive, historical events, such as partitions or estate mergers, which have a major impact on households—an impact that continues to be felt for generations to follow. These events and processes simply cannot be comprehended in the simple, closed domestic-cycle model.

Household Complexity, Household Viability

Nyinba households are large by cross-cultural standards and complex. Comparative data show that most societies have small, nuclear-family households; corporate extended families are rare. Wilk and Netting (1984: 7–9), following Pasternak, Ember, and Ember (1976), attribute large families to the demands of the household productive system, specifically the need to schedule labor simultaneously around diverse productive tasks. Otherwise, they argue, families remain small, because they are more efficient for carrying out domestic functions and have fewer difficulties of interpersonal management.

Nyinba have an economy dependent upon a complex mix of economic specializations that entail major problems of scheduling. They deploy a number of males simultaneously in different places at different tasks—men must be at home plowing, trading in Tibet, and herding cattle—all at the same time. However, one cannot conclude from this that the Nyinba economy causes large households. One could just as easily turn the argument around and say these large, polyandrous Nyinba households demand multiple economic involvements for their support. Similarly, there is no greater logic to the argument that the Nyinba developed their household system to better fit an economy in which males specialized in different tasks than the argument that they developed such an economy to fit large households which comprise more males (see also Yanagisako 1979:173–74). The interest lies not with hypotheses about causality, but rather with how individuals organize such households to meet their economic needs and how they deal with interpersonal conflicts in relatively large groups.

Various sociocultural factors combine to produce the characteristic compositional arrangements we find in Nyinba households. The practices involved include polyandry in conjunction with generational continuity, and the result is a large and compositionally complex household which fits into no conventional category. Because polyandry ordinarily permits only one marriage per generation, there are parallels to the stem-family system of Europe and Japan. The difference is that in these systems only one brother marries, succeeds to headship, and inherits the estate. There are parallels too to the fraternal joint family of India, where brothers remain together for a time. However, in India each brother marries separately and establishes his own family, with partition eventually following. By contrast, Nyinba polyandry includes several brothers within a single marriage, and the restrictions on partition mean that several generations of brothers remain in a single household. Thus the Nyinba household is (generationally) extended lineally and (fraternally) expanded laterally, ordinarily with only one wife present in a generation.

Another factor involved is the concern with viability, or the household's ability to produce adequately for its needs and reproduce itself (Stenning 1958). To be viable a household must include one conjugal couple at the very least, but in order to benefit from available opportunities and for added security, the household needs additional personnel—additional adult men particularly. It is impossible for one man alone to cover all economic bases, because agriculture, trade, and herding have peak labor requirements at roughly the same times in summer and because few men can master the skills of all three activities. Nuclear families with numbers of young children also are disadvantaged by higher dependency ratios than those of households with numbers of polyandrous adult males. This is why Nyinba see large households with high sex ratios to be the most advantageous, and why, all things being equal, they prefer to organize their households along these lines.

In the absense of adequate male personnel, there are two options. First, people can sell their animals and depend on agriculture until the household expands. Land is not sold, except in dire poverty, because it is difficult to acquire again. Alternatively, people can hire servants or casual wage laborers. The problem is that servants never are as reliable as household members and also that the servants they need most—replacements for male labor—are difficult to find. The only other strategies for supplementing male labor—remarriage for widows, nonfraternal polyandry, and informal liaisons—are rare and disapproved. It is far easier to compensate for insufficient female workers by delaying the marriages of daughters, seeking adult daughters-in-law for child husbands, or hiring laborers. Shortages of personnel create more-or-less serious situations of temporary nonviability; shortages of animals are easily remedied, shortages of land painfully so, by heavy labor in clearing brush or saving until the household can buy odd plots. But shortages of the two together create a dangerous situation that may culminate in household extinction.

Households suffer when they get too large, Nyinba say, as well as when they get too small. The former situation occurs mostly when households have deliberately enlarged themselves in preparation for partition and then are riven by discord in the prepartition process. The latter situation occurs when households have trouble producing heirs or are too poor to attract new members. I cite two cases of outsized households below. The first illustrates the problems of a household nearing partition in which discord negates the positive effects of a large male labor force. The second case shows how a household having neither an adequate labor force nor adequate land can be brought to the edge of extinction.

In 1968 a Todpa household included at least eighteen people: two male retirees and one female retiree, four coparcener brothers, and three wives, two of whom had four (or more) children each. The presence of two childbearing wives and two reproducing families within one generation was a mark of incipient partition. The lines were drawn already; people quarrelled constantly, and despite the surfeit of ablebodied personnel, did little work. The household partitioned a year later.

In 1972 another Todpa household included five people: a man who had just assumed the headship, his wife, their son, his retired father, and his unmarried sister. Then the head was caught stealing grain from a neighbor and fled the region. Because it was uncertain whether he would return, his wife attempted to contract an uxorilocal marriage. This uncertainty and the poverty of the estate discouraged potential suitors. Faced with these problems, the wife ran away with a non-Nyinba man. This left three people: a retired father, the unmarried daughter, and a child—a household fragment, lacking an able head and without adequate working personnel. They contemplated merging with another household, but were encouraged to remain on their own because the village had lost too many households in recent decades.

Nyinba guide their decisions about household membership and recruitment by culturally defined strategic considerations. They make use of opportunities for marriage (mostly of women) to add or subtract personnel when this becomes desirable. They resort to employing servants or casual laborers to avoid adding permanent household members who would increase risks of partition. Should they wish to partition, household members form themselves into more than one viable, or productive and reproductively capable, core. The various rules about membership and succession discussed above and these diverse strategies combine to produce households of a special compositional form (or morphology; Netting, Wilk, and Arnould 1984).

Household Size and Composition

Citizen-landholder trongba and gompa households include, on average, over 7 members (table 6.1). This was the case in 1974 and 1983, and at both times approximately 60 percent of such households included between 6 and 10 members.[9] The household of 1983 was marginally larger, and at

[9] If I had included servants and dependent households, Nyinba household size would be even larger. In cross-cultural perspective, Nyinba households are quite large, but the various methods used in assessing household size make generalizations problematic (Goody 1972a:111–16). In addition to this, no one has attempted to compare different types of households drawn from a broad cross-cultural range or to consider the effects of marital type on household size.

Table 6.1 Distribution of Nyinba *Trongba*, 1974 and 1983

Household Size[a]	Distribution of Households in 1974		Distribution of Households in 1983	
	Percentage	N	Percentage	N
2	1.2	1	1.3	2
3	5.9	5	2.7	4
4	9.4	8	7.3	11
5	9.4	8	11.3	17
6	14.1	12	14.0	21
7	10.6	9	16.7	25
8	14.1	12	12.0	18
9	8.2	7	8.0	12
10	14.1	12	9.3	14
11	5.9	5	8.7	13
12	4.7	4	4.0	6
13–18	2.4	2	4.7	7
Total	100.0	85	100.0	150[b]

[a] Mean household size was 7.5 in 1974 and 7.7 in 1983.
[b] This includes a household which has initiated partition, which acts and is counted here as two domestic units, but whose property is undivided and which stands legally as a single trongba.

that time there were somewhat fewer very small, and more very large, households. Experienced household size, a measure which describes the household circumstances of an average individual (Laslett 1972:40) was 8.6 in 1974 and 8.7 in 1983.[10] The reason for the difference at the two points in time seems to be developmental factors—specifically the fact that a number of households had reached a more expansive developmental stage at the second date—but not any changes in those cycles or in patterns of household formation.

Nyinba households include relatively more men and more adults than the households of other societies. In 1983, the average trongba included 4.2 males and 3.5 females (table 6.2). The average large trongba was even more male, with an average of 5.8 males and 4.3 females. This, of course, is one of the consequences of polyandrous marriage and of the preference for a large male labor force which is associated with polyandry. If the

[10] In 1974, I attempted to collect census and genealogical data from all households whose members I knew well or with whom I had a reasonably congenial relationship. In 1983, I followed a more aggressive procedure and approached and collected census data on every Nyinba household. I also collected detailed economic and demographic data from all households (which proved willing to respond) in the smaller villages of Todpa and Nyimatang and from a random sample of households in the larger villages of Barkhang and Trangshod.

Table 6.2 Household Composition, Males and Females, in 1983

Household Size	Males		Females	
	%	N	%	N
All Households[a]				
0	—	—	—	—
1	8.7	13	7.3	11
2	17.3	26	16.7	25
3	16.0	24	28.7	43
4	16.7	25	26.0	39
5	16.0	24	10.7	16
6	11.3	17	6.7	10
7	8.0	12	3.3	5
8	3.3	5	0.7	1
9	0.7	1	—	—
10	1.3	2	—	—
11	0.7	1	—	—
Total[b]	100.0	150	100.1	150
Large Households[c]				
0	—	—	—	—
1	—	—	—	—
2	1.4	1	8.6	6
3	5.7	4	21.4	15
4	12.9	9	31.4	22
5	28.6	20	17.1	12
6	21.4	15	11.4	8
7	15.7	11	8.6	6
8	7.1	5	1.4	1
9	2.9	2	—	—
10	2.9	2	—	—
11	1.4	1	—	—
Total[b]	100.0	70	99.9	70

[a]The mean number of males in all households is 4.2; the mean number of females is 3.5.
[b]Because of the rounding-off of figures, percentages may not add up to 100.
[c]The mean number of males in large households is 5.8; the mean number of females is 4.3.

smaller households include a relatively greater proportion of women, this is because women are so essential for household management and because no household can persist without at least one capable woman. Thus we find trongba continuing for years with widows and children (and suffering considerable hardship), but none with men by themselves.

The average household in 1983 included 4.92 adults and 2.73 children aged fifteen or under: thus 1.8 adults for every child (table 6.3). We would find quite a different pattern in societies where households are organized

Table 6.3 Household Composition, Children and Adults, in 1983

Household Size	Mean N of Children[a]	Mean N of Adults	Child-to-Adult Ratio	N of Households
2	0.50	1.50	0.33	2
3	1.25	1.75	0.71	4
4	1.31	2.69	0.49	11
5	2.00	3.00	0.67	17
6	2.05	3.95	0.52	21
7	2.50	4.50	0.56	25
8	3.11	4.89	0.64	18
9	2.64	6.36	0.42	12
10	3.80	6.20	0.61	14
11	4.23	6.77	0.62	13
12	3.67	8.33	0.44	6
13–18	4.71	9.43	0.50	7
All households	2.73	4.92	0.55	150

[a]Defined as persons born during or after 1968, who ordinarily would not be making a full economic contribution to the household.

around nuclear families—even more so where fertility is high. The difference owes much to polyandry, which produces only one child-producing couple per generation and therefore relatively fewer dependent children for ablebodied adults to support (compare Sahlins 1974:102–5).[11] Another significant fact is that the proportion of children to adults remains roughly constant as household size increases (table 6.3). This suggests that households tend to reproduce their membership and that those with more adults also tend to have more children. This is logical enough, and the mechanisms involved will become clearer in chapters to follow.

In 1974, the mean generational size of Nyinba households was 2.5, or two and a half generations per household (table 6.4). At that time, slightly more households included two generations than three, 51.8 and 44.6 percent respectively. In 1983, the average household included 2.6 generations, and considerably more households had three generations than two: 57.6 and 38.7 percent respectively. At neither time were there any households with just one generation, for example, a lone individual or a married couple without children. At both times very few included four generations, and none included more. These generations almost invariably were linked

[11]The average number of persons per household born in 1913 or earlier was 0.4. Elderly people work hard as long as they can, but few individuals aged seventy or older can manage more than child care or light chores. Adolescents are not called upon for adult work until they are fifteen or sixteen (cf. Acharya and Bennett 1981). Notably, when asked to estimate their household work force, the average response that Nyinba gave was 4.4 persons.

Table 6.4   Nyinba Household Composition by Generations, 1974 and 1983

Number of Generations in Household	1974		1983	
	%	N	%	N
One generation	0.0	0	0.0	0
Two generations	51.8	43	38.7	41
Three generations	44.6	37	57.6	61
Four generations	3.6	3	3.8	4
Total	100.0	83	100.1	106

Table 6.5   Nyinba Households and Developmental Cycle Effects

Households	1974		1983	
	%	N	%	N
Without a married couple[a]	3.6	3	2.8	3
With single children	1.2	1	1.9	2
With widowed parents	2.4	2	0.9	1
With widowed parents and single children	—	—	—	—
With one generation of married couples	49.4	41	50.9	54
With single children	32.5	27	28.3	30
With widowed parents	2.4	2	1.9	2
With widowed parents and single children	14.6	12	20.8	22[b]
With two generations of married couples	43.4	36	42.4	45
With single children	28.9	24	32.1	34
With widowed parents	1.2	1	1.9	2
With widowed parents and single children	—	—	2.8	3
With neither parents nor children	13.2	11	5.7	6
With three generations of married couples	3.6	3	3.8	4
With single children	3.6	3	—	—
With widowed parents	—	—	—	—
With widowed parents and single children	—	—	—	—
With neither parents nor children	—	—	4	3.8
Total	100.0	83	99.9	106

[a] I use the term "couple" for lack of any better term to describe participants in diverse Nyinba marital arrangements.

[b] This includes one case where there were two generations of widowed parents (and grandparents)—thus four generations altogether.

by agnatic ties, the exceptions being the few households with uxorilocal marriages. The reasons for these consistencies across time are obvious enough: first, limitations of the human life span, and second, rules regarding household formation and household membership. Given that, the differences and reasons for them become more intriguing, and some of the answers may be found in a closer analysis of household generational composition.

The differences between household composition in 1974 and 1983 appear to have their source in developmental and demographic fluctuations (table 6.5). These fluctuations, I should note, had no impact on the numbers of generations of married couples living together in trongba and gompa households. At both times, approximately half of the households included one married couple, a slightly smaller percentage included two generations of married couples, and an equally small proportion of households included three generations of married couples. Instead, the differences appear in other features of family composition, specifically in the numbers of older, widowed household members and young, unmarried ones. In 1983, there were more widowed parents living with their married children and more married couples living with children who had not yet married. Thus more households listed under "one generation of married couples" included both widowed parents and children in 1983, and slightly more households listed under "two generations of married couples" included widowed parents, or unmarried children, or both. This would explain the greater proportion of households with three generations at the later date and also may account for the marginally larger mean household size at this time. The question is whether these fluctuations are entirely random or due to some directional change, such as an increase in the average life span.

In both 1974 and 1983, most Nyinba households included one or two generations of married couples and their children. That is to say, households generally contained either a nuclear family or two overlapping families with children. Thus at any given time we are likely to find a substantial number of Nyinba living in nuclear-family arrangements. This should not, however, tempt us to type Nyinba households as predominantly or commonly nuclear. Nuclear families are one of many manifestations of household development: a frequent by-product of developmental processes, but not an intended goal.[12] By 1983, many of the nuclear families of 1974 in-

---

[12] It is not even an intention of partition, although rules guiding who moves off with whom following partition make it likely that one of the newly created households will be no larger (and can be no smaller) than a nuclear family.

cluded two generations of married couples, some with young children. Were we to sample these same households later, we undoubtedly would find many couples of the older generation now widowed and living with their children and children's children.

This shows why it can be misleading to categorize a society's households by types and equally misleading to designate a particular household arrangement as representative of the range of households found in the society. As Berkner notes, citing Hammel: " . . . family structure is not a *thing,* but a *process* [emphases in the original]. The process consists of a succession of phases . . . none of which in itself represents the family structure, for 'a social institution is not its end products, but rather the procedural rules or principles that generate those products under varying constraints'" (Berkner 1975:731).

Some Nyinba households look like nuclear families, while others look like lineally extended stem families. Nonetheless, all are manifestations of a single set of rules of recruitment which have to be adapted to the vagaries of situational circumstances and pragmatic concerns. These include the requirements of maintaining household viability and of compensating for random demographic events. All interact with developmental processes to produce specific household compositions at specific points in time.

The Utility of the Stem Family Concept

The way we think about and classify families still is guided, explicitly or implicitly, by a typology developed by the historian LePlay. This typology contrasted the "unstable" nuclear family, which dissolves with the parents' death, the "patriarchal," or joint family, in which all sons remain with their parents, and the stem family, which permits only one child per generation to marry (Laslett 1972:16–19). Despite its exaggerations, this typology highlights some of the consequences of different modes of handling succession, household membership, and inheritance of property. In a country like Nepal, these differences and their consequences for social structure are unmistakable, for the first mode characterizes the household system of certain Tibeto-Burman tribal groups, the second is the ideal to which Nepali Hindus attempt to conform, and the third most closely fits the Tibetan household system.

Succession in the classic stem-family household characteristically involves several related features: (1) one person assumes headship and estate management; (2) nonsuccessors have to seek their living elsewhere; (3) the estate is maintained intact through impartible inheritance; (4) the estate and the household associated with it continue over a number of generations.[13] The Nyinba and Tibetan trongba system fits this ideal type only in part. This is because trongba brothers succeed as a group, although they act as a single person in managing their property and marrying jointly. At the same time, they are differentiated according to their relative seniority and personal attributes. Goldstein (1978b:327) describes this as providing the advantages of both stem and joint family types: "The Tibetan mono-marital stem family . . . produced the same *result* as the 'normal' stem family in that the corporate family unit was perpetuated without each sibling establishing a separate elementary family within the framework of the corporation" (1971b:71; emphasis added).

The basis for this unique mode of succession and household membership is polyandry. Normative polyandry is responsible for some of the special compositional features of the Nyinba household. It also has the consequence of making the wife and headwoman more central structurally and affectively than in monogamous and polygynous marriages—while at the same time limiting the number of women in those households and circumscribing their economic roles. Chapter 7 considers the operation of this marriage system and its domestic consequences.

---

[13] In the context of attempts to develop a morphological definition of stem families, Verdon rightly points out that impartible inheritance is necessarily associated with, but does not explain, the cross-cultural distribution of stem families.

7

From Polyandry to Partition

The Nyinba marriage system maintains trongba unity and continuity from one generation to the next. The radix of the system is fraternal polyandry, with all brothers in a household taking one wife in common. Polyandry links household men of each generation in their sexual and reproductive interests, as membership in a single household unites their economic and political interests. This provides both the source and the necessity for a degree of fraternal solidarity unparalleled cross-culturally. Commitments to polyandry, however, are not absolute; they may be qualified by factors such as parentage and the numbers of brothers involved.

Polyandry as Type and Process

Nyinba marriage presupposes fraternal polyandry: polyandry is universal and inevitable whenever there are two brothers or more. Not all families have more than one son, however, and not all marriages remain polyandrous. Mortality over the life cycle and less frequently irresolvable interpersonal difficulties reduce the incidence of polyandry as people age. Thus although 70 percent of extant Nyinba marriages began with two or more brothers, only half were polyandrous in 1983. The result is that a cross-sectional survey of marriage displays considerable diversity: numbers of marriages with one husband and occasional marriages with more than one wife—that is, monogamy and polygyny as well as polyandry.

This classification of marriage types, conventionally used by anthropologists, rests very simply on distinctions between the number and balance of the sexes in marriage. For Nyinba the complex patterning of interpersonal relationships in plural marriage calls for a somewhat expanded system of classifications (see table 7.1). Such a system shows considerable

Table 7.1   Distribution of Marital Arrangements in 1974 and 1983

	1974		1983	
	Percentage	*N* of Marriages	Percentage	*N* of Marriages
Monogamy	46.2	55	44.7	67
Polyandry	49.6	59	49.3	74
Simple polyandry	42.9	51	44.7	67
Polygynous polyandry	2.5	3	1.3	2
Conjoint marriage	4.2	5	3.3	5
Polygyny	4.2	5	6.0	9
Total	100.0	119	100.0	150

stability in the distribution of marriages in 1974 and 1983.[1] At both times, 49 percent of citizen-landholder trongba and gompa marriages were polyandrous. While the incidence of monogamy had decreased and that of polygyny had increased slightly by 1983, the differences were small—less than two percentage points. There also were few changes in the incidence of various polyandrous arrangements. "Simple polyandry," the term I use for the customary marriage of one woman to more than one man, was then marginally more common. There were relatively fewer cases of "polygynous polyandry," which occurs when a second wife is added to a childless polyandrous union, and of "conjoint marriage," polyandry with two or more childbearing wives.[2] These distinctions highlight characteristic differences between marriages with one woman and those with more than one woman—and more than one childbearing woman particularly. This is a subject to be explored later; for now the key facts are that marriage with more than one husband is the norm and marriage with more than one woman is comparatively rare—involving less than 11 percent of cases at the time of both surveys.

Describing the distribution of marriages across a sample of households does not adequately represent how men's and women's circumstances can differ in societies with a complex mix of marriage types. Take, for example, a society where polygyny, polyandry, and monogamy exist in equal measure. Necessarily more women would be found in polygyny, more men

---

[1] The data derive from the same sample used to construct the tables in chapter 6. The 1974 data include all marriages on which information is available for these households; the 1983 data derive from marital histories of one woman per household (see appendix C on methods of data collection). I have omitted cases difficult to classify, such as marriages in process of divorce.

[2] Prince Peter, as far as I know, introduced the term conjoint marriage (1965: 198), but primarily to describe what I term polygynous polyandry.

in polyandry, and equal numbers of both sexes in monogamy. Considering Nyinba marriage data from the perspective of individuals makes this clear and better reflects how marriage is experienced—and how it is experienced differently by men and by women. Logic suggests, and the surveys confirm, the concentration of men in polyandry and of women in monogamy and polygyny. Thus slightly over 40 percent of women had one husband (monogamy), approximately 50 percent had two or more husbands (in diverse forms of polyandry), and 20 percent lived with a co-wife (in polygyny, polygynous polyandry, and conjoint marriage) (table 7.2). This was true in both 1974 and 1983. At the same time, less than 25 percent of men were monogamous, almost 75 percent lived in polyandry of one form or another, and slightly over 10 percent had two or more wives. The practice of polyandry produces marriages in which men predominate numerically.

The discussion thus far has relied upon marriage types, and it is simplest to convey the diversity of Nyinba marital arrangements in this way. Types provide a shorthand for description; they can also be useful in framing discussions of how different numbers of husbands and wives and differing circumstances can affect marital relationships. Yet they can also mislead. I have said that marriage composition can vary greatly over the life cycle. In most cases, the changes from one type to another are adventitious and

Table 7.2 Men's and Women's Experiences of Marriage

	Men		Women	
	1974	1983	1974	1983
Monogamy				
Number	55	67	55	67
Percentage	24.6	23.9	41.4	40.1
Simple Polyandry				
Number	139	184	51	67
Percentage	62.0	65.7	38.3	40.1
Polygynous Polyandry and				
Conjoint Marriage				
Number	25	20	16	15
Percentage	11.2	7.1	12.0	9.0
Polygyny				
Number	5	9	11	18
Percentage	2.2	3.2	8.3	10.8
Total[a]				
Number	224	280	133	167
Percentage	100.0	99.9	100.0	100.0

[a] The ratio of men to women in Nyinba marriages was 1.7 both in 1974 and 1983.

incidental to developmental and demographic processes: they reflect no preferences on the part of participants and involve no purposeful changes in the way the marriage is constituted. This must be kept distinct from circumstances where such changes are deliberate and planned.

Developmental-cycle models provide one way of transcending the problems of static typologies. They can describe the processes of change found in the majority of marriages and how these processes are moderated by chance events and individual choice. By adding decision considerations to the model, one can link the rules and cultural notions guiding choices with life-cycle factors. These considerations are critical in explaining the range of forms Nyinba marriages take and the sources of variation that may arise between individuals and over time.

The developmental-cycle model that I have adapted to Nyinba polyandry is by necessity open-ended, like the model created for developmental processes in trongba households. It would miss the point to describe such marriages by a fixed progression of phases; chance and choice factors can bring different marriages through different phases in completely different orders. The model distinguishes between progressions that are inevitable, those that are obligatory, and those that are optional. At the same time, it is sensitive to the fine gradations and the interplay between personal choice and perceived obligation.

We can take the example of a Nyinba widow. Whether she remarries or not is her personal decision, but she will guide that decision by her children's ages, household labor needs, and the availability of suitable men. By contrast, a man with an infertile wife is under strong pressure to take a second wife, but not absolutely obligated to do so; the quality of his existing marital relationship probably will be a major factor in his decision. Finally, a son who has come of age must marry. In the first instance, uxorilocal marriage is discretionary and subject to assessments largely practical; in the second, polygyny is enjoined, yet subject to affective considerations; in the third, marriage has the force of a rule. Thus Nyinba marital configurations must be seen as the outcome of both customary norms and decisions; these decisions must be understood as the outcome of notions about practical matters, kinship, and interpersonal relationships, with all these considerations further conditioned by exogenous demographic events and the factor of time.

1. The Centrality of Polyandry

The linkage of brothers in polyandry is so accepted, so axiomatic, that the Nyinba have no special term for it. There is no term for marriage either, beyond distinctions between uxorilocal (mag-pa) and virilocal (mna'-ma) arrangements. These ideas are manifested in an effective rule: that all pun, or household brothers, initially marry the same woman. Pun, we have seen, refers to relations of siblingship, and pun without any qualifier refers to the children of married partners. It does not matter if the parents are different, so long as they were part of a single marriage. By contrast, children are described as matrisiblings (*ma-spun*) to their mother's children by another marriage and patrisiblings (*pha-spun*) to their father's children by another marriage in a different household. The latter terms also are used for the children of two sisters and the children of two brothers (which does not mean that people think that half siblings and cousins are identical or should be treated the same). The rule is that all male household siblings marry jointly, and I never have seen it broken.

Monogamy occurs by default, when there is only one son. It also can occur at a later point in the marriage, after one or more of the brothers have died. When, as occasionally happens, a brother is born after the marriage's inception, monogamous marriages become polyandrous. There also are very rare cases of a nonbrother subsequently added to a monogamous marriage, with consequences to be discussed.

Uxorilocal marriages normally begin, and mostly remain, monogamous. Residence in the wife's household, however, produces different patterns of domestic and spousal relationships from those in virilocal monogamy and gives the woman greater domestic power and security. Another difference is that any of her sisters may join the marriage later on, and there were two long-lasting marriages involving sisters in the recent past. Today there is one case of nonsororal polygyny. This occurred when an uxorilocally resident woman proved childless. Because she had no sisters, she sought other co-wives and, predictably, chose them herself.

To sum up thus far: if there are no sons, but a daughter, the marriage is uxorilocal monogamy (although a second woman may be added later); if there is one son, (virilocal) monogamy; if two or more, polyandry.

All the brothers in a household join in polyandry, with seven the largest number I know of. Most marriages include two brothers; sometimes there are three, and rarely four or more. The average number of husbands in polyandry is somewhat over two and a half, producing a sex ratio of 2.4 men for every married woman in 1974, and 2.6 in 1983 (table 7.3). The decrease in three- and four-husband marriages and in the average number of husbands per marriage over this nine-year period may be traced to the deaths of a number of co-husbands. That the sex ratio in marriage rose at the same time may be due to the concurrent decline in conjoint and polygynous polyandrous marriages. Additionally, it is rare for a household to

Table 7.3 Numbers of Husbands and Wives in Nyinba Polyandry

	1974[a]		1983[b]	
	Percentage	N of Marriages	Percentage	N of Marriages
Polyandry[c]				
With two husbands	49.2	29	54.8	40
With three husbands	32.2	19	27.4	20
With four husbands	11.9	7	8.2	6
With five or six husbands	6.8	4	9.6	7
Total	100.1	59	100.0	73[d]

[a]The average number of men per marriage in 1974 was 2.8; the ratio of men to women was 2.4.
[b]The average number of men per marriage in 1983 was 2.7; the ratio of men to women was 2.6.
[c]Including simple polyandry, polygynous polyandry, and conjoint marriage.
[d]There also is a marriage classified as conjoint in which only one husband remained in 1983.

raise four or more sons and for a marriage to contain four or more brothers. From the perspective of Nyinba women, that is for the best, and the stated preference is for two or three husbands.

2. Childlessness and the Choice for Polygynous Polyandry

Marriages change from monogamy to polygyny and from polyandry to polygynous polyandry when the first wife proves unable to bear children. This is the response, because wives are invariably blamed for childlessness. Discovering this, I asked several people if there were no sterile men. The response was that there might be, but no one knew of any cases. Another response was to joke about impotence—but the only example was of a low-caste Nepali who worked for Nyinba villagers. In consequence, male sterility is not considered in responses to persistently childless marriages. Practically, this has a certain logic. Virtually all women engage in extramarital affairs, most frequently in the early years of their marriage.[3] If fer-

[3]Men do not approve of their wives' adulterous affairs, but accept that they are likely to occur and do little to stop those discretely conducted. Women have even less right to control their husbands' sexual conduct—and fewer chances to do so in large polyandrous marriages where their nights more often are occupied and their husbands correspondingly more free. Nonetheless, adultery that comes to public attention may be treated harshly and heavily fined (see note 5).

tile, they should sooner or later become pregnant, although this is not a point Nyinba themselves make.[4]

Women's infertility is grounds for neither divorce nor ill-treatment; the reaction is more one of pity. Even a virilocally resident wife ordinarily remains headwoman, and if her marriage is strong, she may be asked to help select the second wife. Of twenty-four polygynous marriages past and present, eight involved the first wife's "household sister" (pun). We have seen the benefits of this: there is more cooperation between co-wives; the senior wife is less apt to take advantage of her authority; the kin relationship mitigates rivalries and lessens hardships for the junior woman. Nyinba say sororal polygyny is better and that they try to arrange it for this reason. Their experiences confirm these notions and presumably reinforce the preference for marriages of sisters.

We would class the marriage of two women to a single man as polygynous and the marriage of two women to two polyandrous men as polygynous-polyandrous. To Nyinba, the number of husbands matters far less than the changes a second wife makes in any marriage. Husbands maintain sexual relationships with both women and must be careful not to show partiality. This is because they wish to have children by the second wife, but already have a close and long-standing sexual relationship with the first wife; they also know the value of her continued contributions to the household. Ideally the two wives' interests will join in concerns about children, for household welfare and continuity. When the marriage is amicable—particularly when co-wives are sisters—this ideal has been met, and I have seen senior wives who dote on their co-wives' children and have taken charge of their care. It is these arrangements which approximate that mythical concept of "group" marriage, where sexuality and parenting are shared between multiple men and women; and the marriages polygynous polyandry has produced have been as successful as any others.

The unity of husbands and wives in polygynous polyandry strongly contrasts with conjoint marriage, which is contracted when one or more brothers are dissatisfied with their marriage. Conjoint marriage is strongly discouraged because bringing more than one childbearing woman into the marriage makes serious domestic discord more likely, breaks down fraternal solidarity by creating separate families, and lays the foundation for partition. This is why it is so rare, involving less than 5 percent of existing marriages at the time of both surveys. Yet such marriages continue to be initiated—quite deliberately—and the proximate reason is to ensure equity in marriage for all brothers.

[4]Childlessness, nonetheless, is rare, which is why only 7 percent of marriages have become polygynous or polygynous polyandrous (table 7.1).

3. Fraternal Equity and Conjoint Marriage

When all wives can have children, their husbands have neither necessity nor obligation to ally with all of them, and the women's own interests are divided by their obligations to the separate families they create. There is no way these women could act otherwise. Each is tied by fundamental obligations to her children and accordingly tries to acquire the largest possible share of household resources for them. At the same time, maternal interests run contrary to generalized ideals of mutual cooperation and concern between household members. The consequence of conflicting obligations is disputes, between the women first and then between their husbands. People in the community may say that this is the women's fault for being selfish and quarrelsome and the men's fault for having taken more than one wife in the first place. The men who instigated the conjoint marriage ordinarily orient themselves toward the new wife, the others toward the original wife; and one of the distinguishing marks of conjoint marriage is separate constellations of men and women within the larger marriage.

This raises the question of whether conjoint marriage is one or many marriages and the larger question of whether polyandry is marriage at all. The latter has been a controversial issue, with much of the early debate bogged down by misunderstandings of polyandry and by ethnocentric biases. The idea of men voluntarily relinquishing exclusive rights in a woman's sexual and childbearing capacities, of not knowing who their children are, and of having to contribute to the rearing of children not their own seemed inconceivable. The solution was to declare that what seemed inconceivable did not really exist, and that polyandry in reality involved only one marriage with one man—an advantage thought to lie with the eldest in fraternal polyandry—while the others were subordinate husbands or simply lovers with lesser rights and fewer responsibilities (see Levine and Sangree 1980:386–89). For Nyinba, however, all men clearly are husbands, although the eldest has more authority in household affairs and initially a certain precedence in his marriage. And as we shall see, despite the complication posed by sexual access of several men, the paternity of children is calculated, and having one's own children is extremely important to all the men.

Conjoint marriage can be nothing but a single marriage, because all the brothers have rights to all of the wives and at any time may initiate a sexual relationship with any of them. While most men have regular sexual relations with just one wife, some may be involved with all of them, and spouses can change their allegiances at any time. I have heard about conjoint marriages with subcouple relationships so stable that they lasted the participants' entire lives, relationships that changed over the years, and relationships that encompassed all the husbands and wives for the duration of the marriage. I also have seen relationships change and the pattern shift between subdivided and all-inclusive during the course of my research.

Nyinba tacitly distinguish between these differing arrangements. When men fail to establish or maintain sexual relations with a wife, it is treated as a renunciation of potential marriage claims. Thus if that wife is caught in adultery, the nonparticipating husband is not entitled to share in the compensation which is his right by Nepali law.[5] Nor are her daughters obliged to contribute to his funeral; and when sons do it is because they are heirs to his property. Regardless of existing sexual arrangements, all husbands and wives meet their household obligations, and they unquestionably are a single household so long as productive activities are joint and the proceeds of agriculture and trade shared by all.

Sexual arrangements tend to be the best indicator of partners' expectations of the future of their marriage—whether they plan to stay together or expect to partition. When marriages are open or inclusive, men have children by different wives, and their interests crosscut the separate matricentric families. In a more sexually exclusive conjoint marriage, the families will be defined by different paternity as well as maternity. This facilitates partition, for the rule that children partition with their fathers would otherwise separate women from their children.[6] All the evidence on marital histories shows fixed conjugal boundaries established or reinforced when partition is being contemplated. It is a symptom of differences perceived as irreconcilable and in itself drives spouses further apart.

The immediate motivation for conjoint marriage may be marital inequities, but the existence of inequities, the perception that they exist, and the inability to tolerate them have sources of their own. Not every man whose needs are poorly met by his marriage initiates a conjoint marriage; those who do either face more serious problems or have greater justification for this than other men. Nyinba see large sibling sets and different parentage of brothers as contributory factors in conjoint marriage. With the former situation, it is a matter of inequities increased. The more brothers

---

[5]Most cases of adultery are privately settled, but those which become a public issue involve heavy fines imposed on the man. This is similar to Nepali practice, and I attribute it to Kalyal influences on Nyinba family law. By contrast, Sherpa impose nominal fines on men and women caught in adultery (Fürer-Haimendorf 1964:68, 82).

[6]This applies to boys and girls over the age of seven. There have been recent cases where mothers were separated from their children, with the tragic consequences described in chapter 8. (The situation changes when the children are adults and themselves responsible for the partition. Then the issue is where the parents are to live—and most elect to live with their children.)

Table 7.4   Effects of Sibling Group Size on Conjoint Marriage

N of Husbands[b]	Simple and Polygynous Polyandry		Conjoint[a] Marriage	
	Frequency	Percentage	Frequency	Percentage
Two husbands	38	55.1	3	12.5
Three husbands	19	27.5	7	29.2
Four husbands	6	8.7	9	37.5
From five to seven husbands	6	8.7	5	20.8
Total	69	100.0	24	100.0

[a]This includes currently surveyed marriages for simple and polygynous polyandry and all conjoint marriages, past and present, on which I have data on sibling group size and declared parentage.
[b]The mean number of husbands in simple and polygynous polyandry is 2.8; in conjoint marriage it is 3.8.

there are, the more difficult it is for wives to meet their obligations to, and mediate between, all the men. With different parentage of brothers, it is a matter of greater sensitivity to inequities or unwillingness to tolerate them.

Marriages with four or more brothers are inherently more likely to disappoint. For one thing, the common wife has to sustain a satisfactory sexual relationship with four or more men, although this tends to be the minor problem. More problematic is meeting each man's expectation of a son from the marriage. It also is difficult to satisfy domestic labor obligations—weaving, washing, cooking, carrying firewood and water—for so many men. While most first wives vehemently resist a conjoint marriage, a woman with four or more husbands resists less.

The data on recent conjoint marriages validate these assessments. Such marriages include substantially more men on average: 3.8 as opposed to the 2.8 husbands we find in nonconjoint polyandry (table 7.4). Conjoint marriages also cluster among the larger sibling sets.

Parentage is important on several counts (tables 7.5 and 7.6). As we have seen, Nyinba place great emphasis on kin relationships and believe that close (*nye-mo*) kin are more loving (*mdza-mo*) and sympathetic (*sdug-sdug*). We have seen in discussions of sororal polygyny that close kinship encourages cooperation and mutual trust. The same holds for men in polyandry; and Nyinba say that the most successful polyandrous marriages involve real (*ngo-rtog*) pun, that is, those with the same mother and father. They also say that those with different parents are more likely to experience failures in fraternal commitments which can end in conjoint marriage. However, having different mothers actually has proven more problematic.

Table 7.5 Parentage and Susceptibility to Conjoint Marriage

	Simple and Polygynous Polyandry (N)	Conjoint Marriage (N)	Conjoint Marriage[a] (%)
Same mother, same father	9	7	43.8
Same mother, different fathers	25	11	30.6
Different mothers, same father	2	0	0.0
Different mothers, different fathers	3	6	66.7
Total	39	24	37.5

[a]This includes marriages where at least half the husbands were aged thirty or older (thus old enough to have initiated a conjoint marriage) and where their parentage is known. As I deliberately sought data on parentage for individuals in conjoint marriage, their numbers here far exceed their representation in the population.

Table 7.6 The Influence of Parentage on Choices for Conjoint Marriage

Men	With Same Mother (N = 52) (%)	With Different Mothers (N = 11) (%)	With Both Same and Different Mothers (N = 63) (%)
With same father (N = 18)	43.8	0.0	38.9
With different fathers (N = 45)	30.6	66.7	37.8
With both same and different fathers (N = 63)	34.6	54.6	37.5

One reason must lie in the difficulties that plague relations between co-wives: their competition for household resources, quarrels over their children, and the resulting sense of rivalry between those children. This is not the case for co-husbands, who are brothers and whose actions are informed by an ethic of fairness to all household children, regardless of parentage—so long as the household remains undivided.

Another factor that may be implicated is the kinship of the parents. We may speak of different fathers, but those fathers are pun, household siblings. This is not so for "different mothers"—only a third of polygynous marriages have involved household sisters. Yet even when co-wives were sisters, it seems not to have diminished risks of sons' conjoint marriage. Two out of six—also one-third—of the conjoint marriages associated with different maternity included the sons of real or household sisters. It seems significant, however, that these were more amicable conjoint marriages and never led to partition. Whether this is because the men were the sons of sisters, or because, as sisters, their mothers had more amicable relationships is impossible to say. Kinship and cooperation in socialization are inextricably intertwined; they cannot be separated out. If it is difficult to disentangle the sources of disunity among men with different mothers, the consequences for marriage are unmistakably obvious.[7]

Tables 7.5 and 7.6 include all the cases of conjoint marriage that I know about, past and present, where I also know the parentage of brothers. The cases are few, but they affirm the effects of different maternity. More than half the Nyinba brothers who had different mothers married conjointly, and another such sibling set was contemplating conjoint marriage in 1983. By contrast, having different fathers lacked any apparent effect. Having both different fathers and different mothers, however, was the circumstance most likely to produce conjoint marriage. Again, this may be the product of notions about kinship or household relationships and probably is the product of both. For men with different fathers and mothers are the offspring of sexually exclusive couples of the previous generation. Their parents' marriages were divided, partition was a possibility, and their fathers and mothers may have discriminated between them from their birth.

When we take sibling group size and maternity in combination, we can see the full effects of these forces for scission in polyandrous marriage. Despite the small sample size, the data are consistent and suggest that the two factors potentiate one another. The larger the sibling group becomes, the more likely brothers are to establish a conjoint marriage; brothers with different mothers are almost twice as likely to marry conjointly; and brothers with different mothers in large sibling groups universally end up in con-

---

[7] It is easier to show how kinship proximity contributes to marital stability in Sri Lanka, where polyandry occasionally links unrelated men and where the parentage of siblings is more easily traced (nowadays, at least, polyandry is not repeated from one generation to the next [Tambiah 1966:287; Hiatt 1980:587]). In the Tibetan case, repetitions of polyandry can produce men whose different fathers may have had different fathers whose own fathers may have been different as well. The sisters in sororal polygyny may have equally complex relationships. While Nyinba keep genealogies, in marriage the primary distinctions are between real siblings (*ngo-rtog spun*), siblings with different maternity (*a-ma logs-su*), and those with different paternity (*a-ya logs-su*).

Table 7.7   The Effects of Maternity and Sibling Group Size in Conjoint Marriage

Number of Brothers[a]	Same Maternity			Different Maternity		
	Becoming Conjoint (N)	Cases (N)	Becoming Conjoint (%)	Becoming Conjoint (N)	Cases (N)	Becoming Conjoint (%)
2 (N = 18)	2	15	13.3	1	3	33.3
3 (N = 23)	6	19	31.6	1	4	25.0
4 (N = 14)	6	11	54.6	3	3	100.0
5 + (N = 8)	4	7	57.1	1	1	100.0
Total (N = 63)	18	52	34.6	6	11	54.6

[a] When the conjoint marriage was initiated.

joint marriages (table 7.7). Even marriages with three brothers appear to be problematic, despite their celebration in origin myths and the preferences people state for them (tables 7.4 and 7.7). Trifraternal polyandry was almost twice as likely to produce conjoint marriage as were cases of bifraternal polyandry. Again I must caution that the sample was small, but it seems undeniable that bifraternal polyandry is the easiest to sustain.

Parentage and sibling group size, however, do not explain all marital choices. Some large sibling groups remain together, while some men with identical maternity do not. As Nyinba note, there also are factors of individual temperament and idiosyncratic interpersonal compatibilities which play a role in the success of polyandrous relationships. Economic factors must be considered as well. Some households can afford conjoint marriage better than others and have less to fear from the attendant risks of partition. Nyinba I have discussed this with say that wealth contributes to marital irresponsibility and that marital irresponsibility may lead to partition; but they deny that wealth is a factor comparable to different maternity in producing marital dissatisfaction and prompting conjoint marriage. This is a complex issue and awaits fuller discussion in later chapters.

Conjoint marriage may be the result of unwillingness to tolerate inconveniences posed by polyandry and preferences for greater marital independence. Yet there are inconveniences to conjoint marriage too—continual dissension, threats of partition, and risks of dividing the household estate. Individuals must balance all the factors involved: the distrust between sons of different mothers, problems of equity and of conjugal access in large sibling groups, and the drawbacks of a property division. All enter into marital decisions. Finally, the factors must be seen as culturally conditioned, from the expectation that sons of different mothers will be rivalrous and the idea that four brothers are too many, to calculations about how much land a household needs to weather partition.

This digression into the sources of conjoint marriage and its consequences for household unity is critical for later discussions of growth and change in the Nyinba community. Yet it has taken us far from the analysis of marriage as a system and a process. Marriages change over the life cycle, because of demographic factors, decisions of individuals, and family developmental processes. The sorts of changes a marriage can undergo are illustrated in the following example, which merges the experiences of individuals in several observed cases (after Berreman 1975):

Three sons married polyandrously in 1945:

1945   △ △ △ = ○   Polyandry

By the time ten years had passed, it was apparent that the common wife was infertile. She had no sisters still single, and the second brother suggested that her parallel cousin (a classificatory sister) would be a suitable choice as junior wife. The other brothers and the wife as well concurred with this choice, and the second marriage went forward:

1955   △ △ △ = ○ = ○   Polygynous
                               Polyandry

The junior wife had her first child in the second year of the marriage. By 1960 there were two sons and three daughters. The youngest brother, however, had no children recognized as his own. He and the junior wife did not get along, and there seemed no hope of improvement in the relationship. He told his brothers he wanted to bring another wife into the household. His eldest brother, unable to persuade the fertile wife to change her behavior and realizing that his sibling's wish was justified, agreed:

1965   △ △ △ = ○ = ○ = ○   Conjoint
                               Marriage

The union remained like this for a number of years. The third wife gave birth to a son and then it was discovered that she had tuberculosis. She died a few years later. Then the youngest brother died in a tragic accident. By 1975, the marriage had become polygynous polyandrous again. In 1980 the eldest brother died from what was diagnosed as typhus. The marriage then was polygynous in form and remains that way still:

1980   △ = ○ = ○   Polygyny

Should either woman predecease her husband, the marriage would
become monogamous:

n.d.   △ = ○   Monogamy

Thereafter if either spouse died and the household's sons had
reached maturity, the person remaining probably would not remarry, but would retire from active life.

This summarizes the sorts of changes that can befall a Nyinba marriage,
most developmentally and demographically conditioned. For Nyinba these
are changes in the personnel of a unitary marriage and not purposeful progressions from one determinate type of marriage to another. The same
sorts of rights and obligations obtain whether there is one husband or three
and one wife or two. The major exception is conjoint marriages with sub-
couples. When Nyinba discriminate between differing marital circumstances, the distinctions they make differ from ours. Their concerns are
virilocal versus uxorilocal marriage and marriages with one fertile wife
versus those with two or more. There is no notion of monogamy as opposed to polyandry. Numbers of husbands matter, but in a different way, so
that there is qualitatively less of a difference between one and three husbands than there is between two and four.

I have categorized marital distinctions as Nyinba make them (table 7.8).
We have seen the norms to be virilocality and marriage of as many brothers
as exist to one woman, and the great majority of Nyinba marriages follow
this pattern. Distinctions between monogamy and polyandry and between

Table 7.8   Marital Types in Nyinba Terms

Marital type[a]	Number of Marriages	Percentage
Virilocal	114	95.8
Uxorilocal	5	4.2
Total	119	100.0
One wife	106	89.1
One infertile plus one fertile wife	8	6.7
Two or more fertile wives	5	4.2
Total	119	100.0

[a] These data derive from the 1974 census.

different numbers of husbands are of less importance. The number of brothers has an impact upon the household economy and interpersonal relationships, but alters neither the way in which those relationships are conducted nor any rights and obligations in the marriage. Having two husbands seems to be the most workable arrangement, although three is economically ideal—the preference of men and many women queried on the subject.

Why Fraternal Polyandry Dominates

There are three bases of support for fraternal polyandry which explain its persistence in a majority of culturally Tibetan areas. The first derives from cultural notions and concepts of kinship. The second relates to household rules of succession and inheritance, which are tied to the goal of maintaining or improving political position in the village. The third concerns the calculus of economic viability. I begin with the issue of economic viability.

Polyandrous marriage is found in most regions of Tibet. Although available data are sketchy, it seems to have been most common in the western regions, somewhat less so in the central regions, and virtually absent in the farthest east and northeast regions (Carrasco 1959). This has been attributed to limited resources in the west and Chinese influences in the east. Polyandry almost certainly was more common among the rich and landed than among the poor and landless and probably was more common among settled agriculturalists than nomads. Aziz's data on south-central Tibet suggests that marriage form is associated less with income than with type of economic adaptation and occupation. Thus polyandry and virilocality are found among agriculturalist trongba, landholding aristocrats, and landholding priest households, while merchants, urban administrators, landless peasants, and outcastes were mostly neolocal and monogamous (Aziz 1978:157–58).

Attempts to explain the existence and persistence of Tibetan polyandry have focused primarily on its economic advantages. In Tibet and the Tibetan borderlands where polyandry is practiced, arable land is scarce, and high altitude, aridity, and poor soils combine to limit the productivity of agriculture. Other alternatives for making a living are few and have their own risks. The assumption has been that without polyandry, Tibetans would be reduced to poverty; and we find this expressed from the very earliest descriptions of Tibetan society onward (see Prince Peter 1963:379, 559–61; Prince Peter 1965; Westermarck 1925:187–88). Today we find similar arguments, supported by fuller data and couched in more sophisticated terms, most persuasively in the work of Goldstein. He argues that polyandrous marriage is valued, not as an end in itself, but for its economic benefits, and that the system is an adaptive and rational response to conditions of scarce resources. Polyandry permits brothers to pool their resources; it provides a means of maintaining family wealth intact over generations, thus sustaining a higher standard of living. At the same time, by limiting the number of marriages contracted, polyandry reduces the numbers of children born and thus inhibits population growth at the societal level (Goldstein 1978b:327–30; Goldstein 1976; Goldstein 1987; see also Ross 1984; Schuler 1987:56).

Nyinba also see polyandry as a practical response to environmental constraints, and they praise its material advantages. However, the importance of polyandry extends beyond the economics of it. First, polyandry has a special cultural value. Nyinba legends and genealogies portray ancestors of both the distant and recent past as brothers linked in polyandry, and there are stories that celebrate ancestors and ancestresses for the harmony of their family life. Second, the solidarity of brothers is one of the core kinship ideals, equivalent to the obligation to support parents in their old age. Third, the trongba system, as it is structured, presupposes polyandry, and its economy, as we shall see in chapter 9, rests on collaboration between several adult men. Fourth, the Nyinba village, as a closed corporate unit, also is structured around polyandry and the nonproliferation of member households. Polyandrous marriage simply is structurally pivotal. Individuals, as well, see polyandry as both socially and economically adaptive. The strength of numbers and a strong, undivided household enhances their political position in the community, just as it sustains a higher standard of living through the coordinated efforts of a number of brothers. Finally, for reasons soon to be explored, most men and women find polyandry a personally comfortable form of marriage and one that suits culturally defined practical goals.

Polyandry thus has economic supports and an economic rationale; but these have been overemphasized at the expense of its kinship, political, and symbolic correlates. Goldstein has refined the image of polyandry as a check against "eternal warfare or eternal want" (Westermarck 1925:187), stressing instead "material markers of affluence . . . social advantage and prestige" (Goldstein 1978b:329). However, neither scarce resources nor individual concerns with maintaining affluence are adequate to explain why a given social system has produced normative polyandry. There are other ways of securing resource conservation through controlled inheritance and marital restrictions—primogeniture and ultimogeniture being key examples. And it is all too obvious that numerous societies in similarly impoverished environments eschew such restrictions. The Nyinba's near neighbors provide prime examples of this.

Given a marriage system centered on polyandry, the questions then become how households secure viability, how their members arrange succession and inheritance when several male heirs are involved, and how participants in polyandrous marriages manage their interpersonal, conjugal, and familial relationships.

Polyandry and Household Viability

Marriage is the primary way Nyinba households adjust their memberships and meet their labor requirements. Marriage, that is, is used as a means for enhancing household viability. Polyandry is seen as the most desirable arrangement, the most apt to assure present viability and future continuity. The problem is that polyandry is not always possible or uniformly successful. We have examined some of the marital arrangements that Nyinba practice in addition to or as a substitution for polyandry: uxorilocal (magpa) marriage, polygyny or polygynous polyandry, and conjoint marriage. These are by far the most common, but there are still other marital options suited to special circumstances.

All these forms of marriage were found in Tibet, together with even more exotic arrangements. The most notorious practice was father-son polyandry. This occurred when fathers of mature sons were widowed. There were strong arguments against marriage for the men of both generations: that this could produce two nuclear families within the household at the same time, with all the conflicts and rivalry for resources we have seen in conjoint marriage, and with equivalent potential for disputes about succession later on. Instead, either the father(s) or son(s) married, with the understanding that the other generation would have sexual access to the wife. Father-son polyandry was rare; Aziz found it in less than 2 percent of marriages. Yet it was considered an acceptable option (Aziz 1978:156). Mother-daughter polygyny in cases of uxorilocal (magpa) marriage was similarly motivated. If the widowed mother were to have married, her daughter might have gone elsewhere; instead they found a man to suit both, and the daughter and her labor were retained for her natal home. Both kinds of cross-generational union were publicly acknowledged, if less favored (Aziz 1978:153–6; Goldstein 1971b: 61; Prince Peter 1963:473). In Tibet there also was the option of sending one of many brothers to a monastery or encouraging him to become a magpa, to reduce potential discord in polyandry with large sibling groups.

None of these options are possible for Nyinba. There is no strong monastic tradition, and the Nyingmapa sect of Buddhism which they follow places less value on celibacy. Uxorilocal marriage never is encouraged openly, because it is regarded as a breach of fraternal solidarity. Polyandry for father and son and polygyny for mother and daughter are accounted incest, because of the prevalence of cross-cousin marriage and the assimilation of all marriages to a cross-cousin model.[8] This is one of the reasons behind the distance and respect characterizing father-in-law and daughter-in-law relations and which discourages them from holding positions of head and headwoman simultaneously.

Fraternal polyandry and the Tibetan practices listed above have the effect of restricting household membership to brothers, their joint wives, and their children. However, some households need to augment, rather than reduce, their membership. This Nyinba accomplish through "added men," "doubling up," remarriage of widows, marrying a woman unable to have children, and through hastening marriages of their sons or delaying marriages of their daughters.

The first way to augment household membership is the "adding of men" (pho-'byar) in nonfraternal polyandry. There are no cases at present, but there were two such marriages of long duration in the previous generation. They occurred when a lone man, incapable of managing his estate on his own, sought the approval of his wife and then added a friend to their marriage. While the added man is supposed to stand as a substitute for a younger brother, he is at a disadvantage, being an outsider to the trongba and lacking coparcenary rights. Because he moves into another man's house and is definitely subordinate to his co-husband, people think of an added man as more like a junior wife; and they note that only a man from an impoverished family would tolerate such a situation. Nyinba stress that men are added mostly for their labor and not for their sexual or procreative contributions to a marriage, although in Tibet, Ladakh, and Lahul, nonfraternal polyandry, known by similar names, is practiced in cases of presumed male infertility (Prince Peter 1963:326, 346, 419). To describe one of these cases reveals how closely the added man is incorporated into the marriage and how far the concept of household siblingship may extend:

> Tshering was a lone husband with a wife and one young son, Dawa, when he decided to add a friend to the marriage. Several years passed and there were no more children, so the men took a second wife. The junior wife had one son, Rangdul, by the added man and several daughters. When Dawa was old enough to marry, he and Rangdul were joined to one woman in an elaborate wedding. The marriage soon ended in divorce, but they married jointly again. Only Dawa produced any sons in this marriage. Dawa died in 1978, and Rangdul now lives alone with the common wife.

[8] Accordingly, spouses and in-laws always are addressed as if an actual cross-cousin marriage has occurred.

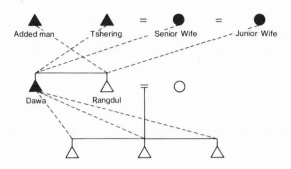

Tshering + Senior wife → Dawa

Added man + Junior wife → Rangdul

All children of junior generation are Dawa's

Figure 7.1   Non-Fraternal Polyandry

It may not be chance that Dawa, the man representing the household's own clan, was believed to have fathered all the sons, or this may be a deliberate fiction adopted to minimize the risk of fraternal disunity. In any event, Dawa and Rangdul, sons of nonbrothers and of different mothers, were regarded as pun and lived out their lives in a stable polyandrous marriage (figure 7.1).

There is a second practice, almost as rare, used to avoid inviability. This is called "doubling up" (from Nepali, *dohorya*); it is not marriage, but institutionalized lovership. When a woman with young children loses her husbands, she is left alone with the responsibility of managing an estate. The situation becomes critical when her parents-in-law are deceased or too feeble to help. A woman in this predicament may try to find a regular husband, but most men are unwilling to become later husbands in another man's home. The only other alternative is doubling up. I know of three cases in previous generations and two nowadays where women found lovers who were neighbors and themselves part of large sibling groups. In the past, the men reportedly moved in, contributed to the work of the widow's household, and helped to rear the children of her marriage.[9] In one of these cases, the widow bore her lover's children too. These children were regarded as illegitimate, but unlike so many illegitimate children, survived, and as the only sons, eventually inherited the estate. Thus the prac-

_____

[9]The present-day cases began in the late 1970s—they are relatively recent and not fully accepted, either by the men's households or the community. This may be why they are conducted clandestinely.

tice of the added man and doubling up counterbalance temporary but severe imbalances in adult male household personnel.

There also are marital solutions to imbalances in female personnel. A very young son may be married to a much older girl (in one recent case, a boy of seven married a girl of seventeen), an older, infertile woman may be added to an existing marriage, or a daughter's marriage may be delayed. But these solutions rarely occur. Most people prefer to hire agricultural workers—and grumble about their unreliability—until the imbalance in female personnel is resolved in the course of household development.

The marital strategies we have looked at have two goals. Some are used primarily to rectify imbalances in adult personnel; others are essentially "strategies of heirship" (Goody 1976). The former strategies include the added man, doubling up, remarriage of widows, taking in a mature daughter-in-law for a young son, delaying a daughter's marriage, and also men's second marriages to postmenopausal or infertile women. The latter strategies include uxorilocal marriage of magpa, which provides for household continuity without proper (male) heirs, and polygynous polyandry, which is practiced solely to produce heirs. There is one case in Barkhang village, mentioned above, which involves both uxorilocality and polygyny and illustrates the importance of heirs produced within marriage. The main figure in this case was the uxorilocal daughter. She first took a magpa spouse, and although she bore one child after another, they all died in infancy. After many years, she added one unrelated co-wife and then a second, but they suffered the same fate. Eventually the repeated child deaths were given a mystical explanation, but at the same time the co-wives were kept on to increase the chances of producing heirs.[10] It would, of course, be far easier to adopt children, but this simply is not done.

Polyandry seems universally to be associated with marital flexibility of the sort described here. To put it another way, everywhere polyandry is found, it is one manifestation of a marriage system encompassing diverse conjugal groupings (Levine and Sangree 1980). Polyandry dominated among landed Tibetans for cultural, social, and structural, as well as economic reasons. It was associated with a household system which included several generations of brothers cooperating economically, where succession was joint, where the eldest brother led, and in which families tried to have more than one son, so that the household would prosper and to provide insurance that it would continue on and, best of all, in the male line.

[10]This was the situation in 1974. By 1983, one of the co-wives had died in childbirth and the remaining co-wife had a son and a daughter. There is one case of adoption. It occurred when the childless freedman wife of a citizen-landholder adopted her nephew; but this is strongly disapproved.

Thus marital concerns, like individual and familial concerns, are accommodated to larger household goals.

The Identity and Differentiation of Brothers

In the practice of polyandry lie two apparent paradoxes. The first is the status of brothers as husbands. On the one hand they are identified with one another: there is unitary succession and a shared marriage. At the same time, the men are separate persons and are regarded as such, differentiated by age and by certain particulars of their relationship with the common wife. The second paradox is the notion of fatherhood. All the brothers father, that is, rear children produced by the marriage, yet they are differentiated as genitors of one child or another. As we shall see, this mix of individuation and unity of men in polyandry is not paradoxical, but a response to men's individual concerns and the facts of fraternal linkage. The system gives each brother an interest in the marriage and binds him more firmly to his household, which is one of the reasons that polyandrous marriage continues to predominate today.

All the brothers in a polyandrous marriage are equally husbands. They have equal conjugal and procreative rights and equal obligations to the wife. They all are expected to work for the good of the household and for the support of the wife and children. In response, the wife is expected to perform domestic chores for all the brothers, to treat them fairly in sexual matters, and thus to give all a chance to father children within the marriage.

For most couples, the problem of sexual equity is handled by having the wife spend an entire night with one husband at a time and with all husbands in more or less equal measure. Because men often are away on trading trips, a strict rota is not feasible, and the scheduling tends to be flexible. A general rule is that a husband who has been away has the first rights to spend the night with the wife. Otherwise the goal is a rough balance, and when all things are equal, the senior brother, the brother who took the principal role in bringing about the marriage, or the brother currently closest to the wife may take precedence.

Because of the openness of these arangements, decisions continually have to be made, and either husband or wife can take the lead in this. Plans may be made early in the day, through glances, an exchange of words, and so on. At night, some women go to their husbands' beds; others think this is too forward and let their husbands come to them. Parents-in-law may try to regulate this too, by literally assigning people to various beds in the house; but this is only when the couple is young, and mostly, it is said, to set a pattern of fairness early in the marriage.

What complicates these guidelines for sexual equity are the vagaries of interpersonal relationships. Jealousy and sexual rivalry between brothers are the exception. The problem more commonly is one of greater and lesser compatibility between specific husbands and the wife. A wife may prefer one of the husbands and let her preferences be known. Relationships change over time, so the neglected husband can hope for the future—while complaining that women are fickle; and preferences are tolerated so long as no one is excluded. Most women initially like the eldest husband more, for the two often are close in age; and it is the eldest with whom most establish the first sexual relationship. In later years a woman is apt to turn to younger husbands with whom she may have a more equal relationship, whose upbringing she may have supervised, and who likely are seen as more sexually attractive. Temporarily neglected husbands are more free to pursue extramarital affairs, while women attempt to control the actions of their favorites (compare Aziz on Tibet [1978:146]).

The eldest brother almost always assumes the principle role in first marriages. At weddings he wears a special turban and performs certain ceremonial functions; his brothers will be given accessory roles if they are old enough and well behaved. The girl's horoscope will be checked first against that of the eldest brother. If the two don't match, signs of compatibility are sought with the second and then the third brother. It must match with one brother, or the marriage will be called off. Poorer households do without the ceremony and simply encourage the eldest son to elope with a suitable girl.[11] In subsequent marriages, younger brothers who have come of age take responsibility for elopements in turn.

All this gives an eldest brother two sources of precedence in most marriages. First, he is eldest and has the greatest household authority. Second, he is the "wife bringer" (*bag-ma 'khyer-ba*), the man who literally brings the wife home or is joined to her at weddings and who initiates sexual relations. This is the case in first marriages and other marriages contracted while his brothers are still young—which means most marriages.[12] Younger

[11] In one village, approximately 40 percent of men's first (and all their subsequent) marriages involved elopements. Men elope with women whom they have been courting and with whom they have established sexual relationships, but only after consultation with their households. Girls complain that boys use the lure of marriage to induce them into sexual relations; but boys say sexual relations are necessary to test the girl's intent and the couple's compatibility.

[12] Sexual intercourse is seen as very important in creating affective bonds, and the priority of the eldest brother as having an enduring effect upon his relationship with the wife. That sex marks marriage is shown in the prepartition strategy of drawing fixed sexual boundaries between couples. As Aziz (1978:145) reports for Tibet, only those brothers who never had sexual intercourse with the common wife can expect to partition with a full share of the property. For the Nyinba, only such men can take away a full share of women's jewelry.

brothers have the opportunity of bringing wives home if they are mature when a second wife has to be added, following divorce or widowhood.[13] This combination of roles usually vested in the eldest may be what led early investigators to assume that the eldest brother was the "true" husband.

While the precedence of the eldest may make him the father of the first children produced by the marriage, it cannot assure him a permanently successful relationship, or continued sexual and reproductive priority. Nonetheless the eldest always has the advantage of respect and deference from his wife or wives. His position contrasts most with that of the youngest brother, whose junior status is so marked that there is a special term to describe it, *kudpu* (*skud-po*). This term implies subordinate position; it is something about which the most-junior brothers are sensitive, and it never is used to their faces. It also does not apply in cases where the youngest is wife bringer, for that gives him a special authority in the marriage.

I once asked a most-junior husband in the presence of his elder brothers what he thought about his position in their common marriage. This prompted an extended discussion in which each brother tried to downplay the special problems of the others. The youngest, in his early teens, felt that the wife treated him like a small boy or ignored him. For some of his friends it was even worse; their wives mistreated and even beat them to retaliate for ill-treatment by their mothers-in-law. He said that the best he could hope for was that the wife would watch over his interests. This disparity of ages, which places the wife in a supervisory role, makes her somewhat like a mother. But this is the only similarity. Wives engage in sexual joking even with husbands who are little boys, and I have seen women tease child-husbands mercilessly. My teen-aged informant concluded that because the wife can be so unkind, the most-junior brother isn't really a husband. But his brothers denied this, and said his age was responsible for his negative viewpoint. They reminded him that since a woman raises her junior husband, she can create a man she later will like best. All the favored youngest husbands prove the truth of this, but it also is true that the youngest husband suffers for a time because of his youth and junior position.

The fact that senior and junior husbands have different positions within the marriage and in relation to their common wife does not mean they are more or less husbands. There simply are differences in their statuses. Diversity in polygynous wives' statuses, based on seniority, rank by birth,

---

[13] For one example, a household had three brothers and three wives. The first was brought by the eldest, but she died in childbirth. The second was brought by the middle brother, but she died later on pilgrimage. The youngest selected the last wife and chose a woman approximately his age.

and so forth, have not been so difficult to comprehend. With polyandry, however, lack of information and androcentric and exotic biases have combined to cloud the issues (see Chandra 1972:80; Levine 1980b:285).

The issue of paternity in polyandry has been even more problematic. Logically it would seem impractical—if not unreasonable—to try to determine the paternity of children born into a polyandrous marriage. However, all brothers are not home at the same time; one brother may be too young for sexual relations and another in disfavor with the common wife. Also, most polyandrously married women have just two husbands, while less than one-third have three and less than one-fifth have four or more. Women keep track of their menstrual cycles and their sexual activity during the month. They believe they are most fertile during the second week of the cycle and that pregnancy is less likely, although not impossible, at other times.[14] Inevitably there are pregnancies where the father could be any of several husbands. Then the parents wait for the birth of the child and compare its appearance to the men to make an assignment of paternity, a practice also reported for West and Central Tibet (see Cassinelli and Ekvall 1969:159; Westermarck 1925:115). Thus the wife holds the major responsibility in paternity designations; the man who is so designated is treated as genitor for all social purposes.

In circumstances such as these, paternity never can be so definite as in monogamous or polygynous societies which heavily guard women's sexual behavior; and this has its drawbacks. I have heard Nyinba privately question a number of recent paternity assignments. First, as people note, multiple conjugal relationships and imprecisions in timing conception often make it difficult to determine who the actual father might be. Second—and this principally is a man's complaint—women may use paternity designations for political purposes: to please a husband who feels himself neglected, to insure that all her children are fathered by the man or men with whom she is likely to partition, and for other, pragmatic reasons. Third, both men and women say that wives can use their rights of paternity designation to mask illegitimacies. This is a subject of frequent gossip, and people whisper of cases where a husband unknowingly accepted another man's child. Commonly cited too are cases where a husband knowingly accepted an illegitimate child, either to avoid scandal or because the marriage was otherwise childless.[15] Only rarely and in the early years of a mar-

---

[14] Accordingly, women may decide to meet their lovers when they are menstruating, to lessen the risk of pregnancy.

[15] In the former instance, the child is apt to be neglected and to die young. In the latter, household members take note of the child's presumed true paternity and openly acknowledge this at a later point in time. The child and its patrilineal descendants are obliged to observe

riage have men rejected their wives' assignments of paternity, which is tantamount to demanding a divorce. Thus while Nyinba place less value on sexual exclusivity and tolerate greater uncertainty about paternity than do members of most societies, they do attempt to determine the paternity of children born in polyandrous marriages.

There are several reasons for the significance attached to paternity differentiation. First, fathers are more important in folk theories of heredity and clanship, as accords with Nyinba genealogical concerns generally and the system of patrilineal descent particularly. Clanship must be determined unambiguously in rare nonfraternal polyandry and when illegitimacy is suspected, to avoid incest between kin and clan fellows. Second, paternity determines rights to household membership, inheritance, and succession.

Having one father acknowledge a child is a prerequisite for membership in a household, a dowry upon marriage for a daughter, and coparcenary rights in the trongba estate for a son. It also entitles the child to support, financial and emotional, from this man and all his brothers within the marriage. The former is described as the child's real father (*a-ya ngo-rtog*). The child is told, sometimes directly, sometimes in indirect ways, who his real father is. This is done by parents, other household members, and/or relatives—practices seem to vary in different families. I don't know when it is considered proper to tell a child, but most children are aware of who their real father is by the time they are five or six years old. This relates to the third value of differentiated paternity, which is emotional. Real fathers and children have special relationships and take special care of one another. Men say they feel that their labors for the household are worthwhile when their child will reap the benefits. They also say they fear being neglected in their old age if they have no real children in the household to look after them. This is why men place such emphasis on having sons "of their own," and why the absence of own children is the most sympathetically viewed reason for conjoint marriage.

The real father is the reference point from which other patrilateral kin relationships are traced. Legitimate children use the terms a-ya and *a-u* to describe the man recognized as their genitor and his brothers; it is extended from them to male agnates of the father's generation. It also applies to husbands of a mother's (real or classificatory) sisters, who themselves are known by the terms used for mother. When an illegitimate child wins an admission of paternity from a man outside his household, he first will refer to and address that man as "father." Later he will extend that term to his

---

rules of exogamy within their natural father's (as well as their mother's husbands') clans, although, as chapter 3 shows, they do not always do so.

new-found father's brothers and adopt appropriate terms of address and reference for all patrilateral relatives. Fathers also are differentiated according to age by modifiers meaning "elder," "middle," and "younger." The reference point for age differentiation is the eldest of the brothers in the household, with those male agnates who are older being "elder father," those younger being "younger father," and so on. The result is that siblings use the same terms for their relatives, regardless of their different paternity or maternity.

Differential paternity rarely is discussed publicly; it is unmarked by any special terms or behavior, unless and until partition is contemplated. Then it becomes a public issue, and fathers begin openly discriminating between their own and their brothers' children. When partition occurs, children aged seven and over go to live with their acknowledged genitors. This is a compelling motivation for adjusting paternity declarations to the exigencies of domestic politics: a woman in a household contemplating partition would be foolish to name anyone but the husband she intends to partition with as the father of her child. Otherwise she risks separation from that child when partition occurs.

Differentiated paternity may be more muted in Tibet. This is what the literature suggests, for no one has reported so careful or comprehensive a system of reckoning paternity there as Nyinba have developed. Nepali inheritance law, which gives brothers equal rights to a share of the estate and allots shares on a per stirpes basis, may play a part in this. Tibetan inheritance, by contrast, was per capita, although brothers leaving a landholding corporate household often did not receive full shares (Goldstein 1978b:328–29). While per stirpes inheritance requires that fatherhood be kept straight, it is kinship concerns which give differential paternity the greater salience in everyday life.

Polyandry persists, despite the disapproval of the dominant Nepali-speaking caste society. We have seen the cultural and social supports for it: ideals of fraternal solidarity, a household system that is organized around several adult males which permits economic specialization and increased income, and finally a social system built upon the nonproliferation of households, which is highly adaptive in a region of limited resources and limited land availability.

The literature on polyandry, however, focuses on its economic dimensions. Thus we find Aziz punctuating a discussion of household labor management with the observation that Tibetans see polyandry as "primarily an economic relationship" (1978:106)—despite her rich data on the powerful values entailed (1978:139–143). By the same criteria, monogamy and polygyny are equally economic relationships. The fact is that marriage in all

Domestic Processes and the Paradox of Partition

societies has its economic aspects, most strikingly where households are the prime productive units and married adults the major contributors to them. Goldstein presents a stronger argument in suggesting that polyandry is inherently problematic for men and is chosen solely for its economic advantages: "Polyandry was a difficult form of marriage which produced stresses and anxieties and which required considerable adjustment by the participants. It was perceived by the thoughtful more as the lesser of two evils than as the prized form of marriage" (1971b:73).[16]

This is not the view that Nyinba men express. I heard no complaints about sharing wives' sexuality, nor of having to reach an accommodation with co-resident brothers. The only complaint, and the chronic problem in Nyinba polyandry, arose when a wife overtly favored one or more men and rejected the others. I know of only one case where a brother was accused of encouraging such favoritism. The cultural ideal is for a brother, particularly the more mature, eldest brother, to stand back and yield his rights to his siblings. He may occupy his time in love affairs with single girls or women whose husbands are away, so his forbearance need not lead to sexual deprivation. What then do we suspect such men might be missing? And why do we presume that sharing a spouse is impossible for men, but not for polygynous women?

If men in polyandry have less personal freedom, this is more because they live in large extended households, which demand considerable mutual accommodation, than because they have to share a woman's sexuality. If younger brothers have less authority, this is because of their junior position in the household, not because of any fundamental, permanent disadvantages in the marriage. Nor can we assume that polyandrous husbands and wives experience more stresses or anxieties than participants in the fraternal joint families common elsewhere in South Asia.

Here I have treated polyandry as the outcome of a unitary marital system, guided by kinship and political, as well as economic, motivations. From the Nyinba perspective, it is not a special type of marriage, but the outcome of a process with diverse resolutions at different points in time. Boys and girls grow up in a society with polyandry the commonest manifestation of marriage, particularly at its outset. They see their elders and respected community leaders living in polyandry at one time, monogamy another time. When boys in their teens marry together with their older

[16]Goldstein's primary data derive from refugees in India and from Limi, a region near Nyinba in Nepal. In both cases—most markedly in the former—major social transformations had led to a decline in polyandry, and this may have colored expressed views on the subject. Aziz worked with a refugee community where the incidence of polyandry had declined as well (1978:146).

brothers, they realize that their positions within the marriage probably will change over their lives. This requires a set of attitudes toward marriage different than those with which we are familiar. Among the more exotic—and necessary—correlates of the system are that sexual exclusivity is not highly prized, sexual jealousy is muted, and paternity is apportioned between a number of men.

For the individual, there are three motivations for maintaining a polyandrous marriage. First, conforming to societal ideals about fraternal amity is important—a person who does so is regarded as the equivalent of our "good family man." As we have seen, different maternity of brothers makes this ideal less compelling, and large sibling-group size makes it harder to sustain. Second, polyandry keeps one in a politically powerful trongba household. Third, it facilitates household management and raises the standard of living. Polyandry in marriage is so integral a part of Tibetan social structure that Nyinba ancestors who migrated south from Tibet certainly imported it and refined it in their new circumstances. Far from Tibetan influence, removed from the constraints of the higher-altitude, arid Tibetan environment, it remained the norm. This is because Nyinba also imported a Tibetan household system and a Tibetan cultural orientation. However, polyandry is not always maintained, either in Tibet or among the Nyinba. Chapter 8 focuses upon partition—the failure of polyandry—and its consequences for social dynamics.

8
Change in the Village: Regulative and Reformative Systems

Nyinba estimate village size by numbers of households, rather than individuals, and they gauge village growth by gains through household partitions minus losses through household extinctions. The concern goes beyond household enumeration, for Nyinba also try to guide the direction village growth takes. Villagers accordingly have helped members of other households through difficult times to try to avert extinctions they considered undesirable, and they have intervened to smooth over quarrels in troubled households in order to prevent partitions, although these efforts have not always been successful.

There are two related rationales offered for actions such as these. First, there is a concern with the consequences of uneven growth across units of village structure, which Nyinba see as impeding effective political and ceremonial functioning. Second, there is a concern with the negative impact of excessive growth or losses in village membership overall. Despite this, changes in village composition proceed inexorably, and when they have occurred, villagers have responded by reorganizing households to achieve a workable balance again. Single partitions or extinctions have posed relatively little problem: they simply have prompted realignments in individual trongbat affiliations. Uneven rates of partition over time have had cumulative, more far-reaching effects and have produced more radical changes, including the restructuring of entire village section systems. Major shifts in population and in patterns of land utilization have produced still more radical changes, including the complete dissolution of certain villages and the creation or reintegration of others. The point to keep in mind is that for Nyinba, village size is a collective concern and collectively managed.

Trongbat alliances provide the most sensitive indicators of changes in village membership and adaptations to them. Trongbat are households sharing a common partition history and which hold certain formal and ceremonial obligations to one another. Because of this, they recapitulate the history of past partitions and the evolution of the village through partitions. Because trongbat alliances are responsive to shifts in village population, their history offers clues to village growth and change over time. Trongbat, however, hold more than a key to the past; they also provide an alternative framework for understanding Nyinba social structure. Through them we are able to see a society more fluid and a village population more variable than either synchronic data or the legends of elders suggest.

Processes of Partition

Conjoint marriage anticipates partition, and the reason is that there must be a married couple to stand at the core of each new household. Despite this, people deny that conjoint marriage is a deliberate strategy for partition. Rather, they argue, particular individuals become involved in conjoint marriage for other reasons and then find themselves embroiled in irresolvable family disputes.

While conjoint marriages do not have to end in partition, once they begin the risk of partition is ever present. This was apparent even within the relatively brief span of my field research. By the time I first left Humla in 1975, ten of the twenty conjoint marriages contracted in recent decades had been severed by partition. By 1984, the end of my second visit, four more had partitioned, and two of the six marriages which had become conjoint in the intervening nine years had partitioned as well. Thus a total of 62 percent of conjoint marriages had partitioned by this time. More partitions can be expected to follow. Significantly, the sons of different mothers always split along the lines of parentage—which, also significantly, was not the case for the sons of different fathers.[1]

The best predictor for partition is sexually exclusive couples who have formed mini-marriages within the marriage and discrete families within the household. Husbands and wives in marriages that remain undivided have a basis for continued unity. They also have reasons for not partitioning— including the welfare of their common children. When the parentage of children is mixed between different husbands and wives, it becomes impossible to divide them neatly into new families. Thus in the case of a mar-

---

[1] Seven of the sets of brothers in these twenty-six marriages were sons of different mothers, and four of these, or 57 percent, have undergone a partition. Of the twenty-one marriages with three or more brothers, twelve, or again 57 percent, have partitioned. Five of the twenty-six marriages ended in widowhood without a partition occurring.

riage that once was sexually inclusive, later became exclusive, and still later was divided by partition, the rule that children go with their fathers can have tragic repercussions. This is clear in the following description of such a situation:

> Lhamo was the first wife in a marriage that later grew to include three women married to four men. Although she eventually allied herself with one of the husbands, she initially was wife to them all and bore children to three. When partition occurred in 1968, her four younger children were taken away by their two fathers, and she moved off with her favorite husband and their daughter. That daughter, however, married in 1970. Lhamo then contemplated leaving her husband to be with her four other children, did so briefly, and finally, unable to decide what to do, returned to her parents' home. Her unhappiness may have aggravated a long-standing illness, and she died in 1974.

We have seen that large sibling groups and brothers who have different mothers are especially likely to begin a conjoint marriage. Once begun, such marriages invariably have problems. Most of the problems are blamed on the co-wives, and the criticisms come from men and women alike.

The fact of the matter is that conjoint marriage is intrinsically problematic. It frustrates many of the expectations Nyinba normally have of their marriages and it creates special hardships for women in particular. First, it brings different women of the same generation together in a single household under conditions of unequal authority. It does so, moreover, in a society where women ordinarily spend only a brief period under the authority of their mothers-in-law and spend their mature years heading their own households. Second, because women stay within the village engaged in agricultural labor, co-wives are obliged to work together and to spend considerable time in each other's company. By contrast, co-husbands are separated by their work. While one man is away on trading trips, the second is apt to be herding cattle in local pasture areas, and the third attending to agriculture at home. Finally, the senior wife, who has the greater control over household stores, can be expected to keep the best for her children. This is notorious as a source of domestic tensions. It is not surprising then to find women the main participants in quarrels, while their husbands, paragons of fraternal solidarity, sit quietly on the sidelines. Yet more may be involved in these quarrels than inequities exacerbated by the irritations of women's daily lives. It also is true that women may voice the complaints their husbands must not voice, lest their complaints shatter fraternal ideals and take disputes past recall.[2]

Co-wives have fewer problems when they are household sisters. Nyinba say that sisters are committed to one another's interests and the interests of one another's children, who are their nieces and nephews. The example people most often give to illustrate the value of sororal polygyny is Yogma household, described in chapter 6. This, nevertheless, is a household which could just as well serve the purpose of illustrating the risks entailed in conjoint marriage. In this case, the risk has extended over four generations.

> There have been conjoint marriages in Yogma house for the last four generations. The first generation included two brothers who were the sons of a single father and a single mother. They wed two sisters, but the marriage was not sexually exclusive, as the paternity of the children in figure 8.1 shows. Their five sons wed three women who were not sisters, one of whom was childless; again the children's paternity is proof of a non-exclusive marriage.
>
> These men had three sons. It was at this point, the third generation of conjoint marriage, that sexually exclusive relationships seem first to have been established. The three sons each took separate wives. The first two were sisters, and they have remained close. They also have excluded the third wife from any power in the household, and this woman's position was further undermined by her failure to produce sons. For a brief period relations between the various husbands and wives deteriorated, partition was contemplated, and they all set up separate hearths. But the brothers and their wives soon were back together again.
>
> The sons of the sisters initially wed polyandrously, but their wife had only a daughter. On account of this, they considered taking a second wife. This was discussed for years; the first wife did her best to try to prevent it; and there were major disagreements among the men. Eventually they did marry again and chose a woman unrelated to their first wife. The newer wife has aligned herself with the youngest brother, and talk of partition has begun again.

The term used for partition is *phewa* (*phye-ba*), which means "to separate." It involves a division of persons and property both, with the latter depending on how the male coparceners realign themselves. Where marriage and family lines are clearly drawn, the division of persons is unproblematic. Men form new households around the wife or wives with

---

[2]Compare Sharma (1980:184) on Northwest India.

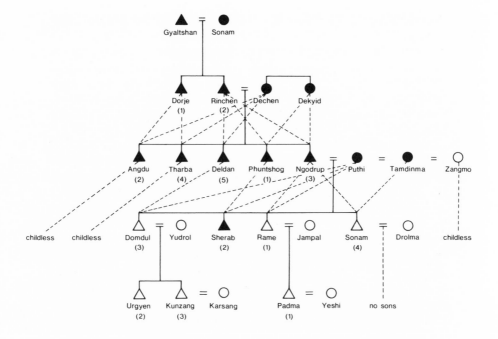

Numbers indicate relative age of siblings

The dashed lines indicate declared parentage

Figure 8.1   Four Generations of Conjoint Marriage

whom they are closest and the children they have fathered. Partition can produce marriages which are polyandrous or monogamous, polygynous-polyandrous, conjoint, or polygynous—it does not matter. However, this is no excuse to add new wives, unless the men wish to risk partitioning yet again.

The step which sets partition in motion is the establishment of separate hearths in different portions of the house. People then divide household food stores, and following that, cooking and eating utensils. Rights to set up housekeeping in specific portions of the house depend upon relative seniority. The eldest brother and his family get the room which served the entire family as its hearth and dining room—that is, the best spot—while the younger brother(s) and his(their) family take the inner storage room and cook on the outer hearth. In the rare event of a tripartite partition, the youngest brother(s) would move into the outer storage room; and were a quadripartite partition ever to occur, the very youngest brother(s) would move to the outer hearth, located at the end of the drafty corridor and stairs that lead to the barn underneath the house and the roof above. This is where all remain until the partition is finalized and separate houses can be built. In cases where a house is unusually large or family resources meager, the partitioning brothers simply may build a wall down the middle of the house and add a second door and second set of stairs to one side. Even so, this is seen as a temporary solution. Eventually the elder brothers and their household will help the younger ones build a new house and then take over the original house for themselves.

The elder brother's household is considered the "inner house," and this may be marked in the name it acquires after partition. Take the example of a household with the (common) name of Gongma. Were partition to occur, the household occupied by the eldest brothers would be known as Gongma Nangma, which means "Inner Upper House," while their younger brothers would form the "Outer Upper House" (cf. Carrasco on Tibet [1959:130]).[3] There is somewhat more prestige in belonging to the inner, thus older, home, but only the village or section founder's home gets any special recognition, and only at a few ceremonies, and at that, no more than special servings of beer.

Rules of Property Division

There are three steps in any property division: (1) determining the size of the share each brother is to receive, (2) assessing the precise value of specific items of property in the estate, and (3) assembling fairly valued parcels of different types of property. Certainly the last is one of the most trying procedures during the entire partition process, and the most difficult task of all is balancing shares in land. Landholdings consist of diverse small plots, varying in size, in altitude, in quality of soil, in distance from irrigation sources, and in angle of exposure to sun, all of which affect productivity. It is virtually impossible to match plot for plot in a fair and equal distribution.[4] One also can imagine the difficulty involved in dividing up an odd number of cattle or in deciding how to apportion the household's single horse; and similar problems arise with heirlooms like enormous brass cooking pots and special wedding costumes. None of these items, however, have anywhere near the importance of land. Brothers may try to balance one large plot of land against one with better soil closer to home, they

---

[3] Partition of households thus is conceptualized in terms comparable to those used in describing lineage segmentation (see the discussion in chapter 3).

[4] Large, newly cleared plots may be subdivided in partition, but the older, more-productive lands usually are considered as being of optimum or, more often, of less-than-optimum size.

may subdivide one field into two smaller ones, and they may trade off a half share in a horse for a prize yak-cow crossbreed. They may also cast lots, and if all else fails, bring in a mediator. Women get to take their dowries with them wherever they go, and if the first wife was wife to all the brothers while the junior wife was sexually exclusive, the former will get a greater share of valuable jewelry to redress the inequity.

Shares are divided according to a unique system of per stirpes reckoning. The uniqueness arises from the complications created by polyandry repeated across generations. These complications and additional, interpersonal considerations may influence property divisions and yield in the end idiosyncratic allocations of shares or divisions identical in form to those produced under a per capita system. Per stirpes inheritance is the rule in Nepal, per capita reckoning in Tibet, and it is possible that Nyinba developed their inheritance system in response to Hindu Nepali influence.

Nepali law follows the Mitakshara system, which is adapted to the traditional Hindu joint family.[5] Two statutes of particular relevance here are phrased as follows.

> (1) Unless otherwise provided for in this law, everybody entitled to inherit the property shall get an equal share;
> (2) Sons of brothers living in a joint family shall be entitled to shares from the shares of their fathers only. (Regmi Research 1976:15)

The poor fit between the second statute and circumstances of a polyandrous extended family system with rare partition should stand out immediately. First, there are problems associated with the legal status of unofficial declarations of fatherhood. We have seen that Nyinba mark the paternity of trongba children and keep track of this information for generations. But paternity remains a private matter until the time of partition. Then paternity assignments become politicized, and in cases where they were clouded by uncertainty, become matters of public contention as well. A second problem lies in deciding which generation of men should be counted fathers in reckoning the shares. Nyinba assess shares either according to the paternity of the partitioners or, if they are soon to retire, according to the paternity of their children. However, there are times when both assessments are equally defensible—and can produce enormously different shares of property for the individuals involved.

There are even more complications than this. For one thing, the ideal of fraternal equity influences allocations of shares in partition too. For an-

---

[5] See Parry's discussion of inheritance in India (1979:164–68).

other, men find it difficult to partition against the will of their brothers, despite their legal right to do so. Thus we can find men squabbling over the paternity of a particular brother or disputing which generation of men are to be accounted fathers for the reckoning of shares. We also can find men effectively bypassing per stirpes rules to provide one brother adequate land to live on or bribing a brother with more land than he deserves in order to gain his acquiescence to the partition. The result is that assessments of shares always are subject to negotiation and can be quite irregular. I shall illustrate this with two cases that followed standard per stirpes rules, yet ended up in effectively per capita divisions, and a third that had to work around positive rules in order to meet the implicit requirement for equity in property divisions between brothers.

    1. Three widowed Todpa men remarried Yudrol, a woman much younger than themselves and only eight years older than their eldest son. Within a decade, Yudrol had several sons of her own, and her stepsons had married and had their own children too. Yudrol and her daughter-in-law quarreled continually over which of their similarly aged children got the best food and clothes. The household was riven by dissension, and partition seemed to be the only solution. It was the general opinion of villagers that there was little that could be done and that this household would partition sooner or later anyway, because there now were two sets of brothers by different mothers.

    The division of persons in this partition was somewhat atypical, partly because the schism crossed two generations. The eldest father and the children of the first wife formed the inner household; Yudrol, her two younger husbands, and her children formed the outer household. The division of property appeared to follow a regular per stirpes (*aya' i skal-ba,* literally "fathers' shares") division, with Yudrol's husbands standing as fathers in the calculations. However, the result was that the two households ended up with roughly equal amounts of property. This was because one man had been favored by both wives and had most of the children, who were distributed equally in inner and outer households. Had the shares been calculated according to Yudrol's husbands' fathers, the result would have been quite different. Since they were sons of different men, each would have received a full share. This would have given Yudrol and her children two-thirds of the property instead of the one-half they actually obtained. The property allocation is shown in figure 8.2.

    2. A wealthy Wutig trongba included four brothers who had a single father and mother. They married jointly; their wife bore them a son and then she died. They soon remarried, but were not

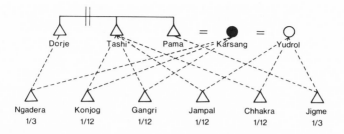

The dashed lines indicate declared parentage

Fractions indicate the size of shares each son was allotted

Figure 8.2   Per Stirpes Inheritance

happy with their new wife and divorced her. This happened several times—in each case they were unable to find a woman acceptable to all the men. Adding to their disappointments were the tragic losses of children from these marriages. Then their eldest son died shortly after his carefully arranged marriage to his mother's brother's daughter, a woman from one of the wealthiest Nyinba households. This ended all attempts at fraternal solidarity, and despite village attempts to mediate and the complete lack of sons and heirs, the brothers partitioned. Each received an equal share, because they had the same father and there were no sons to consider (thus producing what Nyinba call *spun-gyi skal-ba,* literally, "brothers' shares.")

3. A third Nyinba household included four men. While three were sons of one man, the youngest was born of their mother's lover, from a stable doubling-up relationship that began after she was widowed. Despite this, the brothers maintained the fiction that all were the sons of one man, until events of partition arose to challenge it.

The brothers remained in a single polyandrous marriage for many years. Then their first wife died after bearing two sons. Rather than risk producing sons of different mothers, they jointly married an older, infertile woman, primarily for the benefits of her labor and companionship. However, Dondrup, the youngest brother, was dissatisfied with this choice. This was a time when he was heavily involved in high-risk trade and was travelling regularly to India and Kathmandu—thus, people say, exposed to foreign notions about marriage. Whatever the factors involved, Dondrup decided to marry again, this time to a much younger woman and for a mostly exclusive sexual relationship. After the marriage produced one son, Dondrup had a vasectomy. By then it was too late—there already was a son with a different mother — and people predicted this would lead to partition later on. The expected happened within a dozen years. Because the two older sons were adults, they decided to count Dondrup and his brothers as fathers in calculating the shares. For a time, the other brothers schemed to exclude Dondrup from any property at all, citing his illegitimate status. Fellow villagers argued against this, noting that this was an issue that never had been raised previously, that the four of them had lived their entire lives as brothers, and that such an action simply would be legally and morally indefensible. Eventually this attempt to disinherit Dondrup was abandoned.

The plan throughout was that the three older brothers would partition with the two older sons, and Dondrup would move off with his new wife and their son. The trouble was that one of the older sons was fathered by Dondrup as well. With per stirpes reckoning, Dondrup's one-quarter, "father's share" would have to be divided into two parts, giving one-eighth to the older son and one-eighth to the younger one. This meant that Dondrup, his young wife, and son would get only a tiny fraction of the estate's lands, far too little to live on, even with the profits (now dwindling) from Dondrup's trading activities.

In the end, the brothers agreed to follow the fiction that Dondrup's older son was fathered by another brother. That fiction satisfied the proprieties and gave Dondrup's family a full quarter share. The sons in the other household secured three-quarters of the property, the sum of the shares allotted to the fathers partitioning with them, as shown in figure 8.3.

Timing can affect how shares are allocated as well. If Dondrup had left things alone, and if his younger son had waited until the fathers' generation was fully retired and he had children of his own, he would have received a one-third share. But Nyinba see short-term strategies of this kind as unrealistic. Far-longer delays of a generation or more, simply to secure a larger share, are inconceivable. This is what I heard when I asked about the possibilities for such planning in another partition: "If this man had waited till his fathers were dead and he and his brothers had their own children, he would have received a larger share. But who waits when people are quarrelling? Who knows? If they had stayed together, he might have had more children than his brothers, which would have given each of them a smaller share still."

This suggests that partition in polyandry is informed by different notions and expectations than those reported for Hindu fraternal joint families.

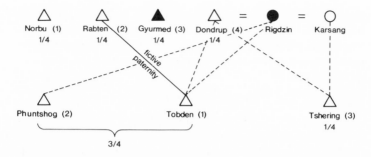

Numbers indicate relative age of siblings

The dashed lines indicate declared parentage

Fractions indicate the size of the shares each son was allotted

Figure 8.3   Fictions in Partition and Property Divisions

There we find men trying to time partition in order to maximize economic benefits to their own families (cf. Parry 1979: 178–94 for an excellent discussion). The difference may exist because having separate families and partitioning are non-normative and rare in polyandry and are situations for which well- or consciously articulated sets of strategies do not exist.

Partition is vehemently disapproved, at the present time at least. To bring a second wife and establish a conjoint marriage is considered profligate; to partition against the interests of one's brothers and desert a first wife and the family's collective children the height of selfishness. This disapproval can last for decades, as the following example shows:

A very wealthy Nyimatang household partitioned in 1956. The outer household formed around the five youngest brothers and the junior wife, who was rather sharp-tongued and openly favored certain husbands over others. In 1969, one of the brothers absconded to marry an heiress in another village. The household was so angry that they sued the heiress, reinterpreting the law against eloping with another man's wife to apply to this elopement with another woman's husband. In 1973, the most-junior husband tried to bring another wife home. The household refused to accept her, and the other brothers and the common wife, as well as kin and friends, were so hostile to the marriage that the couple had to leave the region for a year.

Not only the household, but the community as well, condemned the actions of both these couples. The disapproval continues to this day. When the youngest brother's wife attended a relative's wedding in Trangshod village in 1983, she was taunted so severely that she left in tears. And the heiress refuses to attend such events because of the insults she knows she would suffer.

Constraints in Partition

Individual, household, and community interests ordinarily discourage partition. Partition produces a lower standard of living and loss of prestige for individuals and can impoverish and politically weaken a household. Fellow villagers are concerned that member households remain viable and able to meet collective obligations, such as payment of food levies for, and sponsorship of, local rituals, and that sufficient village households remain to meet governmental obligations, such as occasional corvée labor, and for better defense against depredations on their lands. Villagers worry too that if households partitioned excessively, all would be impoverished and that they might have to abandon the traditions of hospitality of which Nyinba are justifiably proud. The converse—excessive loss of households—would mean that too few would have to fulfill the obligations of many.

The idea that the village as an entity has a stake in its size may derive from Tibetan models. In Tibet, Ladakh, and Bhutan, village size was carefully regulated, although there the regulation was enforced at the level of the state:

> There is a remarkable stability in the number and size of the holdings (in Ladakh). This is achieved by indivisibility through inheritance and by the peasants' relative lack of power to alienate their holdings. (Carrasco 1959:30)
>
> . . . a number of items hint at the existence among the peasantry of a somewhat rigid role of households regulated by the state. Thus we read in the laws of Bhutan . . . the prohibition against combining households . . . (Carrasco 1959:30)
>
> A . . . village such as Samada (south central Tibet) was a corporate entity which consisted of a formally delimited territorial area together with a specified number of corporate families having legal rights to that land. . . . The number of families was always small. . . . (Goldstein 1971a:5)

The rationale for such regulation in Tibet was the government's need for a stable number of households with the resources to meet heavy tax obligations. For Nyinba, the same sort of regulation occurs, but by decision of the community itself, rather than by edict of an overarching political system.

Partition, however, need not be problematic in all situations. Households which own more land than the norm may find certain economic constraints on partition relaxed. Villages suffering declines or imbalances in population may look more favorably upon certain partitions—and worry far more about household extinctions. While people nowadays censure partition and are mostly indifferent about extinction, this was not the case in the recent past, and as recently as the 1970s in Todpa. Thus when one Todpa village household became inviable during my first term of field research, villagers met and decided they should help out. Neighbors and trongbat provided gifts of food and offers of agricultural labor. In the end, the household survived. The reason given for the decision was that the village was too small and could not risk another extinction. The same explanations are offered for why certain heirless trongba properties were transferred to freedmen half a century ago.

Trongbat: Mutual Assistance and Rights to Reinheritance

Elders and village leaders involved in guiding collective decisions describe advantages in more-or-less-stable village populations balanced between enduring section systems. Nevertheless, household partitions and extinctions occur haphazardly and have the opposite effect. While one section is experiencing numerous partitions, the second may be undergoing numerous extinctions, and the third seeing neither partitions nor extinctions during the same period of time. Trongbat, the lowest-level association of trongba households, are the first groups affected by these changes, and their members are first to respond to them.

Trongbat resemble the voluntary household associations found elsewhere among Tibetans. They also share certain characteristics with localized lineage segments and groups based on neighborhood. In reality, they are none of these, although they entail mutual assistance, are founded by agnates, and influence residential patterns. Trongbat are the partitioned segments of a formerly unified household; as we shall see, the obligations between them extend the notions of household members' rights and duties to diverse domains of social life.

Trongbat (*grong 'byed*) means "partitioned households," and this is exactly what they are: households, two to four in number, with a common origin. Trongbat are created in a partition, and the paradigmatic trongbat are the households whose current members partitioned. In everyday speech, the term elides into trongba, so that when people speak of their trongbat, the household related by a partition, it sounds as if they were discussing their own trongba household. This homonym reflects the way in which people think about trongbat—as extensions of their own household. Thus it is trongbat who take over one's estate if a direct heir is lacking and trongbat one calls upon for assistance first at public life crisis ceremonies.

Trongbat obligations are kept distinct from their members' individual kin relationships. Instead of kinship, the idiom of the tie and its rationale are expressed in household terms and summed up in the expression, "split from a single hearth." The strength of these obligations depends upon the number of generations and the number of intervening partitions since the initial split, although the quality of their members' relationships and the way obligations are met depend also on kinship and the personal characteristics of the individuals involved.

Fundamental to trongbat relationships are notions of commonality, mutual obligation, and substitutability—all conceived in household terms. The sense of commonality derives from shared household origins and is said to produce mutual concern and a certain solidarity. Nyinba describe this as a relationship in which "sorrows and joys are shared" (*skyid-sdug gchig-pa*), which also is said about members of a household, kin, and close friends.[6] Mutual obligation is expressed formally on public occasions; and if the households have other bases for cooperation, they may assist one another on informal, everyday occasions. What I describe as the mutual substitutability of households is expressed on public occasions too and is ultimately realized in the right to inherit a moribund trongbat household's estate.

The formal occasions at which trongbat display their relationship are principally weddings and funerals and secondarily other life crisis rituals, exorcisms, household-sponsored feasts, and so on. To begin with, trongbat stand in for, and speak for, one another in arranging betrothals in order to avoid the loss of face possible when direct negotiations fail. They sponsor special feasts for guests at betrothals and subsequent celebrations and are feasted in turn by the other party to the wedding and its trongbat. At weddings—which are exceedingly elaborate events—they work for days behind the scenes and supervise the serving of food to invited guests. The right to do so is highly valued, and it falls first to "close" (*nye-mo*) trongbat. More distantly related households help out in cooking and collecting wood and water. The feasting which follows weddings continues for days, and the first feasts held outside the groom's house take place in the homes of trongbat members.

Funerals are less elaborate than full weddings, but they are far commoner and thus call upon trongbat services more frequently. Trongbat

---

[6] Voluntary associations in Tibet with functions like trongbat are known by this name (Miller 1956).

members take charge of domestic responsibilities for the household of the deceased during the four-day period when pollution and expressions of grief are most intense. They prepare food for villagers who come to mourn at that time and later assist in preparing for the final funeral. Trongbat also help one another at privately sponsored feasts associated with the ritual calendar, at exorcisms, and at life crisis rituals performed by lamas, all of which require extensive preparations.[7] Finally, they act together at local ceremonies, jointly hosting feasts for fellow villagers.

Trongbat perform their work within one another's homes, except when there is death pollution. They usually cook on the outer hearth, in contrast to family members, who prepare their meals in the inner hearth room. In cases of recent partition, the outer trongbat household finds itself cooking on the very hearth they used while waiting for their new home to be built.

These are the everyday rights and obligations of trongbat. Trongbat also hold the ultimate right of inheritance of one another's estates. This right is activated when one of the households fails to produce sons as heirs or daughters who can marry uxorilocally.

Nyinba state that their system of trongbat reinheritance follows Nepali law. In fact it does not, because the law identifies agnates as the proper heirs. By contrast, Nyinba grant these rights to the household or households related by the most recent partition—not to any individual agnates. The key word in this is *hakwala* (Nep.), "one who has a claim" (cf. Turner 1966:628), and the law states:

> The nearest agnate relative within seven generations is known as a *hakwala*. . . . For purposes of inheritance, daughters shall have no title as long as the husband, wife, son, grandson (on the male side) or other *hakwalas* living in the undivided family of the deceased person are extant. (Regmi Research 1976:6–7)

For Nyinba, trongbat are proper hakwala, because the land and other property of trongbat derive from the same source. This stands without regard to kin relationships.[8]

Heirless households do have some control over the fate of their estates, and their members' needs in their final years may supersede the rights of

---

[7] Ortner (1978:106–9) provides a detailed description and analysis of the rituals surrounding funerals and protective exorcisms among the Sherpa of eastern Nepal. Like the Nyinba, Sherpa are Tibetan Buddhists of the Nyingmapa sect, and the ritual practices of the two groups are comparable.

[8] Nyinba also use the Nepali phrase *angsheri bhai*, "brother co-heirs" to describe trongbat, although they are not always brothers or even agnates, because of occasional uxorilocal marriages.

trongbat. Specifically, the last few members of such a household have the right to join another household, with the understanding that they will be cared for in old age in return for the inheritance of the bulk of their property. This is known as "household joining" (*grong-'brel*), and it is rare. I know only of two cases in recent decades. Both involved an elderly widow who moved into the household she joined, lived there in relative comfort until she died, and was given a respectable funeral. One of the two women joined a distant trongbat. She had tried to arrange this with the trongbat closest to her household, but it had too few members at the time and could not guarantee her good care. The second widow moved in with a household that lacked any trongbat connection. The arrangements were made for her by fellow villagers, and the aim was to help the other household—then verging on inviability for lack of land.

The last surviving members in an heirless household ordinarily finish their lives in their own home, cared for by relatives and trongbat. When the last person dies, the house is considered "extinct" (*yal-ba*). Trongbat heirs sponsor the funeral, and then the property is transferred. The distribution follows the order of past partitions. Households produced in recent bipartite partitions inherit one another's entire estates, and households from a triple partition each inherit half the estate. When there are trongbat related by complex series of long-past partitions, claims are less clear-cut, which gives room for maneuvering. A powerful trongbat might take an unfairly large portion. A very poor trongbat might cite its poverty to appeal for more than its share. In the earlier part of this century, when land was less scarce and rights of reinheritance were not guarded so carefully, powerful headmen *thalu* were able to deliver vacant estates to client freedmen.

In summary, trongbat ties derive structurally from the trongba household and are identified conceptually with it. The bond is their common origin in hearth—the center of the domestic world—and land, the key economic resource. If trongbat ordinarily include agnates, this is because partitioners are pun and because patrifilial succession and inheritance ordinarily pass in the male line. Occasional uxorilocality can change this and place potentially marriageable nyen in a trongbat relationship. Irregular successions can bring unrelated people together as trongbat too; and when the successors are freedmen, members of different strata enter a relationship of mutual assistance and cooperation. Despite the constraints on interpersonal relationships (and citizen-landholder resentment at the loss of property to which they were entitled), these obligations continue to be met.

Finally, trongbat are distinguished from relationships based on locality. Newly partitioned households try to build alongside one another, but this is not always possible. If initially possible, it may not be so in subsequent rebuildings—it depends on the density of settlement in a given village. This is why all the trongbat in the small hamlet of Wutig, but only half of those in the full-sized villages of Barkhang and Todpa, are located alongside one another.

There is, in addition, a completely separate concept of neighborhood. Neighbors (*khyim-tshes*) often help one another on a daily basis, but are not obliged to do so. The sole factor supporting their relationship is propinquity, furthered by adjacent yards and connecting roof terraces. This facilitates visiting between households and encourages spending work and leisure time together. Because houses can last a century or more, relations based on neighborhood continue over generations. However, this does not occasion assistance at life crisis, nor confer any inheritance rights. Only small (freedman) households use neighbors to substitute for the ordinary functions of trongbat, which they lack.

Change and Adaptation in Trongbat and Village Sections

Trongbat change over time. A group grown too large from partitions may subdivide. A household that has lost trongbat allies to extinctions may have to forge new alliances elsewhere. Events of partition and extinction over generations can have cumulative effects and eventually create serious imbalances in village section systems. Ultimately, such imbalances can have a negative impact on village functioning—or so Nyinba say, for they generally manage to keep things from proceeding that far. The responses they make are consistent and consistently reformative: redefinitions of trongbat, section, and village boundaries or reorganizations of their memberships.

These attempts at village regulation are consistent with the generalized models of village structure that Nyinba present. When they describe their villages, Nyinba most often speak of trongbat as stable and fixed components of village sections, which they describe as stable and enduring constituents of villages. This, however, cannot be taken as an ideal perpetually challenged by the realities of random partitions and extinctions beyond collective control. Organizational stability is a goal—and it is a reality achieved for limited periods of time.

There is, however, more to Nyinba commentaries on village structure than this. The accounts that people provide are not of a single piece. They are rich and they are various. In message they follow two general patterns, which can be described as alternative models or levels of models of social structure. At one level, we can find the conventionally expressed, simplified statements about stable trongbat, unitary foundings of villages, and the like. These tend to emphasize structural relationships and tend to be synchronically oriented. At another level are more esoteric models of village structure that consider processes of change over time and embrace, rather than gloss over, irregularities in household origins, successions, trongbat arrangements, and so on. Younger Nyinba usually are conversant only with the former, while knowledgeable elders cite both. I tended to hear the former mostly at earlier stages in my fieldwork and more often elicited the latter towards the end of my stay. The different types of narrative also serve different functions: the first charters village unity, and the second keeps clanship straight, ensures that people worship the correct deities, and validates inheritance claims.

Elders are expected to keep in memory accounts of how serial partitions generated present-day villages and to mark cases of trongbat and section memberships which do not follow normal patterns. That is, they are expected to know both village-wide genealogies and the genealogies marking village households' past partitions. These past partitions, one should note, are seen retrospectively in a positive light, because they laid the foundation for present-day village structure. This is similar to the way in which histories of origin glorify immigrant ancestors, while immigrants nowadays are held in contempt. The general form of processes of village generation through household partition can be illustrated with a conventional genealogical diagram (fig. 8.4).

When describing the development of their villages, elders pay particular attention to household foundings and the initial partitions from founding households. They begin with the immigration of the ancestor or ancestors who founded the village and established the household(s) standing at the apex of village structure. The next structurally significant events are the first partitions, which Nyinba conventionally ascribe to the village founders' sons. Following this are an indeterminate number of partitions between section founding and the present day.

In the first partition depicted in figure 8.4, the innermost, founder's household, labeled 1, passes to the eldest son, and the two brothers in households 1 and 2 become trongbat. When the descendants of 2 partition, their households, 2 and 4, become trongbat to one another. When 4 partitions, it becomes the primary trongbat to 6, which puts 2 in the position of being a more distant trongbat to both of them. When 6 partitions, the trongbat again subsegments. Households 6 and 8 now have the closer relationship, and 4, now of less importance to its former ally, may reinstitute a fuller cooperative relationship with 2. While 2 would be the primary trongbat to 4, and 6 would be the primary trongbat to 8, all these households also may act together in collective activities and all retain rights— although in different degrees—in one another's estates. The notion of

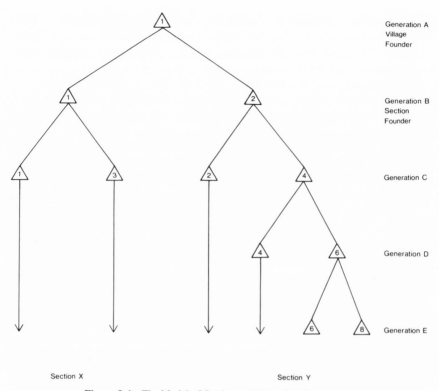

Figure 8.4 The Model of Section and *Trongbat* Generation

graduated rights and the potential flexibility in trongbat relationships are well expressed in a diagram my Nyinba assistant drew (fig. 8.5).

As he described it, the first partition creates a trongbat of households 1 and 2. Later partitions make trongbat of 1 and 3, or 3 and 5. However, barring the extinction of household 3, 1 and 5 would not have a strong, cooperative relationship on their own. It is the absence of appropriate trongbat partners that leads people to forge alliances with households related from long-past partitions. This is illustrated in figure 8.6.

In this example, we see household 1 obliged to reinstate a long-lapsed trongbat relationship with household 2. It has the option of so doing because all partitioned households are potential trongbat and trongbat in the widest sense of the term. They may forever reactivate rights and obligations of mutual assistance. Thus the trongbat relationship is inherently flexible, which facilitates adaptations to inevitable changes in the balance and numbers of village households. We also can find in trongbat relationships

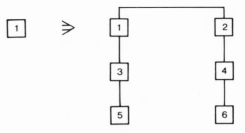

Figure 8.5 Dynamism and Change in *Trongbat* Relationships

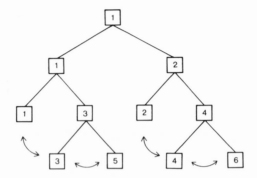

Time A: Existing Trongbat Relationships

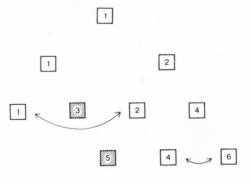

Time B: After Extinctions

 Trongbat Relationship

Extinct Household

Figure 8.6 Changing *Trongbat* Relationships

the partial crystallization of the village's past partition history, upon which the ghostly traces of extinct households still exert an effect.

I can describe the circumstances of four trongbat in Todpa village that illustrate such flexibility and the way in which households reorganize in the course of village change.

1. Two Todpa households, which we may call A and B, partitioned more than nine generations ago. Later each underwent another partition and let the initial trongbat relationship lapse. A's trongbat later became extinct, and B's partitioned once more, leaving its former partner more strongly committed to another household. So B sought out A and reinstituted their relationship. This was facilitated by the marriage of A and B's household heads to sisters especially fond of one another.

2. Nai, Todpa's innermost, or founder, household, lost its only trongbat in the early 1950s. The last survivor in this case was an elderly widow. Because Nai itself was virtually moribund at the time, she decided to join her property to, and spend her last years in, another, distant trongbat household which could properly care for her. As a result, Nai lost its right to full reinheritance and its trongbat relationship as well. Its response was to ally with an unrelated neighbor experiencing similar problems in viability. Now with a vigorous young head and fine lands, Nai's economic situation has improved, but its trongbat situation still is a makeshift one.

3. A third Todpa household lost its two trongbat to extinctions well over a hundred years ago.[9] Because it has a partition history different from those of the other households in the village, it had no former trongbat to turn to. Instead it joined with two other households, themselves the last representatives of a former village section. These three are still trongbat today.

4. Todpa includes two temple households located near one another several hundred feet above the village. They belong to different village sections—each belongs to the section from which the temple founder originally came. They have, nonetheless, preferred to rely on one another, rather than on their true trongbat. There are two reasons for this. First, members of temple households have greater familiarity with the special rituals each has to follow than lay persons do. Second, their relationships with true trongbat had foundered.

The first of these cases involves a fairly routine adjustment to the vagaries of unpredictable household partitions and extinctions. The second

---

[9]This happened prior to the tax registration of 1868, which fails to list these households.

case is more unusual, involving two almost fatally weakened households clinging to one another because they could not meet trongbat obligations to anyone else. The third case illustrates anomalies in section membership, which will be discussed presently. The fourth case shows how special needs may lead a household to establish relations of mutual assistance with neighbors. By 1983, I should add, the two temple households had mended relations with their true trongbat and were beginning to seek them out in formal, ceremonial contexts. All other Todpa villagers had conventional trongbat relationships, that is, relationships with the household or households they most recently had partitioned from. In the main, what these cases show is that trongbat are managed at individual household discretion and that relationships by kinship, friendship, and neighborhood may be called upon to supplement trongbat in exceptional circumstances.

By contrast, imbalances in sections and villages affect larger groups and thus become a matter of collective concern. Such imbalances may be rarer than those in trongbat, but they are also more difficult to remedy, for they require coordinated action and involve numbers of households.

Alterations in section systems are uncommon, and none have occurred in the recent past. Evidence of such events can be found only in village and household genealogies and in the narratives and oral histories given by Nyinba elders.[10] Relying on such materials is problematic, for it rarely is possible to assess their authenticity. In consequence, the reconstructions of changes in sections and villages which follow should be regarded as exploratory and inferential. At most they relate past events as Nyinba choose to recollect them. At least they provide an index to Nyinba understandings of social structure, village development, and the processes of change over time. If nothing else, the reformative practices these accounts describe are consistent with what I have observed on a smaller scale in the present day. Thus, if they do not describe real events, they describe responses which are reasonable in these sociocultural contexts, which Nyinba villagers might have made, and which they certainly might make in the future.

1. Barkhang: Restructuring Village Sections

Barkhang villagers tell of an ancestor who came from Tibet, founded the village, and had three sons. These sons partitioned and in so doing formed

[10]Elders with whom I discussed these subjects were primarily men and women from politically prominent households, several of them former headmen or thalu. The oldest person I regularly consulted was born in 1897 (he died in 1980); the rest were born in the first years of the twentieth century. I should note that whenever historical records were available, they supported elders' accounts.

the nuclei of village sections. Elders add that a man belonging to Khyungba clan, a clan found throughout Tibet, later joined the village, and that he was followed by a man from a neighboring Tibetan-speaking community—thus effecting a degree of openness to migration completely at variance with Nyinba norms today. Some villagers dispute the account of a unitary, or single, founding and argue that the village was founded by two brothers and a third, unrelated man. They find proof of this in present-day clan structure: descendants of the two men presumed to be brothers are joined at a higher-level, named lineage and intermarry with the descendants of the third man.[11] While Nepali law permits individuals seven or more generations removed from a common agnatic link to marry, in no other Nyinba clan is endogamy tolerated—regardless of the number of generations elapsed.

Whatever the relationship may have been between these men, there is no doubt that the sections associated with them have expanded at different rates. Households linked through sequential partitions to the eldest brother or the third, unrelated founder (depending upon the version one follows) now number five. By contrast, there are ten (twice as many) households linked with the middle brother and fifteen (three times as many) households linked with the youngest brother. Elders say, and household genealogies confirm, that this is a long-standing imbalance that began centuries ago. Elders also say that this is the reason behind the complete reorganization of the section system, which seems to have occurred at some point between 120 and 180 years ago.[12]

The section reorganization proceeded as follows. The five households associated with the eldest brother remained together and were joined by most of the households tracing succession to the middle brother. This created a sizable section, which now numbers thirteen households. The large section associated with the youngest brother was divided in two. One part was joined by the *tso,* or section founder's household, for the middle brother; the other part retained its own *tso.* To the latter also were added households tracing origins to the Khyungba clansman and the subsequent

[11] The former are known as "White Druwa," in contradistinction to the descendants of the other man, who are known as "Black Druwa." At the next-lower segmentary level, the lineages are known by their founder's name.

[12] The section reorganization had to have been completed before 1868, the date the tax rolls were compiled, because they show it to be already in place. It had to have been completed after a particular partition occurred, because the households produced in the partition were assigned to different sections in the course of the reorganization. We know that this partition occurred six generations ago and that present-day generations average 30.2 years in length. Figure 8.7 shows how these households, known as Thagtara, were split between different sections.

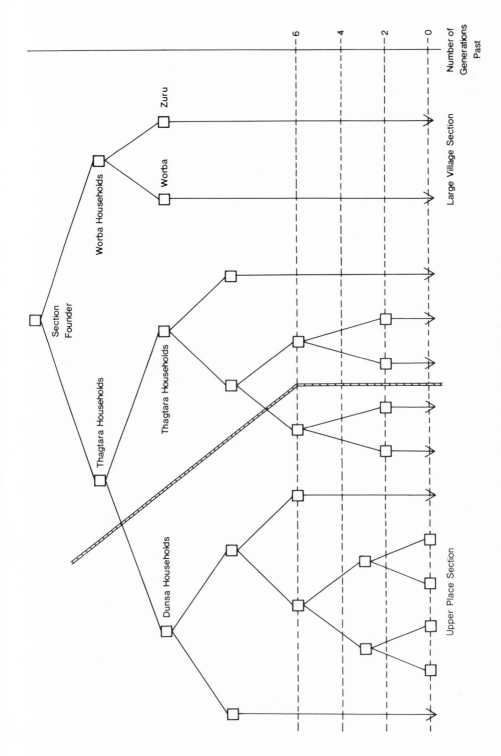

Figure 8.7 Barkhang Village's Section Reorganization

immigrant. In 1983 these sections numbered thirteen and fifteen households respectively.

Figure 8.7 illustrates the complex bisection of the youngest brother's section; it also shows how irregular partitioning can lead to enormous disparities in different village segments' rates of growth.[13]

I am not aware of the logic behind this section restructuring. There may have been political considerations we know nothing about today. One possibility is that the new groupings followed patterns of neighborhood. Most of the households in what came to be known as the "New House" section are located in the northeast, those in the "Large Village" section are located in the southwest, and those in the "Upper Place" section are located in the center of the village. However, it is equally likely that section memberships and trongbat alliances influenced where people built their houses and therefore are responsible for the settlement patterns we see today.

2. Trangshod: Continuity in Households and Sections

Compared to Barkhang, the structure of Trangshod is a model of clarity. The village is organized into four sections: three are traced to the partitioning sons of the founding ancestor, and the fourth is traced to a member of the Khyungba clan who immigrated from Barkhang. What is special about Trangshod is the close relationship between its sections and clan memberships. At present, 63 percent of household heads live in the section founded by their clan ancestor, from whom they claim direct descent. In the other three villages, it is less common to find household heads tracing descent from their section's founder: this occurs in only 31 to 41 percent of cases. Trangshod villagers are proud of this stability and the lines of patrifilial succession unbroken by uxorilocal marriages. This, coupled with the fact that Trangshod is the largest village, supposedly the first founded, and with several extremely politically powerful households, may be why Nyinba view it as the model for the rest.

3. Nyimatang: Change at the Level of the Village

Until approximately two hundred years ago, there was no village of Nyimatang. Instead, there were two smaller villages situated about fifteen hundred feet lower than the present-day village, near to which stood the scattered homesteads of new immigrants. The two protovillages reportedly included twenty-seven households at the height of their strength, in addi-

---

[13] Missing from the illustration are four households whose points of partition origin are insufficiently clear.

tion to the half-dozen immigrant households on their borders—exactly the number of Nyimatang trongba today. Six or seven generations ago— around the time of the Gorkha conquest of Humla in 1789—these villages effectively ceased to exist. The reasons given are repeated household extinctions due to heirlessness and emigrations due to Kalyal harassment. Kalyal remained in control of Humla after the conquest and reportedly were particularly hostile to members of these villages because they had fought on the Gorkha side. This was to the advantage of the immigrant households, who acquired control of the vacant lands.

A generation or two later, these households and other, newer immigrants began reclaiming higher-altitude lands. Nyimatang elders attribute this to the pressure on lower-altitude land from They, a neighboring Nepali village. At first there was a two-tiered settlement pattern. People kept their main homesteads at the lower-altitude settlement and occupied them through fall and winter, for sowing barley and millet and for grazing in the cold season. They moved to the higher altitudes in summer, for summer-planted crops and pasturage. Over time, more of the low-altitude fields were lost and more high-altitude land reclaimed, and this led to the establishment of Nyimatang as the main village. The process was complete by 1868, the time of the survey on which current tax rolls are based.[14] Although no other Nyinba village has included dual settlements within living memory, they are not uncommon in Nepal and other alpine regions, because they facilitate cultivation at a broad altitudinal range.

Unlike other Nyinba villages, Nyimatang recognizes a number of founders. There are the founders of the two extinct, protovillages whose property now is held by others, and the later immigrants who established new households on the protovillages' borders and cleared higher-altitude lands. The section system nonetheless collapses all of these households into three groups. The first section includes the households that acquired most of one protovillage's lands plus the temple households that serve Nyimatang. The second section includes the households that acquired most of the other protovillage's lands. Each of these sections is named after the extinct village whose lands its members hold. The third section includes households of the latest immigrants. It is aptly named "Families on the Side," which recalls their former marginal status. Nonetheless, in Nyimatang—and only in Nyimatang—households worship the household god (pho-lha) associated with the man who founded their household and not the god of the estates they inherited.

---

[14]Nyimatang elders describe five listings of households for tax purposes since the Gorkha conquest of 1789. The dates of the first two are uncertain, but the third reportedly occurred in 1852. The fourth definitely took place in 1868 and the last in 1889. Nyimatang reportedly became the recognized tax unit in the second or third listing.

4. Todpa: Merger of Protovillages and Sections

The idiosyncracies in Todpa's village structure are easy enough to explain. I have discussed Todpa's history of origin in chapter 2 and described its anomalous trongbat alliances above. If I have more details on Todpa, it is because there were more knowledgeable elders willing to devote time to discussing village legends and household genealogies with me and because they were especially precise in their accounts.

Todpa is said to have been divided into three territorially discrete sub-villages in the distant past, which is also said of Barkhang and Trangshod. While Todpa people can point to ruins of houses not far from the present-day village to support these claims, it is quite possible that all Nyinba settlements were more dispersed in the past, in contrast to the pattern of large, politically dominant main villages and subsidiary hamlets today.[15]

Todpa elders also assert that members of the earlier villages were of different descent than the Pal clan members of the present day and that all but one of these households died out. In consequence, this household lacks true trongbat and, as we have seen, had to develop an alliance with two households which were in a comparable predicament. These two were the sole households remaining in an otherwise extinct section. The village response to this was to dissolve the section and attach the survivors to another, more-populous one. Thus Todpa legends tell of three initial villages, their virtual extinction, a village refounding, a division into three sections, and a later collapse into two, all followed by the growth of a hamlet alongside the main village today. In this, two themes predominate: the radical consequences of massive population shifts and the cultural theme of movements between tripartite and bipartite schemata in models of village social structure. Yet changes such as these are not implausible, given Nyinba villages' small populations, their long-standing exploitation by politically more powerful neighbors, and their exposure to epidemics, wars, and conquests over centuries. Of far greater importance here, however, is the fact that Nyinba understand their history through such processes and their present-day village structure as the recapitulation of such events.

We have seen that villagers rearrange their trongbat relationships in response to partitions and extinctions and manipulate section systems in response to uneven rates of growth and decline. The aim is to achieve a workable balance in the memberships of these groups. This is what people

---

[15]The movement between nucleated and dispersed settlement patterns may shed some light on the vacillation between themes of unitary and multiple village foundings in Barkhang's and Todpa's legends. Practically, I should note, hamlets facilitate utilization of far-flung agricultural lands and, like dispersed village settlements, may be the residential arrangement of choice when population has increased.

Table 8.1 Composition of Nyinba Village Sections in 1974 and 1983

Village[a]	Number of Households			
	Section A	Section B	Section C	Section D
Trangshod				
1983	10	11	12	18
1974	9	11	12	17
Barkhang				
1983	13	15	13	—
1974	11	14	13	—
Nyimatang				
1983	7	11	14	—
1974	7	11	14	—
Todpa				
1983	16	10	—	—
1974	14	9	—	—

[a] Missing from this list are five households in Barkhang hamlets whose section affiliations are unclear (being linked with Trangshod for some purposes and Barkhang for others), the two Trangshod temple houses, and one Nyimatang household that recently joined the village.

say, and there is no questioning the outcome (table 8.1). Barkhang, which restructured its section system over a hundred years ago, has the greatest equivalence in section memberships, followed by Trangshod, which for Nyinba is the model of regulated growth. Trangshod has just one outsized section, a disproportionately large one, and it is the section that combines all later immigrants' households. Although Todpa sections seem uneven in size, seven (six in 1974) households in the larger section belong to the hamlet of Wutig, which manages certain of its affairs independently. Within Todpa, the two sections are as balanced as they can be, nine and ten households each. Nyimatang, which, as we shall see, is the village now experiencing the greatest growth, has the least balance. I have heard people express their discontent with the section system, and it may have to be reorganized in future.

Changes in village population have led to a variety of adaptations—their scope varying with the circumstances. Minor changes have been met by adaptations within existing structures, such as realignments of households in trongbat or the transfer of one or two households between sections. Larger-scale, cumulative changes have prompted reorganizations of village sections, as in Barkhang, or the joining of one depopulated section to another, creating a two-section system out of three, as in Todpa. Major population shifts and changes in land utilization have given rise to complete reconstitutions of villages, changes in settlement patterns, or the redrawing of village boundaries. Examples include the creation of Nyimatang and also the transfer of the hamlet Wutig from Nyimatang to Todpa.[16] None of these, however, could be considered a radical change in social structure. None, after all, involved the elimination of trongbat or sections or their replacement by some other system for organizing villages. If this ever occurred it is not recollected, or perhaps simply not reinterpreted in light of present-day models of social structure.

[16]Considerations of space have led me to relegate this to a footnote. Briefly, in the past Todpa was situated further west, while one of Nyimatang's immigrant settlers was living west of the protovillages and near present-day Wutig. Wutig's founder is thought to have partitioned from this Nyimatang household. This makes Wutig's association with Todpa anomalous. Although it rarely is mentioned, it is marked in the hamlet founder household's worship of this Nyimatang household's god (pho-lha).

Part 4

Stasis and Change: Polyandry and Alpine Economics

9
Husbands, Husbandry, and the Economic Balance

Like many highland groups in Nepal, Nyinba have a diversified economy. They engage in agriculture, trade, and animal husbandry, ranked in that order of importance. The emphases in other highland groups differ, varying according to local environmental constraints and cultural traditions. Nyinba, however, manage more extensive involvements in the different economic sectors than most other groups do and are able to do so simultaneously. What makes this possible is their large households, which include numbers of active adults, adult males in particular. This, in turn, follows from their system of polyandry.

The principles guiding polyandrous marriage, household formation, and household management combine with cultural constructions of gender and associated notions about men's and women's suitability for different types of work to produce a unique domestic economic system. Households prefer a large, male membership and try to maximize the number of men and to minimize the number of women—a preference provided additional support by concerns about household unity. Economic strategies accordingly involve men specializing in diverse productive tasks. Household women, by contrast, concentrate on tasks involving agricultural labor near home.

In consequence, men's economic contributions are more extensive and more diverse than those of women. They also are more highly valued and given more public recognition.[1] The paradox is that households depend

---

[1] These notions of contraposition between male and female work, the greater power accorded to those who contribute more to their households, and the ready substitutability of women are expressed in three proverbs Nyinba are fond of using: (1) A man's skills derive from his traveling for trade; a woman's skills derive from her hands at home. (2) Whoever does more work has more power. (3) As you change the sole of your shoe, so can you change your daughter-in-law (or wife).

greatly upon their female workers, and high sex ratios from polyandry contribute to chronic female labor shortages in many households. The long-
standing response has been supplementation of female labor: in the past
through slavery, today through hired workers. Underlying this is the notion
that much female labor is routine and simple—if physically demanding—
and can be delegated to workers who are not household members. By contrast, most male labor is seen as requiring special expertise, and for trade
particularly, it is considered unwise to entrust it to people outside the
household.

Finally, this is an economic system subject to diverse forces for change
over the last few centuries. Nyinba have experienced the progressive loss of
lower-altitude fields to their neighbors and have had to clear less-productive,
higher-altitude land to replace the fields they have lost. Those neighbors
have also been expanding into forest- and wastelands, and the result is diminished pasturage for everyone. At the same time, political changes in
Tibet have destabilized the traditional salt-grain trade, and improved communications in the south have made Indian salt readily available and thus
less profitable to import. The consequence is that Nyinba earnings from
trade have declined precipitously. People have responded to this by inten-
sifying their trading involvements: traveling farther and working harder for
less income. As we shall see, polyandry has played a role in domestic
adaptations to these changes.

Agriculture and the Division of Labor

Nyinba households depend on agriculture to meet a major portion of their
subsistence needs, and some households depend almost entirely on agriculture. In truth, there is no place in northern Humla better suited to agriculture than the Nyinba region. The major valleys face south; they are broad
and gently sloping. This and low rates of village growth have made Nyinba
wealthier on average than members of almost any other Humla group.[2]

During my first stay in Humla, I often heard Nyinba describe agriculture
as the basis of their prosperity and the pillar of their economy. But in 1982,
people's confidence in agriculture had been shaken by a series of disastrous
harvests (in 1976, 1980, and 1982). Many began speaking hopefully of
opportunities for increased salt-grain trading. The recent history of trade,
however, provides reason for caution. In the 1960s particularly, upheavals
in Tibet led to serious economic reversals, which prompted increased emi-

[2]The sole exception to this is Limi, whose traders profited from changed conditions in Tibet
(Goldstein 1974).

gration and seem to have contributed to an increased pace of expansion into higher-altitude lands.

Reclamation of higher-altitude lands has been going on for over a century. Until recently, the major force for change seems to have been pressure on lower-lying land from the Nepali villages that stand beneath Nyinba ones. These Nepalis settled alluvial-fan and valley-bottom lands alongside the Karnali River and its tributaries. When their populations grew, they had little choice but to expand up the hillside, where land already was under cultivation by their Nyinba neighbors. Nepali villagers who could afford to do so bought Nyinba fields, while those who were poorer worked for Nyinba for payment in land. Nyinba who resisted selling claim they were harassed by pilferage of crops and by cattle deliberately released into fields ripe with grain. Most eventually gave in and sold the land. Thus Nepalis have been pushing Nyinba out of their lower-altitude lands, and the two groups have been moving in tandem up the hillside.

Nyinba now depend more on more-marginal lands, which give less return for labor, and have had to accommodate themselves to diminished pasturage and depleted forests near their villages. Animal husbandry has suffered, timber for houses is scarce, and fuel must be sought at locations progressively farther from home.

Despite these problems and the recent harvest failures, agriculture remains central, economically and symbolically. As we have seen, the defining feature of trongba status continues to be the estate in land. While involvements in salt trading fluctuate with changes in the composition of the domestic work force, households always cultivate their own lands. For men, however, involvements in agriculture are sporadic, and the demands of trade take many away from the village for months at a time. Thus the major responsibility for agriculture commonly falls upon women.

This is not to say that men's contributions to agriculture are insignificant. Men are responsible for plowing and planting seed at regular intervals throughout the agricultural season; they also build and maintain terrace walls in slower months. Household men do the major part of carrying heavy loads of grain from the fields and of the strenuous work of threshing just-harvested buckwheat in the fields—if they are home at the time. However, women, as table 9.1 shows, engage in a broader range of agricultural tasks. These are the tasks requiring regular labor for protracted periods, such as weeding, and those considered distasteful, such as preparing and applying compost. Weeding is particularly time-consuming. To give a point of comparison with men's work, the same field it takes a day to plow and plant takes a woman from five to fifteen days to weed thoroughly; and some crops require two, or even three, cycles of weeding. Women are en-

Table 9.1 The Sexual Division of Labor

	Tasks Performed By	
Male	Either Sex	Female
Agriculture		
Plowing	Preparing fields for planting	Drying grain
Constructing terrace walls	Constructing irrigation	Kitchen gardening
Seed planting	channels	Clearing fields of stones,
Carrying harvested grain	Irrigating fields	brush
	Slash-and-burn cultivation	Applying compost
	Selecting seeds, except	Weeding
	millet	Selecting, harvesting oil
	Harvesting grain, except	seed and millet
	millet	
	Threshing grain	
	Bagging grain	
	Gathering hay	
	Protecting crops from	
	animals	
Food Processing		
Drying meat		Roasting, milling grain
		Storing grain
		Winnowing grain
		Drying vegetables
		Husking grain
		Pressing oil
		Making liquor
Animal Husbandry		
Castrating animals	Breeding animals	
Butchering	Milking	
Shearing	Preparing dairy products	
Medical treatment		
Gathering		
Collecting distant wood	Collecting nearby wood	Gathering edible food
Home Manufacturing		
Spinning coarse wool	Plastering walls	Washing newly woven goods
Sewing	Carrying earth for buildings	Spinning finer wool
Leather work		Weaving
Making rope		Dyeing cloth
Carrying stones		
Building, repairing houses		
Construction of watermills		
Washing wool		
Domestic activities		
		Child care
		Fetching water
		Cooking and serving food
		Washing dishes, pots, and
		clothes
		Infant care
External Economy		
Long-distance trading	Agricultural labor, paid in	
Salaried employment in	kind	
the district capital	Collecting food loans within	
	the district	

Note: Classification categories after Acharya and Bennett (1981:340–44).

gaged in agricultural work throughout the year except deepest winter, when the ground is covered with snow. Then they spend more time in food-processing tasks left over from summer and in preparing cloth for the family.

There also is a range of agricultural tasks shared by women and men—much of it work during the harvest, when the demand for labor is most intense. In this we might infer a concession to practicality—one particularly advantageous where household composition can vary so widely (Berreman 1978). Otherwise and as a general rule, men are responsible for activities requiring greater strength, while women concentrate on activities requiring slower, sustained labor and finer work.[3] This is the explanation given for women's work in weeding, which is tedious, and in havesting millet, which drops from its stalk if handled roughly. However—quite tellingly—the fact that women are responsible for unpleasant or polluting tasks is explained by their lower status (table 9.1).

In figure 9.1, we see the phasing of agricultural labor performed by women and men and how it is coordinated with the annual ceremonial cycle. These ceremonies are scheduled around agricultural events, primarily the sowing and harvesting of grain; they also celebrate them. At the same time, they address a multiplicity of religious and secular concerns; and we find a major segment of the Buckwheat Harvest Festival, the major agricultural festival of the year, concerned with trade and the welfare of traders, soon to be off on their long winter journeys. The very name of this festival, *Tralha,* involves a play on words, for it can be interpreted as either "a thanksgiving for buckwheat" (*bra-bo*) or "a reinforcing of male (traders') personal gods" (*dgra-lha*).

Because of this division of labor, households cannot survive without adult women. Men rely on women not only for certain kinds of agricultural work, but also for the processing of food and its preparation and other domestic activities that must be performed on a daily basis throughout the year. Men do undertake some of these tasks in the face of serious female labor shortages, but not very happily, particularly if they have to be seen at it by fellow villagers. (I should say that women too complain about being saddled with men's work when their husbands are away from home.) Although certain aspects of women's work may be denigrated, men and women alike note that the industry and skill of a household's women can make the difference between wealth and poverty. These ideas are reflected in legends about how ancestresses raised their households to wealth and in

[3] Although household rules and strategies among landed agriculturalists in Tibet seem to have been largely similar, the division of labor may have been more flexible (Aziz 1978:108).

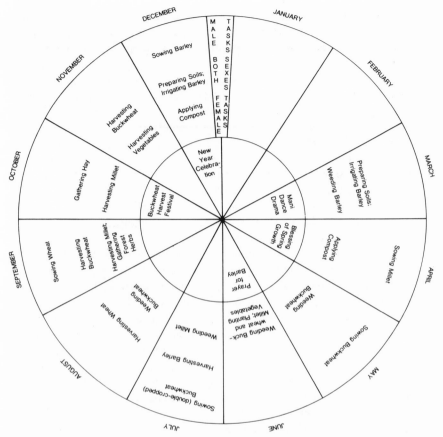

Each field of millet is weeded two to four times; barley is weeded once and buckwheat is weeded once or twice

The scheduling and names for agricultural festivals vary by village

Figure 9.1   Nyinba Agricultural Calendar

the veneration of "Grandmother Goddess of Harvest Prosperity" (*A-'bi 'Ong Lha-mo*) at annual agricultural festivals.

Conditions of Alpine Agriculture

Agriculture in hill regions is physically very demanding. Plots of land are small, as small as one-twelfth and usually smaller than one-quarter of an acre. Households own many such small plots, separated from one another by up to two miles, and 2,000 feet in altitude. This means considerable expenditure of time and energy simply in traveling to, from, and between separate agricultural sites. Today most villages stand roughly in the center of their lands, more or less equally distant from their lowest and highest fields. Barkhang, at 9,500 feet, is the lowest-lying village, and it has fields ranging from 8,500 feet to 10,400 feet. Todpa, at an altitude of 10,250 feet, has fields located between 8,900 and 11,000 feet. The advantage in having fields lower than the village is the ease in carrying loads of compost down to them, although this means that loads of harvested grain must be carried back up to the village. The problems exist in reverse for higher-altitude fields.

Fragmentation of landholdings in alpine regions may seem counter-productive, but it does have certain advantages. First, it gives individual households shares in the range of microniches created by variations in altitude, degree of incline, exposure to sunlight, soil conditions, and availability of irrigation water. This permits diversity in crops grown, which increases the self-sufficiency of individual households. Second, the use of small parcels of land at different altitudes and in different locations spreads the risk of climatic aberrations and crop failures. In autumn, I have seen crops above a certain altitude battered by hail or damaged by frost, while those below benefited from gentle rains and increased moisture. The following spring I have seen those same low-altitude fields parched by drought, while the ones above escaped damage because their seeds had not yet germinated. Finally, fragmented holdings accommodate staggered scheduling of work, so work may be distributed more evenly over a longer period, and a longer growing season (Netting 1981:17–18; Rhoades and Thompson 1975).[4]

Thus despite the relatively high altitude and temperate climate, Nyinba are engaged in agriculture from March through January. They are able to cultivate some of the lower-altitude fields with millet, amaranth, and beans, which require a longer growing season, and double crop others with barley and buckwheat; they can rotate wheat and buckwheat in middle-altitude fields; and they can plant the highest-altitude fields with buck-wheat, although many have to be left fallow in alternate years.

Whatever the advantages to be derived from dispersing fields over a broad range of altitudes, there are numerous disadvantages as well, most notably the increase in labor time. At present, fragmentation of landhold-ings may have passed the point of diminishing returns. What Nyinba say is that their plots of land have become too small and too dispersed and that

---

[4] However, as Orlove and Guillet caution, assuming that alpine productive arrangements are necessarily adaptive risks functionalist tautologies (1985:10).

they spend too many hours trudging back and forth between them. This is especially true for the poorer, recently partitioned households which secured only one of each type of land from the original estate, and therefore only one field in each of the widely separated agricultural zones. Partition also has led to the subdivision of the best lower- and middle-altitude lands. Although the ideal field size is one that takes a day to plow (equivalent to approximately 0.3 acre), there are very few fields which have remained that large. I recall once having been cajoled into making a lengthy detour just to see several contiguous one-day fields. The sole solution to this problem is to avoid partition. For local people, the reduction in field size provides another argument against partition.

While Nyinba take advantage of a range of altitudes and agricultural conditions and grow a number of crops, they grow buckwheat more than anything else. This is in spite of the fact that it is the food grain of last choice. There are several reasons for the predominance of buckwheat. For one thing, it can be grown anywhere and is reliably productive. Its yields are high at all altitudinal ranges, in shade and sun, and in poor and rich soils, and it is free of the diseases that damage other crops. For another thing, buckwheat requires less work—and significantly, less women's work. A field of buckwheat takes about half the time to weed as a field of millet. Unlike barley, it does not require irrigating and the upkeep of irrigation channels. Nor does it require much fertilizing. In the distant past, barley, which is much preferred, may have been grown more often, or so a network of ruined irrigation channels at high altitudes suggests.

Buckwheat also is the crop of choice in newly tilled land, and is thus the basis for most attempts at agricultural expansion. While potatoes may have served an equivalent function among the Sherpa of eastern Nepal, only a few Humla villages to the south grow more potatoes than buckwheat on new land.[5] Perhaps their soils are better suited to potato cultivation; perhaps some other feature of local agricultural conditions is involved. Elsewhere in Humla and among the Nyinba, there is prejudice against potatoes, as there once was in Europe (Netting 1981:160). Potatoes are used as a vegetable and in sauces and are grown in kitchen gardens, but they are not accepted as a staple carbohydrate food. People explain that eating potatoes in quantity is unhealthful, and they also dismiss potatoes as the food of the poor.

Estimates of agricultural yields place bitter buckwheat among the most productive crops (table 9.2). However the measurements used are imper-

[5]Fürer-Haimendorf (1964:8–11) states that the introduction of the potato supported a major population expansion, and similar arguments have been made for communities in the Swiss Alps (Netting 1981:159–68).

Table 9.2 Productivity of Major Crops

	Tre Harvested Per Plow-Day[a]		*Tre* Harvested Per Measure Sown	
	Estimate for a Good Year[b]	1982 Production	Estimate for a Good Year[b]	1982 Production
Barley	300	202	15	9.8
Wheat	240	114	12	5.6
Millet, mixed varieties	400	166	40	28.4
Buckwheat, mixed varieties	—	285	—	16.4
Sweet buckwheat[c]	180	—	11	—
Bitter buckwheat, single-cropped	440	—	25	—
Bitter buckwheat, double-cropped	320	—	20	—

[a] A *tre (bre)* equals approximately 1 liter; a plow-day refers to the amount of land a yak-cow crossbreed can plow in one day, which is equivalent to approximately .30 acre.
[b] Estimates were provided by key informants; actual productivity derives from economic data collected on 126 households.
[c] Varieties of buckwheat were not differentiated in productivity assessments for 1982.

fect, and the estimates of productivity require further qualification.[6] First, measurements by number of days plowed are imprecise, because workdays are shorter in late fall when barley and wheat are planted and longer in spring and summer when millet and buckwheat are planted. Second, measurements by seeds planted can be misleading, because fall crops are sown more thickly to compensate for loss of seedlings to animal foraging over winter and because smaller-seeded crops, especially millet, extend further in sowing. This is why measurements by seeds planted show millet to be so very productive. Third, measurement in terms of *tre* harvested are problematic, because the different grains produce different amounts of edible food. The buckwheats have a hard hull and lose up to half their bulk in processing, whereas millets lose up to about a third, and barley and wheat lose very little. With this taken into consideration, barley and wheat become about as productive as buckwheat. Barley and wheat, moreover, are much preferred as foods. Nonetheless Nyinba put more land into buckwheat, because more

[6] Nyinba ordinarily estimate productivity in terms of yields per plow-day, and measurements by day are the standard in Nepali tax schemes for highland areas (M. Regmi 1976). By contrast, Tibetan tax rolls specified seeds sown (Goldstein 1971a). While Humla people say they once measured production by the size of threshing area required (Nep. *khalo;* Tib. *yulsa*), this system is not in use today.

land is suited to it, it is more reliable, and it requires the least work—
which is particularly important in labor-short households.[7]

The result is that people eat more buckwheat than any other grain, and
poor people with marginal lands probably eat the most buckwheat of all.
Wealthier families have buckwheat pancakes at least once a day and rice
imported from salt trading or locally produced millet, wheat, or barley at
other meals. Nyinba also grow small amounts of amaranth, kidney beans,
soybeans, and lentils, but do not value them as foods and either use them in
sauces, or in snacks, or give them away to locally resident Nepali untouchables. The vegetables they produce include daikon radish, turnips,
potatoes, peas, cucumber, pumpkin, and Hubbard squash. People have
been slow to adopt new vegetables, and cauliflower was grown in the
nearby district capital for ten years before any Nyinba household planted
it. Most people continue to prefer and mainly prepare sauces based on
radish.

The daily diet of bitter buckwheat pancakes and radish, which is often
eaten raw and seasoned with chilies purchased in low-altitude villages,
may be partly responsible for perennial complaints of indigestion. People
would rather eat meat and would like to have more milk and butter to give
their children, but local production is simply inadequate. As a result, all
but wealthy Nyinba get little meat except in autumn or on special occasions, and all households use the less expensive vegetable oils for cooking
instead of butter. Oil is not produced in adequate quantity either and has to
be imported from villages of other Humla communities. Some households
keep bees for honey, some have walnut trees, all have apricot trees, and
most have apple trees. People gorge upon fruit in season, but there are no
attempts to preserve it for year-round consumption.

In consequence, the diet is high in carbohydrates and calories and comparatively limited, consisting largely of one grain and one vegetable. After
childbirth, women are provided with a higher-protein, but even more limited, diet, consisting of little more than barley, meat, and butter for about
one month. While I lack detailed data on food intake and nutrition, a recent
study by Macfarlane on a Gurung village in central Nepal offers possible
points for comparison. Macfarlane found that men, on average, consumed
one and a half pints of grain daily and took in a total of 2,226 calories and
88.6 grams of protein, while the average woman consumed somewhat less
(1976:164, 176). Nyinba may eat more than this; they say young working
women need about two pints of wheat or rice per day, and men working

[7] Buckwheat occupied 39 percent of field days in 1982 and 54 percent of the measured yield
in seeds.

hard up to three. People not so heavily engaged in physical labor are said to consume about one-third less. Healthy young people are quite plump here, and despite its limitations, the Nyinba diet probably is better than that of many highland Nepalese.[8]

Salt-Grain Trading: The Flexibile Option

The salt-grain trade probably has figured in the Nyinba economy for centuries, as it appears to have done throughout the Nepalese-Tibetan borderlands (Fürer-Haimendorf 1975; Fisher 1986:87). It is one of the major ways of making a living in high altitude, agriculturally marginal regions. In northwestern Nepal, all groups that live in the agriculturally marginal highlands—Nepali-speaking high-caste Hindus, Tibeto-Burman-speaking Byansis, and ethnic Tibetans—trade in salt.

A special lure of salt trading is that its profits are in rice, the grain which is preferred and which is ritually significant for Hindus. While this should make salt trading especially attractive to Nepali speakers, their involvements tend to be limited. There are two reasons for this: they are unable to speak Tibetan and accordingly are less effective in dealing with Tibetans at the northern end of the trade, and they tend to live in small nuclear-family households. Nyinba, by contrast, live in large, polyandrous households, where there typically are a number of co-resident adult men, one or more of whom can engage in salt trading full-time.

Salt trading is virtually a year-round occupation. There are nomadic Tibetan speakers in Humla, known as Khampa (or 'Khyam-pa, meaning "wanderers"), who support themselves by salt trading alone. The entire society spends the year traveling from one trading point to the next. Among Nyinba, only men trade in salt, and the number of men available determines the extent of their household's trading involvements and how many pack animals they keep. In some households, certain men do nothing but engage in trade; in others, several men may be equally competent and take turns by season or year.[9] Some Nyinba hire shepherds to help, but consider them unreliable and no substitute for household members. Therefore when

---

[8]The average adult Nyinba man weighed 57.9 kilograms (128 pounds) and was 161.9 centimeters (5 feet 4 inches) in height. Women weighed 51.3 kilograms (113 pounds) on average and were 150.9 centimeters (almost 5 feet) tall. I measured all the adults I came across who permitted this (not including pregnant women); the total was 57 men and 56 women of diverse ages.

[9]Occasionally newly married women accompany their husbands on the salt-trade circuit in winter, and wives sometimes meet their husbands in summer camps in Tibet.

January	February	March	April	May	June	July	August	September	October	November	December
Trade at Indian border salt market											
		Trade Indian salt for rice in middle hills									
			Trade salt for rice southwest of Humla								
				Return home with rice from winter trade							
				WEDDINGS							
					Go to Tibet for first salt trading						
						Go to south Humla to exchange cattle for barley					
							Go to Tibet or Limi for salt, cattle, wool, and trade goods				
									Go southwest of Humla to exchange salt for rice		
										WEDDINGS	
										Go south for the winter salt trade	

Figure 9.2 Salt Trade Calendar

there are no men available for salt trading, households sell their animals and look to agriculture for their primary support.

The pack animals, I should add, are goats and sheep. This is the pattern throughout northwestern Nepal and in the neighboring districts of Almora and Garhwal in India (Fisher 1986:89; Srivastava 1958:17). They are the only animals agile enough to negotiate the narrow, precipitous trails found in these regions, trails which link Humla with the middle hills. These goats and sheep are special rugged breeds which tolerate the extremes of temperature encountered, from the cold of high passes into Tibet to the heat of Indian border towns (Fürer-Haimendorf 1975:249–50). The problem is that they are small and carry only small loads. Castrated rams can manage no more than twelve and castrated goats eighteen liters of grain or even smaller quantities of salt. Female animals carry less. Where the roads are better, as between northern Humla and Tibet, people use yak, yak-cow crossbreeds, or horses as pack animals. These are the principal pack animals in central and eastern border regions of Nepal.

The annual salt-trading cycle includes four major and one minor segment and traditionally has revolved around three kinds of exchange. The exchange of grain for salt predominates; it is conducted in conjunction with subsidiary exchanges of grain for wool and grain for cattle. A recent addition has been trade in goods manufactured in India and Tibet. The distance of Humla from modern markets and the limited capacity of carrier animals make such commodities scarce and expensive: their cost in Humla is three to four times the price of the same item purchased in Tibet or at the Indian border. Only recently have Humla people had the cash to purchase the simplest manufactured goods—which now makes this trade possible—but what has made it even more attractive to Nyinba are declining profits from salt trading.

Figure 9.2 depicts the scheduling of the trading cycle. The map in Figure 9.3 follows the paths traders take as they lead their carrier sheep and goats from Tibet to India. I begin the description of this cycle in June. This follows a month-long rest after the long winter trading journeys and after the spring weddings that must be provisioned by imported rice. June is when the new annual cycle of trade begins, with the so-called Spring Trade (*sos tshong*).

Spring Trade is the simplest segment of the annual cycle and involves only a brief trip to Tibet. Traders stop off at rich, high-altitude pastures near the Tibetan border to set up herding camps for female animals, kids, and lambs. Some men stay there as shepherds throughout the summer season: others proceed with male goats and sheep to the town of Purang.

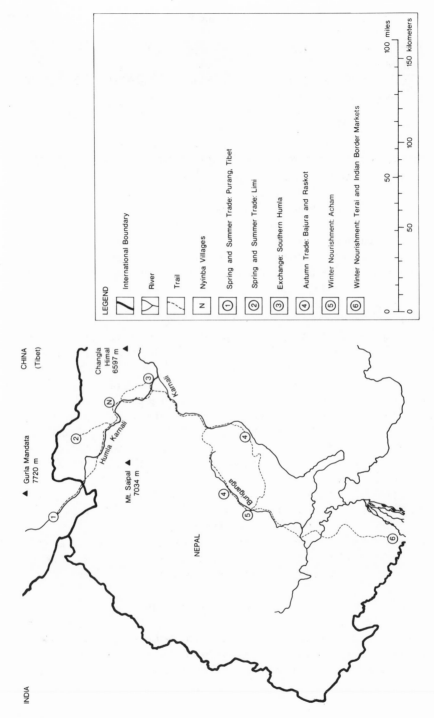

Figure 9.3 Major Routes of the Salt-Grain Trade

There they exchange homegrown grain or imported rice for Tibetan salt. Then they return home to store the salt.

The next segment is named "Exchange" (*tshab*) and it involves trade in yak-cow crossbreeds. Nyinba purchase crossbreeds in Limi or other northern Humla communities which have extensive pasturelands and engage in large-scale cattle raising; occasionally they cull surplus animals from their own herds. The animals then are taken south, where pasturelands are limited and the altitude too low to keep yak, and exchanged for grain. The profits are considerable, and traders can expect to earn three times the price they paid for an animal. This is because grain is relatively inexpensive in southern Humla and animals expensive—the reverse of the situation in the north.

These trading relationships with northern cattle-breeding and southern Humla grain-producing communities are of long duration, as is indicated by the complex, archaic system of pricing, which is based on Indian silver rupee rates of exchange prevailing a century ago. What this also indicates is the long-standing interdependence between pasture-rich and agriculturally marginal northern Humla and agriculturally self-sufficient and pasture-poor southern Humla.[10]

Households with fewer animals and less involvement in the salt trade may skip the first two segments altogether. None, however, miss "Summer Trade" (*dbyar tshong*). This is the time when traders from all over northwestern Nepal converge on Purang, setting up camp in long-established sites outside the town. Nyinba bring grain—the profits of trading or their own stores—to exchange for Tibetan nomads' salt and wool. Nepalese Byansis from villages near the Indian border bring goods from India, and Tibetans bring Chinese goods from other market towns, goods Nyinba can buy with cash or grain. In the 1960s, a few men began buying Tibetan antiquities, which they then sold in India. The trade was high risk and high profit; it mostly has come to an end now, because high-quality antiquities are rarer and much more expensive. Nyinba sometimes also travel to Limi to purchase wool or items Limi men were more successful at finding and exporting from Tibet.

During summer trade, men concentrate on exchanging grain for salt and also try to exchange grain for wool. Those who lack sufficient grain work for nomadic herdsmen and shear their sheep for payment in wool. This

[10]The trade in crossbreeds has another northern dimension, for they also are sold in Tibet where it is too cold to keep the common cow for breeding purposes. Crossbreeds are desirable as plow animals and are far better milk producers than yak females or cows, but the males are sterile, so they cannot reproduce their own kind.

wool is of very high quality and far superior to what local carrier sheep produce. Nyinba import wool mostly for their own needs and they use it in all their better clothing. They also may promise payment in wool (ordinarily the poorer-quality local wool) to attract casual agricultural workers in times of labor shortages. Finally they use bits of wool to pay for fruits or other special foods grown in southern Humla. While wool exchange has its own complex networks linking groups in Tibet and Humla, they are much narrower than those developed around salt-grain exchange.

Before leaving for home, traders buy Tibetan sheep, which also are prized for their meat. Imported lamb traditionally was a staple of the diet in autumn and was the focus of a system of food exchanges between affines. This ended when the government in Tibet restricted the export of sheep in the mid 1960s. When the restriction was lifted in 1980, Nyinba did not lose a year before they resumed their autumn food exchanges again.

Almost immediately after returning home, the traders travel to rice-growing areas eight to twelve days' walk to the southwest, to the regions of Bajura and Raskot. This is the "Autumn Trade" (*ston tshong*), and like every segment of the salt-grain trade, it has become increasingly less profitable over the last half century. Nonetheless, it still holds certain attractions. These communities not only have grain in surplus, they also produce a coarse cotton fabric which Nyinba exhange for the equally coarse (unprocessed) wool of their carrier sheep. This cotton is ideal for summer clothing and is much in demand in Humla.

By the time the animals return home in November laden with rice, the harvest is over. Grain, milk products, and meat are more plentiful than at any other time of the year, so that major weddings and final funeral ceremonies are scheduled for this month. Salt traders, however, do not get to attend, because within a week or two after returning from Autumn Trade they leave for "Winter Nourishment" (*dgun gyar*), the longest and most complex segment of the salt trade.

The first stop is at villages with grain surpluses, that traders pass along the road south. In these they deposit some of the salt they are carrying in exchange for rice promised when they return in spring. The animals then proceed with lighter burdens to their winter camping grounds in Acham. Female and young animals are left there to graze, while the males are taken eight days farther south to the area of Rajapur near the Indian border. Most traders make at least two trips to the border, but will limit themselves to one if the animals are not doing well, and add a third if they wish greater profits. Aging animals are sold at the border, and the money used to buy salt at a market established in the 1960s. Men also make brief trips to bazaar towns to buy cloth and manufactured goods. The salt then is taken back to Acham, where it is exchanged for rice or sold. In recent years, rice has become less, and salt more, plentiful in Acham, with predictable consequences for trading profits.

Sometime in late winter or early spring, the male animals are laden with Indian salt and led north. Traders stop at villages along the way to barter salt for rice and occasionally for other grains. They also stop to collect rice from villages where they had deposited Tibetan salt in autumn. Now both male and female animals are carrying heavy loads, and traders have no choice but to proceed very slowly. They finally arrive home in April. In bad agricultural years the rice comes at a critical time and replenishes dwindling food stocks. In better years it can be stored or used in spring weddings.

If no more, this description should indicate how much time, work, and discomfort the salt-grain trade involves. The larger the herds, the greater the number of shepherds required: up to four, five, or even more men are needed to manage a large herd in winter. The critical question is whether salt trading repays the investments in it and whether it is as profitable as agriculture. I cannot assess productivity against labor inputs, but I can compare profits from agriculture and salt trading. In 1982–83, approximately two-thirds of Nyinba households engaged in the salt-grain trade.[11] This brought the average household Rs 15,040 worth of grain and Rs 2,496 worth of salt. Agriculture, by contrast, provided Rs 16,902 worth of grain for those same households. When all Nyinba households are considered, average agricultural income totaled Rs 14,780.[12] The problem for comparison is that 1982 was a bad year for agriculture. In a good year, households might have made half again as much grain (table 9.2). At the same time, one of the special advantages of the salt-grain trade is that it provides an alternative source of grain in bad agricultural years.

I have selected three examples to illustrate the range of individual households' involvements in and profits from the salt trade.

1. The largest herd in all the Nyinba villages is held by a Nyimatang household. The animals include about 340 sheep and goats, of which approximately 150 are males. In 1982, this household earned the following profits, above and beyond any costs incurred in trade: Rs 57,024 worth of rice, Rs 13,440 worth of bar-

[11] These are households of all social ranks whose members responded to a detailed economic and demographic survey (see chapter 6, note 10).

[12] All grain and salt values are calculated in terms of prices prevailing in autumn 1982. Part of the reason for the high value of the grain obtained in the salt trade is the high cost of rice locally. As these figures suggest, salt-trading households tend to be wealthier in land as well.

ley, and roughly Rs 4,000 worth of salt.[13] Two household men were employed virtually year-round, aided by up to four shepherds at a time. Household men also traded in manufactured goods and earned, very roughly, Rs 25,000 in cash from that. Total salt-trading profits thus were approximately Rs 99,464, or $7,593 at 1982 exchange rates.

2. A Todpa household owns approximately 110 sheep and goats, of which some 50 are male. In 1982 they brought home Rs 12,864 worth of rice, Rs 2,240 worth of barley, and Rs 3,200 worth of salt. One man worked on the salt trade year-round; his brother joined him in winter. In conjunction with the salt trade, they bought and sold manufactured goods and earned an additional Rs 11,000 from that. Salt-trading profits thus totalled Rs 29,304, or $2,237.

3. Another Nyimatang household, considered a small-scale herder, owns approximately 40 animals, of which 15 are male. In 1982 they brought home Rs 7,200 in rice and Rs 5,760 in salt. This kept one man busy virtually year-round. He did little other trading and earned no more than a few hundred rupees in profits from selling wool and some manufactured Chinese goods bought in Tibet. Thus the household gained somewhat more than Rs 13,000 from the salt trade, or around $1,000.

Although there is a clear relationship between the number of carrier animals and profits in grain and salt, trade in commodities depends upon the interests and skills of individual men. This is a recent development, an example of salt-trade intensification, but it has not become the reason for engaging in that trade. Its primary purpose remains to bring grain home and feed participants along the way. For the larger holder, this means feeding hired shepherds, for whom food is one of the attractions of the job. For the smaller holder, the food consumed provides another dimension of profit. In the third case above, the lone trader undoubtedly consumed food equal to half his take-home profit in grain. The opportunity for profit and for bringing large amounts of grain home differentiates salt trading from temporary labor in grain-surplus areas of Humla and south of it. Wages from casual labor are so low that most are spent on daily subsistence, and laborers return home with only what they can carry on their own backs.

Large holders bring home tremendous amounts of food, some of which they sell, some of which they consume themselves, and some of which they use to sponsor lavish feasts. This is one of two forms of conspicuous consumption Nyinba engage in, the other involving purchases of jewelry

---

[13] Rice and salt cost Rs 12 per *tre*, ana barley Rs 7 per *tre* in 1982.

and clothing to display on such occasions. Otherwise the rich live frugally, wearing clothes only slightly less tattered and threadbare than those of their poorer neighbors. Houses of the rich and all but the poorest Nyinba are similar, furnished in similar style and with identical items. If there is any difference, it is in the size of the home and the number of dishes, pots, and pans owned. The rich do eat better food—more rice, barley, meat, butter, and honey. Much of their better diet is due to imports from the salt trade.

Households without herds cannot manage to sponsor feasts or hold weddings, and they must borrow or buy rice for funerals. If they have adequate lands, they may be comfortable economically, but never as comfortable as salt-trading households with equivalent amounts of land. Anyone can enter into the salt trade at any time, although households with other resources can enter into it more swiftly, simply by buying sheep and goats. Most poorer households have no choice but to send their men out to work as shepherds for pay in herd animals. Nonetheless, the basic requirement for entering the salt trade and transcending the limitations of local agriculture is similar for both: adequate male household personnel.

It is not uncommon to find households moving in and out of the salt trade and changing their levels of involvement in each generation. Disengagement and reinvolvement often proceed over a period of years. Household men find themselves unable to care properly for their own animals, they entrust them to others, and because of negligence, the herd slowly diminishes in size. When the household again has enough men, they begin to buy animals or work as shepherds for others. If they are competent, natural increase will augment herd size. I relate two such examples of herd buildup.

  1. A Barkhang household partitioned about four decades ago. One of the brothers split off by himself and, predictably, found that he could not manage salt trading on his own. However, he had three sons, and when they grew up, he hired one or more of them out at a time as shepherds. The middle brother proved extremely skillful at sheepherding and in fifteen years had built his and his brothers' annual shepherd's salary of three sheep each into a herd of 240 animals. Even then he was not satisfied. Only one-third of his herd were carrier males—as opposed to 40 percent on average in other herding households. This stemmed from his desire to increase herd size, even at the expense of current profits. One of the brothers had taken a job in Simikot in the 1970s, but quit it in 1982 to rejoin the salt-trading enterprise because this promised the greater profits.
  2. Three Nyimatang brothers were orphaned at an early age. The middle brother was placed with a wealthy household and

served them, first as cowherd and then as a shepherd, for many years. About a dozen years ago, he left them to manage his own herd. Today that herd includes approximately 30 males and 50 females, and he is planning to expand it further.

Thus salt trading is an option for any household with the requisite manpower. It also is seen as the most sensible investment for excess household capital. Land is very expensive, it is rarely sold, and only marginal lands are open to new cultivation. Casual labor in southern Humla is seen as degrading; it also is poorly paid. Nyinba, furthermore, are qualified only for menial, poorly paying jobs in the district capital. Finally, pasture for cattle, as we shall see, is limited and continues to be reduced by expansion of agricultural lands.

Salt trading accommodates to the demands of changing household size. It is readily expandable when there are enough adult men and simply discontinued when there are too few. It is ideally suited to a polyandrous household system, in which there may be five brothers in one generation and only one in the next. This is part of the reason there is far greater variance in herd size than in landholdings. The largest herding household owns over three hundred goats and sheep, while one-third of households have six or less (too few for profitable salt trading), and one-quarter have none at all. By contrast, the biggest landholder has twelve times more land than his poorest trongba fellow.

In the face of repeated bad harvests, people have turned to salt trading to solve their economic difficulties. Yet previous years were marked by pessimism about the trade's future (also see Fürer-Haimendorf 1975:264–65). Further pessimism is justified. The past half century has witnessed a continual decline in profits for Nyinba and other Humla people who engage in salt trading—and at every trading juncture. The decline has been more severe in the south, in part because of the increasing availability of Indian salt and in part because of increasing population and rising demands for grain at home. Easier access to Indian salt can be traced to the regularization of Indian-Nepalese relations and settlement of the border area known as the Terai. The Nyinba response to the weakening market has been expansion and intensification of the salt trade—increased work to offset decreased profits.

To give a more precise picture of these losses, I can compare exchange rates of fifty years ago with those of today. At the former time, Nyinba received four measures of salt per measure of rice in Tibet and had to pay two measures of grain for the wool of one sheep. Nowadays they receive three measures of salt per measure of rice and have to pay three measures of grain for the wool of one sheep. These are current government rates, and although people can obtain better rates by dealing directly with Tibetan nomads, this is illegal and not always practicable. Fifty years ago in Raskot, the area visited in autumn and spring, Nyinba received three measures of locally grown rice for one measure of Tibetan salt. This brought a total profit of 1200 percent. Nowadays the rate is one to one, and the profit has declined to 300 percent. Raskot people do give twice as much local cotton for wool as they used to, which compensates minimally for these losses. In Acham to the south, Nyinba used to receive three or even four measures of rice for their one measure of salt. Now the rate there is one to one as well.

To counterbalance the decline in profits, Nyinba began going to the Indian border for additional salt when it first became readily available there. A few traders went for the first time in 1963; the others followed their example and went in 1964. Between 1963 and 1983, the cost of salt there rose 500 percent (Rs 14 to 70 per sack). However, the price of the sheep Nyinba sell to buy salt at the border has risen as well.

The Nyinba response to the erosion of their profits has been to put more animals into trade and to travel more and farther distances. People say that today's small herd was more than adequate for any household's needs in the past. The salt trade was simpler then too, centered on areas nearby in Tibet and in Nepal's middle hills. Now it extends from Tibet to the Indian border, requiring more work and more road-days for men and animals. Increasing population and conversion of forest- and wastelands into farmlands also has made it harder to feed animals on the road. The intensification of trade, moreover, has aggravated competition between various salt-trading groups, all of whom have had to increase their efforts for the same reasons as Nyinba have.

Although the decline in profits has been less severe in Tibet than in Nepal's middle hills, the future of trade here seems to be even more uncertain. The Chinese have introduced improved seed varieties suited to Tibet's climate, artificial fertilizers, and modern agricultural techniques, all of which promise to lessen Tibet's reliance on imported grains—grains, that is, imported by Nyinba and other salt-trading middlemen.

Further declines in profits can be expected in the middle hills. When roads are extended farther north, there will be little need for the Nyinba's carrier animals. Even before this happens, it may become increasingly more difficult to use those animals, because of the loss of roadside pasturage. The problem is that Nyinba and others in Humla now are increasing their involvements in the salt trade. Beginning in the late 1970s, people deserted settled agricultural communities in Humla to become Khampas—

nomadic herders who live off the salt trade (Rauber 1982a, 1982b). When the salt trade breaks down at one end or another, as it surely will, those groups who depend entirely or partially upon it will suffer serious economic reversals. I am not sure what solution Nyinba will find then to supplement their agricultural production.

Supplemental Herding

Nyinba claim that they had larger cattle herds in the past and that the conversion of good, high-altitude pasture into farmland led them to reduce herd sizes. Nonetheless, pasturage in this region of Humla always has been limited, and Nyinba apparently never took their cattle herds to the more extensive grazing lands several days walk to the north. In consequence, community members may never have owned that many cattle—the situation seems more one of small-scale herding becoming smaller scale still. Today winter pasturage is so inadequate that animals require supplementary hay, and the hay is so inadequate that animals spend the winter hungry, and some starve to death before spring comes. Summer pastures are steep and rocky, and numbers of animals often are lost in falls from cliffs. This explains why the average Nyinba household makes do with only four yak or dzo (yak-cow crossbreeds) and two cows. As more pasture is converted into farmland, these numbers may decline further.

Although cattle herding is limited, it still is significant economically. When asked why they keep cattle, people answer that cattle are useful for their manure in compost, for meat and milk products, and also as pack animals. Butter is an important component of the Tibetan way of life, both in the diet and for religious offerings. Yet butter is too rare and too expensive for most Nyinba to eat. In 1983, it costs Rs 80 ($5.63) per kilogram. It also could be sold in Limi or Tibet for cash, of which many households have few other sources. Yak females (properly known as *'bri*) produce an average of eight kilograms of butter per summer, a crossbreed female (or *dzo-mo*) twelve, and a cow three. Most households keep only about two kilograms of butter and sell the rest. Some of this money is used to buy mustard seed oil, apricot oil, or walnut oil—substitutes for butter at half the price.

Cattle herds also are inadequate to meet the demand for meat. However, neighboring high-caste Hindus, who of course do not eat beef themselves, seem to have no compunction about selling their older animals to Nyinba.[14]

[14]The slaughter of cows and yak is illegal in Nepal, but is unofficially tolerated where Buddhists live.

This keeps beef relatively cheap, but not cheap enough to consume daily. Milk is not consumed regularly either; it is readily available only in spring and autumn in the village and in summer for those who stay with the animals in the high pastures. Some people keep chickens, primarily to sell or for eggs to offer to guests. As I have said, overall consumption of milk and meat products is low, peaking in autumn when cattle return to the village and sheep are brought from Tibet.

During the winter, when animals are stabled in the village, small children or retired men take the cattle out on mild days to graze. In summer, an otherwise unproductive household member, more often a man, sometimes a young girl or elderly woman, goes to the high pasture. Households with very small herds join forces with others, preferably kin or affines in similar circumstances, with whom they alternate herding responsibilities. Wealthier households tend to keep larger herds in order to make more compost for their more extensive landholdings and to support a better diet. Wealthy households also can afford to hire a shepherd if there is no household member available for this.

The importance of manure should not be underestimated in a region where land is double cropped and only the most marginal lands are left to lie fallow. People without cattle go so far as to follow the paths animals take to pasture and collect dung fallen on the road. Thus while cattle raising may be unproductive in the sense that it provides little food directly, it may contribute indirectly to the production of grain.

Supplementation of Labor

Many Nyinba hire laborers to help with herding, salt trading, and agriculture. The wealthiest households keep servants, and a few continue to support freedman dependents; households with middling or larger herds use shepherds; and almost every household hires casual agricultural workers at some time during the agricultural season. Nyinba mostly hire impoverished Nepali speakers of high or low caste whose villages are nearby, lower down on the hillside. A few Nepalis have established permanent or semipermanent residences on the edge of Nyinba villages, in order to have easier access to employers and their work sites. Finally, Nyinba occasionally hire Tibetan refugees, Tibetan speakers from neighboring communities, and poor Nyinba.

Casual workers are needed often. In autumn 1982, the average Nyinba household hired agricultural workers for 23.5 full days. Autumn may be the period of peak demand for agricultural labor, but summer is said to follow closely after. In summer, most of the need is for women's work; in

autumn, workers are needed both to supplement household women, especially for bringing in the millet harvest, and to help harvest other crops,
work Nyinba assign to either sex. To an outsider, this would seem in-
controvertible proof of a need for more household women. However,
Nyinba questioned on the subject of their household work force consistently expressed greater concern about shortages of male labor and described an ideal household even more disproportionately male than their
households already are (table 9.3).

There are several traditional arrangements for supplementing household
labor in agriculture. The commonest is casual labor (*rog 'chol-ba,* literally
"employed assistants"), which can be contracted for as little as a morning
or as long as employer and employee wish. The pay includes meals for the
day and one tre of grain or, in autumn, wool, or Raskot cotton worth approximately Rs 10.[15] Nyinba households with greater than average labor
needs also keep up traditional hereditary relationships (Nep. *lāgi-lohār*)
with Nepali untouchables, following the conventions of the local Nepali
jajmani system. The untouchables, who usually are ironsmiths, are expected
to make tools for their employer, and members of their households are
obliged to work a certain number of days at plowing, weeding, and harvesting. The system of payment is very elaborate, involving fixed numbers of
baskets of grain and measures of wool at specific times of year. Women who
are friends also may establish cooperative labor exchanges (*rog-rog byed-
ja*), working for one woman's household one day, another the next, and
eating together at the home they worked for that day. Households with
greater needs do not bother with this; they maintain dependent households,
employ servants, keep up arrangements with untouchables, and hire additional workers at peak seasons. These are the very households that would
have kept slaves in the past. People with smaller landholdings or lesser labor
needs work together with friends and hire casual workers at peak seasons.

Poor unmarried women from Limi, a community of Tibetan speakers to
the north, used to spend the winter weaving cloth in Nyinba villages. Limi
women are skilled weavers, and Nyinba households hired them because
their own women simply were unable to meet family needs for cloth. While
weaving is highly esteemed and provides a way for women to express their
artistry, it also involves slow and tedious work. Limi women stopped com-
ing in 1980, partly because bad harvests limited the amount of food Nyinba
had to pay winter workers and partly because they reportedly found better
employment elsewhere. The consequence was that Nyinba were wearing

[15] Men who are hired to help plow and women hired for wood collection or washing newly
woven wool cloth are paid two tre of grain plus their meals.

Table 9.3 Household Labor Needs

	Male Workers[a]	Female Workers[a]
Mean number of workers in 1982	2.5	1.9
Ideal household work force	3.6	2.4
Percentage of households[b] desiring more workers	68	49

[a] This is derived from people's own estimates of their household's work force. The households include both trongba and non-trongba.
[b] There were 126 households surveyed.

fewer homemade woolen garments in the second period of my fieldwork, and the price of woven garments had soared. Instead of wool people wore more imported cotton and corduroy, and the men and some young girls had taken to wearing western-style clothes. This is another product of the central contradiction of the Nyinba domestic economy: minimizing the number of women in the household, while relying greatly upon them.

The Valuation of Labor

The presence of impoverished Nepalis and other Tibetan speakers who are willing to work for low wages has proven critical in supporting simultaneous Nyinba involvements in different economic sectors. Nyinba can usually find the casual laborers they need for agriculture, although they have to promise more attractive wages in the peak harvest season. They ordinarily have very little difficulty finding sufficient numbers of shepherds for a season or a year. The flexibility this offers is enormously advantageous, especially for sheep herding, where it permits seasonal readjustments of the work force to continually changing herd sizes. In effect, the availability of hired labor means that households can find workers when they are essential and dispense with them when their needs have been met. Hiring labor also is more cost-effective than maintaining households of dependent freedmen—unless a reliable source of labor is needed year-round. First of all, hired labor allows households to manage multiple economic involvements without increasing the size of their memberships. Second, it helps households maintain reasonable levels of agricultural production when they lack

sufficient personnel. Finally, it makes it possible to keep the number of
household women perpetually low—while ensuring that the work assigned
to women continues to be done.[16] This was the need that slavery seems
most to have served, and this seems to have been the critical fact around
which the entire slavery system was structured. At the same time, polyandry provides the point of articulation for household men, the basis for their
domestic cooperation and the rationale for their unity. In this way, systems
of marriage, gender, and social hierarchy have traditionally been linked to
a special system of household management. One of the practical consequences and manifestations of this is that women stay home and concern
themselves with local agriculture, while men specialize in diverse productive tasks.

Above all, men's labor interests center around salt trading, an activity
readily adaptable to changing household size and changing household
needs. Thus while men can be deployed in any economic sector, they alone
engage in the one activity that frees households from limited resources at
home. This is the fact that Nyinba, men and women alike, cite when explaining why men provide greater economic benefits to their households
and why the more men a household includes, the greater its chances for
economic success.

In virtually all intensive agricultural societies, women's work seems to
be valued less than the work of men. These notions may be compounded in
virilocal fraternally polyandrous systems. Polyandry (barring regular polygyny) places several adult and economically active household men alongside a single woman. Among the Nyinba and in traditional rural Tibet,
these men were employed in diverse economic sectors, which served to
protect their households against losses in any one such sector. If people
thought little of this before, instability in the salt trade in the 1960s and
repeated famines over the last decade certainly brought the value of diversification home. There is, however, more to the matter. Nyinba, men and
women alike, say that men's work generally requires greater skills and
harder work and is more important to a household. This is not to say that
they deny the important economic contributions women make—for they
do not—although women are more apt to point to their contributions than
are men. Nonetheless, the greater emphasis and the dominant theme in
conversation is the value of men's work.

From an observer's perspective, women's work seems undervalued.

---

[16]I should note that this same goal has been met in other Tibetan-speaking groups in Nepal
by using the community's own unmarried, or "surplus," women as casual laborers (Schuler
1987:152; Goldstein 1976:229).

Women undoubtedly contribute far more time than men to agriculture, which is the primary source of income for non-salt-trading households. Even for salt-trading households, agriculture was the source of more than half the year's income in food grains in 1983. The need is to ground these impressions: what contributions do women actually make to agriculture and to household income generally?

Evaluating the economic worth of different types of work is a complex matter. It is made even more difficult in a subsistence economy, where the products of labor have no fixed economic value. Most items the Nyinba make are not sold but consumed at home or exchanged for other home-produced goods in nonmonetary transactions. There also are problems in determining what counts as work and in assessing the relative productivity and intensiveness of different types of work. Most Nyinba women, for example, husk their own grain. However, some notoriously lazy women hire casual workers to do this for them. The problem is that they have to watch the worker, usually landless and impoverished, lest he or she steal from the grain, and the result is that two individuals come to be doing the work of one. Both husking grain and watching while a paid worker does it clearly are work, but one costs the household more than the other.

A recent multicommunity study in Nepal examined the division of labor and the time spent on work in rural households. The study considered a range of types of work: directly productive activities, such as agriculture; other activities related to subsistence, such as food processing; and also housework and child care. Although the latter sorts of work tend not to be counted in national surveys of economic productivity, they are essential to household functioning and occupy time that could be spent otherwise. This, moreover, is the sort of work that typically falls to women. The study found that women contribute 80 percent as much time as men to agriculture, animal husbandry, manufacturing of goods, and paid employment. When subsistence activities, food processing, water collection, and so on were added, women's work levels rose to roughly equal to those of men's. And when domestic work was added, women were found to be working 44 percent more hours daily than men (Acharya and Bennett 1981:156–60).

There is no doubt that Nyinba women work longer hours in the village than men. It is a fact obvious to anyone, which all acknowledge. However Nyinba claim that men engaged in salt trading work as hard as or harder than women do at home, because the work is unending and strenuous and the hours are long.[17]

---

[17] I have never traveled with the salt traders and have no way of evaluating these statements.

Another finding from the Nepalese study is that girls of almost all ages work longer hours than boys of the same age. An earlier study of children's economic contributions in a Nepalese village came to the same conclusion: girls do more work than boys in almost all age groups (Nag et al. 1978:296). Both studies attributed the lesser work contributions of boys to their greater attendance at school.

Nyinba say that girl children begin working earlier and work harder and longer hours than boys of equivalent ages. A boy is allowed to play until early adolescence, while his sisters begin doing work such as fetching water at approximately age six and begin weeding along with their mothers at approximately age nine. Mothers expect their small daughters to help care for younger siblings, which frees the mother for other productive labor. Almost all boys are sent to school, although not all go—some preferring play to learning—whereas girls are kept home for work. Schools are very new here and have not led to any lesser expectations of work from boys. Boys did not work in the first place, and the reason so many resist going to school is that it takes them away from play. Nyinba explain their expectation of more work from girls by their lower valuation of women in general (expressed as *rngan-chen*, disrespect or disregard) and their greater concern and "love" (*snying-rje*) for boys.

The problem is that no matter how many hours little girls work for their households, they are valued less than boys. This Nyinba justify by the fact that parents never benefit from rearing girl children, since they join other households shortly after reaching adulthood and their full work capabilities. Yet the work of adult women in their marital households is devalued as well, no matter how many hours it involves, nor how much it contributes to household income.

The work that Nyinba glorify now is trade, which only men do, while the work depreciated is agriculture, which is what women mainly do. Whether Nyinba are similar to other Tibetan-speaking populations in this regard is uncertain. It is clear that regional variations and class factors have a bearing upon Tibetan women's involvements in trade (Aziz 1978:108; Schuler 1981). Among Nyinba and the other Humla Tibetan communities I have studied, women engage only in minor exchange transactions outside their home communities. Rather, they are trained for and assigned to work which mostly is seen as drudgery, yet at the same time is absolutely critical for household prosperity.[18]

[18] In their study of diverse ethnic groups in Nepal, Acharya and Bennett (1981:301–2) found that where women as well as men were substantially involved in the wider market economy, they had greater input into household decision making and presumably greater power

Economic Differentiation and Social Stratification

Nyinba downplay differences of wealth in everyday life. Constraints on displays of wealth are echoed in concerns about envy and the attacks of witches and reaffirmed in the various themes of legends and in the courtesies of daily life, all of which express trongba equality (Levine 1982a). Wealth, nonetheless, influences household members' prestige in the larger community in fundamental ways: it affects their marriage choices, has an impact upon intracommunity political alliances, which, in turn, are shaped by marriage alliances, and has, it need not be said, appreciable effects on standards of living. Another effect of wealth—and one of the most profound—is on internal domestic organization. While contrasts in the domestic lives of rich and poor may be more stark among the freedman population, there are differences among trongba as well. For one thing, wealth is positively correlated with household size, and larger households both facilitate and necessitate greater involvement in diverse sectors of the economy.

Nyinba evaluate a household's wealth primarily by the extent of its landholdings. As they put it, land gives a household a "name." In arranging a marriage, the girl's parents look first to landholdings and second to levels of engagement in the salt trade. This is because landholdings presage a household's economic future, while salt trading involvements stand mostly as an index of present income and standard of living. After these considerations comes ownership of valuables: money, gold, jewelry, brass utensils, carpets, silk, and special clothing. The number of cattle matters, but is less important, since animals die so often and the area is not well suited to livestock raising. Wealthier households do tend to have more milk animals, in part because of the contribution milk makes to the diet. This is not a trivial matter where food choices are so limited, but a household lacking cattle that has other wealth can easily acquire cattle.

The relationship between the different forms of productive wealth and household size is shown in figures 9.4 through 9.6. Since land is rarely bought and sold, and since there are so few opportunities for bringing new lands under cultivation, landholdings must be regarded as more contributor to than consequence of household size; thus I have treated land as an independent variable in these calculations. Sheep and goat herds and cattle herds,

---

and authority. Perhaps participation in the wider economy is valued in these groups too because it expands economic horizons and frees households from reliance on a fixed resource base at home.

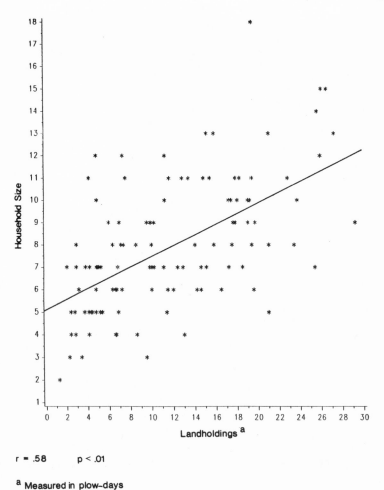

r = .58   p < .01

a Measured in plow-days

Figure 9.4   Relationship between Household Size and Landholdings

easily expandable and contractible as circumstances demand, would seem
to be more the outcome of the available household labor force; thus they
are treated here as dependent variables.

These figures show a moderately strong and consistently significant
positive relationship between the size of households, their landholdings,
and their sheep and goat herds. They show a somewhat weaker but still
significant and positive relationship between household size and cattle

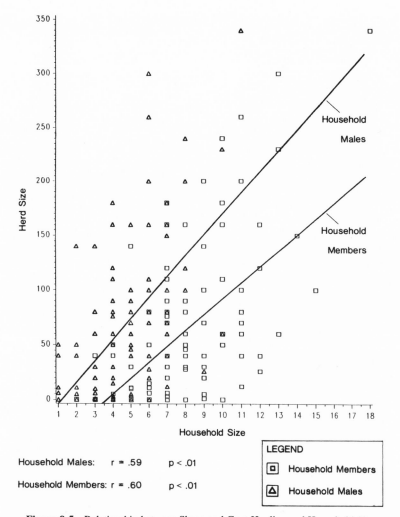

Figure 9.5   Relationship between Sheep and Goat Herding and Household Size

herds. We also find considerable variation: some small households own a
large amount of land and some large households have no sheep or goats
whatsoever. The fact of the matter is that such variation is the reality of
life. There always will be households that suffer tragedies of heirlessness
which no amount of wealth can remedy and others with a wealth of sons
that are delayed by poverty from entry into active salt trading. These fig-

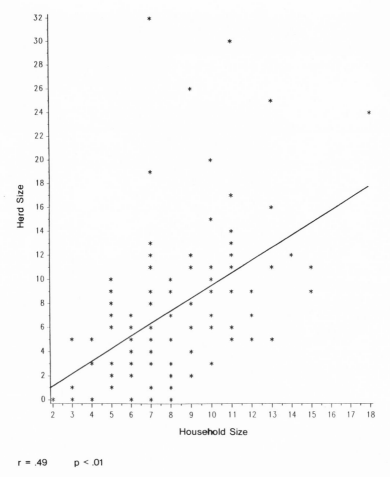

r = .49   p < .01

Figure 9.6 Relationship between Cattle Herding and Household Size

ures also affirm the relationship between diversified productive strategies
and household size, lending support to the argument that larger households
permit multifaceted domestic economies, as well as call for them.

Culture, Social System, and Economic Adaptations

Fürer-Haimendorf explains the emphases on trade found in so many
Tibetan-speaking groups in Nepal in terms of environmental and cultural
factors. First, these Tibetans tend to occupy higher-altitude regions, where

self-contained peasant communities cannot manage on agriculture and animal husbandry. Second, and perhaps more important, they live at the inter-
stices of two complementary economic zones: the arid Tibetan plateau to
the north and the middle hills of Nepal to the south. The Tibetan plateau is
grain-deficient; in Nepal, there are shortages of salt, wool, and pasturage
for breeding livestock. Fürer-Haimendorf goes on to argue that Tibetans'
proficiency at trade cannot be explained simply by the poverty of their environment and features of their location, for also implicated in this is a set
of distinctive attitudes and social arrangements. These are societies which
encourage commerce and entrepreneurship through, as Fürer-Haimendorf
has it, a stress on individualism, independence, social egalitarianism, and
opportunities for economic mobility (1975:286–89).

For Nyinba, the major factor supporting involvements in trade is the
household system, formed as it is around a core of polyandrous males. The
lifelong co-residence of brothers permits specializations, not only in trade,
but also in agriculture and animal husbandry to the degree that pasturage
permits. In a region like Humla, where famines are common and trade unpredictable, economic diversification appears to be a virtual necessity. One
might conclude then that Nyinba became trading middlemen partly because they occupy a narrow valley system and partly because land-hungry
neighbors have progressively encroached on their territory. One might say
that their efforts at trade are facilitated by their location at the edge of two
economically complementary zones. Finally, one might argue that they became adept traders because of the positive value given to independence and
egalitarian sociality. However, the fact of the matter is that Nyinba were
able to maintain such extensive involvements in trade in addition to other
economic activities only because of the presence of a large pool of domestic, servile, and casual laborers at home. Other Humla Tibetan speakers
place less emphasis on sustaining polyandrous marriage and in consequence find themselves less able to sustain multiple economic involvements. This has not led them to reform their social systems in what might
be seen as more adaptive directions. The sole consequence is that they are
poorer than Nyinba.

However much Nyinba glorify trade, it is a relatively small-scale enterprise. Humla has not been a region where major fortunes in trade could be
built, except perhaps at the height of the Malla kingdom over six hundred
years ago. The Chinese takeover of Tibet created certain opportunities for
trade in antiques, but only for a brief time. There are no major markets
near at hand, and until recently few commodities were available beyond the
salt, grain, and wool that Nyinba barter in communities located between
India and Tibet. It is possible that economic circumstances in Humla will

improve in the future, and when that happens, Nyinba may be able to capitalize on their expertise to become major traders like those found in other Himalayan border areas of Nepal.

A final point is that Nyinba form a part not only of the regional system of trade, but also of the regional system of labor exchange. Individuals from northern Humla communities long have moved south in winter to work in the agriculturally more productive middle hills. Nyinba do not move themselves, but traditionally hired workers from communities to the north in winter and still hire workers from nearby communities year-round. They do so to supplement an insufficient female work force and to better adjust the male work force to productive needs. Nyinba say they prefer to have many household men and to have fewer household women, and they generally manage this. The result is fewer childbearing women in trongba households and the production of only one family for each set of brothers. This lessens the chances for partition and has created a society which has maintained a rough balance in the number of its households and which has lower rate of population growth than might otherwise occur.

10
The Logic of a Low-Growth Population

The Nyinba community is atypical in Nepal and in the developing world for having experienced only moderate growth over the last century. A number of factors seem to have contributed to this. First among them is the traditional system of household management. This limits the number of marriages contracted and produces self-sufficient households that remain undivided from one generation to the next. Second are village attempts to regulate household partitions and extinctions, which follow assessments of village needs and how they are best served. A third factor is community closure, which is grounded in ideas about kinship and descent and effected through obstacles to immigration. This is countered by prevailing constraints on emigration—paradoxically, embedded in the same cultural logic, but with antithetic effects. Finally, rates of population increase are now and seem to have been in the past relatively low.

The household system rests upon a delicately balanced polyandry, which gives each brother a claim to equal rights in the sexual and childbearing capacities of the common wife. Household positions formalize the patterning of interpersonal relationships, and individuals' progressions through these positions over the life cycle provide personal rewards, although these are deferred for some and limited for others. The reward shared by all is the stake in a continuing, economically sound and politically effective trongba. Nevertheless, polyandrous marriages are not always satisfactory, and their failure means household partition and village growth. Among the reasons for partition are breakdowns in fraternal solidarity, which are attributed to the divisive effects of different maternity, and difficulties inevitable in marriages involving large sibling groups. Different maternity seems to create a legacy of mistrust between men, while sibling groups of three or more brothers make the balance and equitable treatment which polyandry demands more difficult to sustain.

Partition also seems to be influenced by village political considerations. Ordinarily community opinion stands in support of households that remain united. However, fears of population decline or the perception that village management would be better served by additional households may make community members more sympathetic to—or simply less critical of— partition. Logic alone tells us that some partitioning is necessary. If polyandry were maintained uniformly and if partition never occurred, then the Nyinba community would be no larger than those few founder households which have produced heirs in every generation. This in fact is one of the messages of origin legends, which depict frequent partitioning early in village history. Today, partition seems to be better tolerated when numbers of village households have become extinct and when households have fallen heir to extinct estates. As we shall see, extinction and reinheritance have their own dynamic and may motivate subsequent partitioning, while partitions, by producing households prone to problems of viability, often end in extinctions and reinheritance.

Household management and decisions about partition are affected by further considerations. Access to adequate resources—from a household's own estate, from reinheritance of a vacant estate, or from land newly cleared—removes one of the major constraints upon partitioning. This at least is my interpretation, although Nyinba omit this factor from their accounts of partition decision-making processes. In the end, however, none of these factors, alone or in combination, is sufficient to explain partition. There are cases of men in small sibling groups with inadequate land who partition despite community disapproval, of men with ample resources who live out their lives in a single polyandrous marriage, and of men in large sibling groups apparently content to share a wife. The availability of land may make it easier for a man to support himself on his own, but it does not eliminate existing kinship ties between brothers or political constraints on partition. Similarly, the lesser trust among men with different mothers is not compelling enough on its own to consistently override the advantages of remaining in a politically strong, wealthy, and unified trongba.

Growth in the Village

Attempts to chart Nyinba village growth over time rely upon household registers, the earliest of which was compiled in 1868. There are few other data available. National censuses have been conducted every ten years

since the second half of this century (Krótki and Thakur 1971), but results
for the Nyinba community were not tabulated separately and in any event
are incomplete, because of faulty methods of data collection (see Kansakar
1977). Nor is there any system for registering vital events in Humla district. Thus the data are limited and must be treated as only suggestive. And
what they suggest is a pattern of moderate and regulated growth extending
over the last century and more.

Nyinba community growth has been moderate, overall and relative
to that of other Tibetan-speaking groups in Humla, as shown by comparisons between the number of registered taxpaying households in 1868
and the number of households in the same villages and communities in 1983
(table 10.1). Lists of taxpaying households were, by necessity, highly accurate—so much so that they still are used as the basis for determining tax
obligations and rights to land among every Humla community I have studied (see appendix B). I confined my comparisons to Tibetan speakers, because other ethnic groups in Humla have quite different sociocultural systems, and many have experienced far higher levels of community growth.
Simikot, for example, a predominantly Chetri-caste village and Humla's
district capital, increased fourfold over this same 115-year period.

Between 1868 and 1983, the Nyinba community grew more slowly than
any other community of Tibetan speakers on which I have data. Only one
Nyinba village, Nyimatang, experienced greater growth than a non-Nyinba
village. That slow-growing village is Khalos, which has lost much of its
population to emigration in recent years. Overall the number of Nyinba
households increased at an average rate of no more than 0.26 percent per
year. At this rate, it would have taken more than 250 years for the community to double its size. Trugchulung, a community one day's walk to the
north, has more than doubled in size during this same period, and Limi
may have done so as well. Goldstein (1981:725) suggests that Limi is now
experiencing very high rates of population growth—the projected doubling
time is thirty-one years—while Ross (1981:108) suggests that the population of La (Dinga) in Trugchulung may be increasing by more than 50 percent per generation. Tsang (Dozam) is another matter. Locked in a narrow
valley inhospitable to agriculture, it has been exporting its population in
considerable numbers; its rate of emigration is probably as high as that of
any other Humla Tibetan community.

Rates of population growth in Nepal as a whole are estimated to have
stood at 1.2 percent per year during the early part of this century and to
have risen to over 2.6 percent per year today (Nepal 1985:13). Household
data suggest that many villages in the country increased fivefold between
1850 and 1950 (Macfarlane 1976:203–4). By contrast, no Humla commu-

Table 10.1   Growth in Humla Tibetan-Speaking Communities

	Trongba[a] 1868	Trongba[b] 1983	All Households[c] 1982	1983	Increase from 1868 to 1983[d] (%)
Nyinba					
Barkhang	39	46	55	55	18
Nyimatang	21	33	37	37	57
Todpa	18	26	27	27	31
Trangshod	44	53	60	58	20
All villages	122	158	179	177	30
Trugchulung					
Chadog	11	24	24	24	118
Khalos	18	24	26	24	33
Khamgung	26	61	55	55	135
La (Dinga)	18	—	38	38	111
Sangrag	25	—	42	46	68
Tamkhyim	13	—	25	25	92
Yabka	24	—	65	65	171
All villages	135	—	275	277	105
Limi					
Dzang	5	13	50	50[e]	160
Haldzi	14	—	—	66	—
Til	4	—	—	35	—
All villages	23	—	—	—	—
Tsang	33	54	49	50	64

[a] This is the number of households listed in the 1868 tax registers.
[b] This is based on my own censuses.
[c] This is the figure submitted to the government. In the Nyinba case, it includes small, former-slave households which had not been listed in 1868. In Trugchulung, newly partitioned households are excluded from the government list (and household taxes) for several years. Thus my figures are lower in the former case and higher in the latter.
[d] This is based on my figures, where available.
[e] Limi is unusual in having large numbers of non-trongba households, which were not listed in 1868 (but were included in the government figures for 1983). Therefore, I am able to estimate increases in numbers of trongba only.

nity of any ethnic group I know about increased quite so much during this period.[1] And for Nyinba, present-day demographic data suggest an intrinsic rate of natural increase between 1 and 1.5 percent per year. Thus the population is growing, but much less rapidly than the rest of the country (see appendix C).

[1] Humla villages in general may have grown more slowly than those elsewhere in Nepal. Humla, of course, is a long-settled region, where agriculture is made difficult by the steep

Partition, Extinction, and the Balance of Landholdings

The relatively lower growth rate in Nyinba villages can be attributed to the rarity of partition, which is confirmed both by household registers and household genealogical data. I examined these for all the village households known to have partitioned since 1868. In the first eighty-one years, there were fifteen "successful" partitions—that is, partitions which persisted beyond a generation (table 10.2). There were six more in the decade of the 1950s and eleven in both the 1960s and 1970s. Thus far in the 1980s only two partitions have taken place. When I left Humla in December 1983, another household had begun the process of partition—it had split into separate families and had established separate hearths—and a second household was said to be contemplating partition. However, at last report the former have reunited and the latter remains undivided.

1. Partition and Risks of Inviability

The problem with partition is that it creates households which are more vulnerable—immediately so—to problems of viability. I was able to observe two households struggle with and eventually succumb under the weight of such problems. These households initially partitioned between 1940 and 1950, and they were extinct and reabsorbed by their trongbat by 1983. Another household that had partitioned at the same time was gone before I ever reached Humla. Because failed partitions are of neither political nor kinship significance, they tend to be dropped from household genealogies and quickly forgotten. Thus, it is likely that additional households were formed by partition in the past but failed and were so rapidly taken over by rightful trongbat heirs that no traces of them remain. This may be one reason for the apparently low incidence of recalled partitions prior to 1950.

The causes of inviability in newly partitioned households are all too obvious. These households are more apt to suffer deficiencies of personnel or deficiencies in resources and suffer most where both deficiencies occur. Two present-day cases serve to illustrate this:

---

terrain, high altitude, and low levels of rainfall. Villages in the more recently colonized, lush hills of eastern and central Nepal may have expanded more in the recent past, because of both intrinsic rates of natural increase and immigration. Today most mountain and hill regions are experiencing population losses, because of opportunities for settlement in the Terai, the region bordering the Indian plains (see United Nations 1980:19).

1. In approximately 1950, one of Barkhang's three headman households underwent a partition. It had a very small land base to begin with, because of repeated partitioning in previous generations, and the new partition produced two households with very inadequate amounts of land.[2] The elder brother and his wife had to work extremely hard, but they managed to persevere. Fortunately, in the early years of their marriage they had two sons, the eldest of whom became a policeman in the eastern Karnali Zone and sent a portion of his earnings home. The younger brother had quite the opposite experience. He was plagued by ill health and frequently unable to work. He married several times, but one wife after another left him. Not until he was sixty-one years of age did he produce a son and heir. Shortly afterwards he died, leaving an orphan and an estate in decline. The widow found herself unable to maintain the estate and soon abandoned it. She then supported herself and her child by working for others. This provided an opportunity for her husband's brother's family. They slowly bought back the land, effectively merging the partitioned estate with their own. The widow's trongba is most often described as extinct now, and this is how I have treated it in calculations here.

2. A wealthy household in Wutig, Todpa's hamlet, partitioned in 1978. Prior to the partition, the household experienced a series of tragedies, summarized in chapter 8. Tragedies continued to befall both households after the partition, and this may result in the extinction of both.

Formerly this household included four brothers who initially married polyandrously, but their common wife died after bearing a son. Following this, the brothers could not agree upon a common wife, so they began bringing home wives individually and in subgroups. All the male children produced in these marriages died. Then the lone son from the brothers' first marriage died. This made an end to any pretence of household unity, and the brothers partitioned. The two older brothers went off with the longer-resident, older wife, and the two younger ones went off with the newer wife.[3] The older two brothers still have not produced an heir. The younger two both died in freak accidents shortly after their wife bore them a son. Like the widow in the previous case, she finds herself unable to manage and may have to abandon the estate.

[2] This is one of the "Dunsa Households" depicted in figure 8.7.

[3] I should note that this is not always the case, and there is no regular pattern of selecting partners in partition by age. In one Trangshod household, the reverse occurred. The younger two brothers partitioned with a wife respectively twelve and seventeen years older than they, while the two older brothers stayed with the younger wife, who was the contemporary of the younger two brothers.

Table 10.2 Incidence of Partitions, from 1868 to 1983

Village	1868–1949	1950–59	1960–69	1970–79	1980–83	Total
			Time Period			
Barkhang	2	2	3	4	0	11
Nyimatang	3	1	4	2	0	10
Todpa	2	0	3	2	1	8
Trangshod	8	3	1	3	1	16
All villages	15	6	11	11	2	45

Partition fragments a large household into two or more parts and creates new households with a fraction of the work force that supported the old one. Thus thirty-three out of the forty-five cases of partition described in table 10.2 produced at least one household with a single brother—to whom fell responsibilities once shared with a number of men. In only six of the partitions did all the new households include two brothers or more (in the remaining six cases, the composition of households following partition is unknown).

A man who has partitioned off alone invariably finds himself in difficult circumstances. It is impossible for him to engage in trade and cattle herding as well as agriculture simultaneously—he cannot be in Tibet trading salt and in the high pastures with his cattle and at home harvesting buckwheat all at the same time. I have watched a man who partitioned with little land try and fail to juggle all three. His solution was to hire himself out as cook to the visiting anthropologist and sneak away at times of peak agricultural labor. With adequate land, a man could stay at home farming, make a single annual trading trip to Tibet, and hope for several sons who would be able to diversify economic activities in the next generation. Without adequate land, there is a good chance that his household will not make it to the next generation.

Failed partitions, however, may be due to more than simple deficiencies in land or personnel. Such households also may find it difficult to maintain stable marriages, they may be unable to secure heirs when those marriages prove sonless, and they may find little help from fellow villagers in the course of crises of inviability. We know that Nyinba have an extraordinary number of strategies for producing household heirs. Men in childless marriages may take second wives, and households that lack sons but have daughters may select one to marry uxorilocally. Widowers who wish to perpetuate their trongba have the option of remarrying quickly, and widows from prestigious and wealthy trongba may either remarry or develop an informal liaison with a neighbor.[4] Households that are poor or recently established, however, find it more difficult to attract second wives or second husbands or uxorilocal spouses for daughters, and other Nyinba may be less willing to help maintain a household that brought its difficulties upon itself by partitioning against community disapproval. It also is possible, although I never heard this view expressed, that members of recently partitioned households may struggle less against extinction and being reabsorbed by the closely related trongbat household from whence they so recently came.

2. Extinction and Community Interventions

Overall, the rate of heirlessness and extinctions among Nyinba households seems low. In preindustrial populations with relatively low rates of growth and large families like the Nyinba, we could expect to find approximately 20 percent of couples with only daughters and between 10 and 20 percent with no children at all (Goody 1976:133–34). Nyinba marriages are far more successful than this at producing male heirs. We know that less than 7 percent of present-day trongba marriages are uxorilocal, that is, occur in households without sons to serve as heirs. While my listing of extinctions for the last 115 years may be incomplete, it is reliable for more recent decades, and the rate over the last generation hardly approaches 10—much less 20—percent. The fact that there are so few heirless and daughter-only households can be attributed to the flexibility of Nyinba marriage, which provides a number of strategies for households trying to produce sons.

The relatively low number of extinctions also owes much to Nyinba practices of intervening to help households suffering crises of inviability. We have seen the logic of such interventions and how they are sensitive to concerns about the direction of village growth. Thus, while villagers have turned their backs on certain households, they also have acted, singly and collectively, to help others surmount such crises and survive to the next generation. I have described one such intervention in Todpa, saw another in Barkhang during the course of my field research, and heard of four more in recent decades.

If households suffering crises of inviability were left to weather them on their own, more might fail and the rate of extinctions might match more closely the rate of partitions. However this is not the case, nor is the situation that simple. For, as we shall see, extinction and the inheritance of va-

[4] There are four cases now of widows who have remarried and brought their new husbands to the former husbands' homes. Less formal relationships between widows and married men in their villages, known as "doubling up," have been described in chapter 7.

cant estates have their own effects: among them a relaxing of constraints on further partitioning.

3. Consequences of Extinction: Occupations and Mergers

In theory, the estate from a household that falls extinct should pass to true trongbat, with property shares allocated according to the distance from a common partition origin. In fact, the claims of proper trongbat heirs often are set aside and extinct estates delivered to households with no rights whatsoever in them. In the twenty-eight extinctions known to have occurred since 1868, twelve, or 43 percent, involved occupations by nonheir households (table 10.3). Five of these were impoverished trongba suffering serious problems of viability. The property secured in the occupation provided each with greater economic security and may have prevented further extinctions—and thus the loss of additional households to the village. The other occupants of extinct estates were landless people—recently emancipated slaves and immigrants—and in this case occupations revitalized marginal households and returned functioning trongba to the village.

A closer look at events of extinction reveals that different Nyinba villages have responded quite differently to them. In Nyimatang, villagers have tended to give vacant estates to nonheirs, while in Trangshod, extinctions almost always led to property mergers with actual trongbat heirs. Not only that, but Nyimatang gave away three vacant estates to immigrant outsiders during this period—something no other village did even once. (One

Table 10.3 Incidence of Extinctions and Their Consequences, from 1868 to 1983

Village	Extinctions		
	Resulting in Mergers	Resulting in Occupations	Total
Barkhang	4	2	6
Nyimatang	2	6	8
Todpa	2	3	5
Trangshod	8	1	9
Total[a]	16	12	28

[a] In addition to partitions and mergers, other events changed the numbers of households in villages between 1868 and 1983. For example, Nyimatang gained a new temple household and a household from a Barkhang hamlet which had lost most of its land to the neighboring Nepali village of They. Todpa gained two temple households which were only hermitages occupied by celibate lamas in 1868.

Table 10.4 Average Village Landholdings in 1983

Village	Double-Cropped Land[a]	High-Altitude Land	Combined Land Value[b]	Number of Households[c]
Barkhang	4.0	4.8	10.4	34
Nyimatang	3.3	5.9	10.5	32
Todpa	4.0	9.9	15.5	23
Trangshod	3.9	3.2	8.7	37
All villages	3.8	5.6	10.9	126

[a]Landholdings are measured in plow-days.
[b]Each lowland field is treated as worth 1.4 times a highland field. Lowland fields may be double cropped and are approximately that much more productive than highland fields.
[c]This includes households of all categories.

of these immigrants was a man from a neighboring community who was married to a Nyinba woman and who had long served a wealthy Nyimatang household as shepherd, one was a Tibetan nomad who had worked for villagers, and the third was an immigrant lama.) In Todpa, occupations were marginally more common, while in Barkhang, they were slightly less so. One of the most plausible reasons for these differences is the relative availability of agricultural land in each village and associated notions of how many households it can or should accommodate.

Average landholdings vary markedly among the different villages (table 10.4). Todpa villagers own the most land by far, and the most high-altitude land particularly. Todpa, notably, has allowed more occupations of vacant estates than mergers. Trangshod villagers own the least high-altitude land and the least land overall. Significantly, Trangshod is the village that has permitted the fewest occupations of vacant estates and has enforced most often trongbat rights of reinheritance. The fact that Nyimatang villagers today hold, on average, no more land than the villagers of Barkhang may be due to their far greater prodigality in the past—that is, to the higher rates of trongba occupations and higher rates of trongba partitions. These actions may have been encouraged by a more favorable balance of landholdings then, for we know that Nyimatang villagers fell heir to vacant lands from the two protovillages that died out around the time of the Gorkha conquest of Nepal.

Manipulations such as these of trongbat rights follow from the notion that villages collectively have a stake in the size of their memberships. Concerns with village size are phrased not in terms of a determinate goal or an ideal number of households. Rather, there is the general notion that more or fewer households would serve village needs better. During public gatherings and celebrations in Todpa in the 1970s, I heard community leaders say that more households would be desirable, because now ritual and festival obligations fell too heavily on too few. Todpa elders discussing the recent past also told me that the occupations of half a century ago had gone unopposed because land at the time was in ample supply. In Nyimatang, the reason I overheard for granting a vacant estate to one new immigrant was that he was the sort of person who would persevere, build up the estate, and reliably meet community obligations. In the early part of the twentieth century, as one Nyimatang elder told me, vacant estates were plentiful, and it was not easy to find people to take them over and meet what then were extremely heavy tax obligations. Such perceptions about village needs must be subject to continual revision as the number of village households changes, as the balance of households within village sections shifts, as economic opportunities open, or as community and government obligations are redefined.

4. Mergers, Occupations, and the Likelihood of Partition

Individual households have responded to their good fortune and the receipt of additional property through mergers or occupations in quite different ways. Several factors seem to have been implicated in these differences. First is the social status of household members—that is, whether they were citizen-landholders, immigrants, or freedmen. A second factor is the type of inheritance—whether it was an occupation or a merger. Finally, village membership—and presumably village opinion about expansion—seems to have influenced whether the recipients of mergers chose to partition again.

Household status undeniably had an effect on reactions to occupations. Among the occupying households, five were citizen-landholders, five were newly emancipated slaves, and three were recent immigrants (table 10.5). Some of these citizen-landholders acquired vacant estates almost immediately after partitioning—in each case to supplement shares of land inadequate for their support. Others lived on the edge of poverty for a generation or more before their inadequate landholdings were supplemented by receipt of a vacant trongba. The immigrants and freedmen were previously landless; what they gained from their occupations was land minimally adequate for household support.

One can imagine how dramatic a change the acquisition of a fully functional estate—consisting of a house, land, animals, and various material items of daily life—meant for the recipients. Their standard of living improved overnight. Freedmen moved from a tiny house consisting of two rooms to one more than four times its size and rose from landlessness to

Table 10.5   Characteristics of Households
Occupying Vacant Trongba

Village	Citizen-Landholders	Emancipated Slaves	Immigrants
Barkhang	—	2	—
Nyimatang	3	1	3
Todpa	1	2	—
Trangshod	1	—	—
Total[a]	5	5	3

[a] One extinct trongba was divided between an immigrant and a
recently emancipated slave.

being counted among the village's primary landholders. Changes in political status may have met more resistance and proceeded more slowly. Nonetheless, these freedmen had trongbat for the first time—citizen-landholder
trongbat at that—and found themselves with obligations to the wider
community. The change for immigrants was equally dramatic. For citizen-
landholders, the net effect was to raise the household's economic level to
the standard of kin and fellow villagers and to compensate for the losses
from prior partitions. Thus their landholdings were doubled and their prestige in the community accordingly enhanced.

Another difference for the freedmen and immigrants was that they came
from groups where monogamy and partition between brothers were the
norm.[5] Thus it should not be surprising to find that all instances of partition
following an occupation occurred in freedman or immigrant households,
while none occurred among citizen-landholders. Not only that, but both
immigrant households that were able to partition—that is, that had more
than one brother in a coparcenary generation—did so. Four out of five freedmen households have included more than one brother in a coparcenary generation. Although only two of them have partitioned, one has subdivided
its estate among its four sons, in effect partitioning three times.

It might seem that giving vacant properties to freedmen and immigrants
in preference to mergers with true citizen-landholder trongbat fueled village growth. However, in the end it may have made less difference than one
might imagine. Mergers seem simply to have laid the foundations for sub-

[5] One of the immigrants who occupied a vacant estate came from Tarap in Dolpo, where
polyandry is extremely rare (Jest 1975: 261); the second was a Tibetan nomad—nomads reportedly are rarely polyandrous—and the third came from Tsang, where partition is very
common nowadays. The former two occupations occurred three or more generations ago; the
last occurred less than a decade ago.

Table 10.6   The Effect of Property Acquisition on Partition

Village	Partitions			
	Following Mergers (N)	Preceding Mergers (N)	Following Occupations (N)	Total (N)
Barkhang	—	2	1	3
Nyimatang	1	—	2	4
Todpa	1	1	1	3
Trangshod	3	1	—	4
Total N	5	4	4	13
Percentage of Partitions[a] (N = 35)	14.3	11.4	11.4	37.0

[a] On which this information is available.

sequent partitions. Even the hope or expectation of mergers to come seems to have precipitated partitioning. Of the thirty-five cases of partition since 1868 on which information is available, five followed mergers and four preceded them (table 10.6).[6] There were only sixteen mergers to begin with, which means that a total of 56 percent of recorded mergers can be linked to partitions. (And since three of the sixteen mergers took place after 1970, additional partitions may be yet to come).

Mergers may have had so powerful an effect on citizen-landholders because they provide the recipient household with a second full estate. The household acquires a second set of agricultural plots at different altitudes, a second herd of domestic animals, and a full complement of farm implements, pots and pans, and all the requisites of daily life. When the extinction and reinheritance follow soon after the initial partition, the reinheritor receives all its old property back again, plus whatever the extinct household had managed to acquire in the meantime. Mergers also make the village and one of its sections a household smaller. Unless villagers had felt that there were too many households to begin with, one would expect less opposition to subsequent partitioning.

Reactions to mergers seem to have been influenced by village membership as well. In Todpa and Nyimatang, every merger that occurred was associated with a partition. In Barkhang, two out of three were, while in

[6] Three of these mergers followed so closely upon the partition that the forthcoming inheritance must have been a consideration. In the fourth case, the merger followed by several decades. However it involved an estate held by an aged, childless couple who clearly were going to die without heirs.

Trangshod only four out of seven mergers were associated with partitions. As we have seen, Todpa and Nyimatang are the smallest Nyinba villages, and they are the villages whose members have shown an interest in further expansion in the more-or-less-recent past.

Events of occupation and merger, however, have been implicated in little more than a third of partition events. The great majority of households which have partitioned since 1868 did so without having received a vacant estate and without any hope of receiving one. Moreover, some of the households which occupied or reinherited a vacant estate chose not to partition. This is because partition is not a regular practice, and there is no factor that can predict it with absolute certitude.

Partitions following mergers may be seen as part of still another village reformative process, bringing village households to their previous balance again. Mergers too may be seen as constituting one point in a cyclical process of movement between partitions and extinctions. Partition often produces households which lack adequate property or personnel and which are more likely to lapse into inviability and extinction. Mergers provide trongbat heirs with a second full estate, which thereupon sets the stage for partitioning again. Inasmuch as the units involved are households whose interrelationships are understood in domestic terms, we may see the movement between partition, extinction, and merger as a kind of suprahousehold developmental cycle. This reminds us that villages are little more than supradomestic structures, similarly centered around kin and affines. From a demographic standpoint, such processes—and approximately 25 percent of the partitions since 1868—are inconsequential. They do not promote growth or decline in the village, nor do they produce any change in constituent units of social structure.

Mountain Agriculture: The Domestic Economy and Partition

The ways in which Nyinba manage their domestic economy also have implications for partition decisions. Mountain agriculture generally is quite intensive and demands heavy inputs of labor for relatively little productive output (Guillet 1983). Most households find it difficult to meet their labor needs under ordinary circumstances and find this increasingly difficult as their landholdings increase in extent. Nyinba also say that productivity declines when holdings get too large. Thus people asked to describe their ideal estate in land (*dud-tshang*) spoke not of one unimaginably large, but rather of one easily managed and highly productive, composed of a good mix of well-located and high-yielding fields.

This may be a consideration in partition decisions among households

Table 10.7 Landholdings and Partition in Trongba

	Landholdings[a]		
	N of Lowland Fields	N of Highland Fields	N of Cases
All trongba			
Partitioners			
Prior to partition	6.05	7.99	22
After partition[b]	3.04	3.89	33
Nonpartitioners	4.53	6.93	79
All households, 1983	4.09	6.04	112
Citizen-landholder trongba			
Partitioners			
Prior to partition	6.24	8.36	19
After partition[b]	3.24	4.11	29
Nonpartitioners	4.53	6.95	77
All households, 1983	4.18	6.17	106

[a] Landholdings are measured in plow-days.
[b] Data are not available for all partitioners.

with larger-than-average landholdings. Households that partitioned owned approximately one-third more lowland fields and up to one-fifth more highland fields than their nonpartitioning neighbors (table 10.7). The effect of partition, however, was to produce households with landholdings much smaller than average. Among citizen-landholder trongba, partitioners were left with 72 percent as many lowland and 59 percent as many highland fields as nonpartitioners. Among all trongba, freedmen as well as citizen-landholders, partitioners were left with only 67 percent as many lowland and 56 percent as many highland fields as their nonpartitioning neighbors. The table substantiates what Nyinba say: that people who partition suffer economically for it and have to make do with lesser landholdings. It also suggests that freedmen in trongba start out with, and are willing to make do with, less than citizen-landholders.

Hamlets and the Agricultural Frontier

Partitioners' reduced landholdings would be less of a problem were new land readily available. Land is important in ways not immediately obvious: it is necessary for trongba status, as well as being critical to household subsistence and providing a household's principal source of support when salt trading fails. The problem is that it is very difficult to acquire additional land. Land ordinarily is not for sale, and the best areas were put into production generations ago. Nowadays there are few lands left to be cleared which are not marginal, high-altitude, or too distant from home to work efficiently.

The situation is somewhat better for members of the newer hamlets. Most hamlets are located near forest areas, which have been and are being cleared and converted to farmland. These areas may be less well favored than village lands—they are at higher altitude, or too shady, or on steeper slopes, but they are able to produce tolerable yields. Nyimatang's hamlets are the exception to this: they stand on the sites of its protovillages, which were settled earlier and which also have lost much land to the Nepali Hindu village beneath them. For other village's hamlets, the opportunity to clear new land and thus to compensate for land lost in partition seems to have contributed to higher rates of partition and higher rates of hamlet growth. The histories of three of the most rapidly growing hamlets can be illustrated.

Before 1868, Langlo gompa was the local branch of a prominent monastery in Tibet. Its frescoes, now faded and peeling, are uncommonly fine and the finest in this area. At the time of the major land registration of 1868, Langlo was occupied by a Tibetan lama and his nun sister. The registration listed house site and forests in both their names and described this as a part of Barkhang village. However, it made no mention of the agricultural land, which was held to be Tibetan property. In the 1889 registration update, a powerful Trangshod man took advantage of the situation to register the agricultural land with his own village. This infuriated Barkhang villagers and led to a dispute that lasted for generations.

Both the brother and sister stayed on at Langlo. He later married a Nyinba widow, while she bore an illegitimate son by a Nyinba man. Her son's son neglected and later abandoned the estate. It then was given to a freedman household which expanded their landholdings and whose children have undergone three (sequential) partitions.

At the time of emancipation, village headmen travelled to the zonal capital of Jumla to collect money to buy the freedom of villagers' slaves. This provided the opportunity to examine local land records. The headmen found the greater portion of the forests near Langlo still unregistered and, after a carefully negotiated agreement, listed half of them with Barkhang and the other half with Trangshod, the villages between which they lie. Freedmen from both villages later settled on these lands and cleared large sections of the shady hillside, creating the present-day hamlet of Madangkogpo.

Thus what in 1868 was only a temple occupied by a monk and nun on a forested hillside of pine, rhododendron, and azalea now includes two villages of five households each, surrounded by cleared fields. These households include the descendants of the lama (one household), the descendants of the freedman who occupied his sister's lands in Langlo (four households), and five small households in Madangkogpo.

Wutig, Todpa's lone hamlet, offers another, if less dramatic, example of expansion. In 1868 it consisted of four households. Three partitioned, and today there are seven. What supported Wutig's expansion was the reclamation of high-altitude land directly above the village. This land has proved especially productive in growing buckwheat.

The land above Wutig had long been used by Barkhang villagers for pasturage. In the 1940s, Todpa began to reclaim land for cultivation there. Barkhang tried to halt this; relations between the two villages deteriorated, and highly placed thalu of Kalyal descent were brought in by both sides. After a bitter fight, Todpa villagers won and established permanent fields in this area, a substantial portion of which fell to Wutig.

Both Todpa and Nyimatang are relying more now upon higher-altitude lands. This is because they can do so, having ready access to such lands, and because they had to, being pressured out of their low-lying lands by the Nepali Hindu village below. Barkhang's attempts to expand have been checked above by Todpa and below by that same Nepali village on one side and rocky, marginal lands on the other. Trangshod also has densely populated Nepali villages beneath it and to its west. Above are steep rocky slopes, ill-suited to cultivation. Thus Barkhang could only expand toward forestlands to its west, and Trangshod could only move east, where the two met to battle over Langlo and Madangkogpo. This scarcity of land and constraints on expansion undoubtedly have contributed to the lower amount of growth in Barkhang and Trangshod villages and to their patterns of decisively favoring mergers and legitimate trongbat reinheritance over occupations of vacant trongba.

In Barkhang and Todpa, hamlet growth has far outstripped village growth (table 10.8). In Nyimatang, where hamlets stand on the sites of the two protovillages that became extinct, the rates of partition are identical in hamlet and main settlement.

This should not suggest that opening up new lands is an easy job, undertaken lightly. In reality, it is enormously difficult and considered mystically

Table 10.8   The Effect of Hamlet Residence on Partition

Village and Hamlets	Population in Trongba	*N* of Partitioners	Partitioners as Percentage of Population
Barkhang	40	6	15
Barkhang hamlets	7	5	71
Nyimatang	23	7	30
Nyimatang hamlets	10	3	30
Todpa	19	5	26
Todpa hamlets	7	3	43
Trangshod	53	10	19
Trangshod hamlets[a]	0	0	—
All main villages	135	28	21
All hamlets	24	11	46

[a] I have listed all households in Langlo and Madangkogpo with Barkhang.

dangerous. Like all Tibetans, Nyinba believe that deities dwell in land and water sources and that it is hazardous to disturb them. People who do so are apt to fall ill, and an angry deity may send other misfortunes upon their households. Agriculture in general is considered sinful, because it destroys small forms of life. This does not stop Tibetan agriculturalists from opening up new fields when they need to, but it means that they prefer not do to so unnecessarily. Opening up new fields also is backbreaking work, and it takes years of manuring and careful cultivation to bring the field to high levels of productivity. Nyinba villages put their best lands under cultivation generations, even centuries, ago and have tended them carefully since. Most land opened to cultivation in the last generation has been marginal in one way or another—too shady, high altitude, steep, or stony for high yields. But this land is all that is available now, and the hamlets and the higher-altitude village of Nyimatang have been able to take advantage of such opportunities as exist.

Residence in hamlets, in itself an expansionary move, seems to have encouraged further expansion. There are two reasons for this. First, access to new lands seems to be perceived as providing an exemption from the ordinary economic constraints upon partition. Second, practices of allocating new lands positively advantage partitioners. This is because putting large areas into cultivation becomes a village-wide enterprise. Villagers collectively undertake land reclamations and they divide the rights to new lands equally among all member trongba. While unified households receive only one portion of land in such distributions, partitioned households receive two.

In the end, although hamlet residence provided the opportunity to compensate for losses of land in partition, and although partitioners could take greater advantage of the new land available, not all hamlet households which had two or more brothers in a coparcenary generation made the decision to partition. This underscores the fact that material factors do not decide partition, just as they are not the critical determinants in marital and family arrangements. It is more accurate to speak of hamlet residence making partition more manageable. The result is that sons of different mothers, those in large sibling groups, and husbands and wives who simply do not get along may partition without fear of prolonged economic hardship.

We have seen that decisions about whether to stay in polyandry or to partition depend on a composite analysis. The relevant factors include the strength of fraternal relationships, whether the household has or anticipates acquiring adequate lands, and whether it can expect to remain politically effective. Of course partition only can occur in generations where there are two or more brothers. Were the sample of households larger, one could attempt multivariate statistical analyses to determine the weight of the various factors involved and how they interact with one another. However, the number of households for which we have information on all the factors that appear to be relevant—maternity of brothers, sibling-group size, stratum membership, landholdings, expectations of a merger, opportunities to clear new land, size of and attitudes toward expansion in the village concerned—is simply too small to make this feasible. What we have then is a collection of factors the importance of which is unranked and which appear to make households more or less partition prone.

Partition is non-normative, yet it is as central to Nyinba social structure as is the corporate trongba. Without partition, villages today would include no more than the households of immigrant founders. Without partition, villages could not maintain their size in the face of inevitable extinctions. Partition is one option, today strongly disapproved, in a household system that is responsive to village politics, economic needs, and interpersonal relationships, which in turn are shaped by notions about kinship obligation and mutuality.

Migration and Economic Marginality

Nyinba discourage immigration and emigration both, and few people permanently enter or leave the community. Given the limited marital opportunities for women, the constraints upon partition for brothers unhappy in their marriages, and the poverty of many freedmen and some citizen-landholders,

one might expect to find more frequent emigration. Nyinba, however, reject emigration today for the same reasons that slaves chose not to escape
and freedmen stayed on after emancipation: that is, ethnicity and culture.
Nyinba fit comfortably into neither Tibetan nor Nepali Hindu worlds.
High-caste Hindus regard them as inferiors by caste and as "Bhotia"
beefeaters, an irremediable disability. Tibetans differ in dialect and dress
and tend to dismiss people like Nyinba as *rongba*—rustic, lower-valley
dwellers.

Nyinba also regard themselves as a unique ethnic group, with few points
of cultural and social linkage to the wider societies around them. They live
their lives within a Nyinba world and measure their achievements by
Nyinba standards. Status within the home community is the pressing concern. Thus while traveling, Nyinba live in the simplest conditions tolerable. Shepherds—not hired ones, but herd owners—eat the worst food on
the road, in order to bring more rice—the prestige grain—home to offer to
kin and friends at hospitality events. The emphasis upon endogamy within
the community and the great shame attached to having daughters marry
outside of it is another manifestation of this. The community is to large
extent a closed one, socially and culturally as much as, if not more than,
demographically.

Demographic closure, nevertheless, is incomplete, and some immigration and emigration continue to occur. Today immigration is by far the less
common phenomenon. Only five outsiders joined Nyinba villages over the
past two generations.[7] By contrast, twenty-six citizen-landholders and
eight freedmen emigrated—and are believed to have emigrated permanently—over the last twenty-five years. This may seem like a large number
of individuals, but it makes for a rate of emigration of about .1 percent per
year. There were another three citizen-landholders and three freedmen who
were gone during 1982–83 but expected to return.[8] It is not uncommon for

[7] These immigrants included two women and three men. One woman, now deceased, came
from Limi; the other came from Tamkhyim, one of the villages of Trugchulung. One of the
men, now deceased, came from Chadog, another Trugchulung village, and two men came
from Tsang. In addition, wealthy households include servants of non-Nyinba origin. There is
a man from Chadog and two Tibetan nomadic pastoralist women in Todpa and one Tsang
woman in Trangshod. These long-term servants have made Nyinba villages their home, but
are not considered members of the community. There also are a number of high-caste Nepalis
who take up servant posts for years at a time, but maintain homes elsewhere.

[8] Of course it is impossible to determine the permanency of any case of migration until there
is no chance of the migrant returning, that is, when he or she has died. In 1973–75, I collected a similar list of emigrants expected not to return, yet two of them have done so—much
to everyone's apparent surprise. The same thing may happen with people on my present list.
This list probably did not miss many individuals. During the course of my 1983 census, I

Table 10.9 Migration by Village, Gender, and Stratum

Village	Male		Female		Total
	Citizen-Landholder	Freedman	Citizen-Landholder	Freedman	
Barkhang	3	3	2	1	9
Nyimatang	5	0	5	0	10
Todpa	2	0	3	1	6
Trangshod	5	1	1	2	9
All villages	15	4	11	4	34

young men eager to see the world, and young couples who have gotten themselves embroiled in messy cases of divorce, to leave for a year or two. Permanent migration, however, is more likely to occur among members of marginal households, and it may bring to extinction those suffering from problems of viability.

If we consider emigration from the point of view of village, gender, and social stratum, we find that Nyimatang lost ten citizen-landholders to migration, and that this was more than any other village lost (table 10.9). Seven of the ten were from poor hamlet households, the eighth was the daughter of a man in an adjunct household, and the ninth was from a poor temple household. The tenth emigrant was a woman from a wealthy home who had special reasons for leaving: she was deaf and mute and unable to find a husband locally, so she married a man in the neighboring community of Tsang. Most of the freedmen emigrants came from Barkhang and Trangshod—the villages with the largest numbers of freedmen—and all but one came from small households. Four of Todpa's six emigrants came from two households mentioned in chapter 8. These households were suffering problems of viability so severe that only they were willing to serve as trongbat to one another.

The commonest explanations given for emigration by the household members left behind are marriage outside the community, the search for a hidden valley paradise—Shangrila—and the desire for a better living (table 10.10). I should pause to note that these only are partial accounts.

---

cross-checked household membership against my census data from 1974 and against the census carried out in conjunction with land reform. I also interviewed elders on this topic and asked about migration in the questionnaire I administered to 126 households. If I missed anyone, it may have been the poorer freedmen, whose household memberships are less stable. Because migrants tend to be forgotten and dropped from genealogies, I have considered migration over only a twenty-five year period.

Table 10.10   Reasons for Migration

Reason Given	Male		Female		Total
	Citizen	Freedman	Citizen	Freedman	
Medical treatment[a]	0	0	1	0	1
Marriage elsewhere	0	1	6	3	10
Search for Shangrila	4	0	3	1	8
Search for a better living	4	2	1	0	7
Pending criminal prosecution	1	1	0	0	2
Religious training	1	0	0	0	1
Reason unclear	5	0	0	0	5
Total	15	4	11	4	34

[a] There are an additional two men who died while being treated for tuberculosis in urban hospitals. Both were older, with families, and presumably would have returned when cured.

They describe simple proximate causes and not the complex reasons and chains of circumstance prompting a given individual's decision to leave the community. Ultimately our concerns lie with the circumstances underlying the proximate events: why a particular woman decided to marry an outsider, when others did not; why a certain couple decided to listen to predictions about the opening of a Shangrila and accepted the risk and hardship of trying to find it, while their neighbors remained in the village; and why certain men left their homes and kin to seek a better living elsewhere, while most made the best of their circumstances at home.

Economic disadvantage seems to figure in many men's decisions to emigrate. This may be why not a single male freedman trongba member chose to abandon his good fortune and new-found estate. This should be seen as more than a matter of income, for small householders are politically disadvantaged as well and have to face numerous indignities in daily life. Although more of the citizen-landholder men who emigrated were poor, some were from quite-wealthy households and left for other reasons, to be detailed below.

Marital disadvantage lies behind many women's decisions to emigrate, and women who emigrate generally do so in the course of their marriages to outsiders. It is polyandry that is responsible for the generally unfavorable marriage market for women, and the result is numbers of what Nyinba describe as leftover women, those in their twenties and thirties who have not yet married, or who were married, then divorced, and have had difficulty remarrying. There were a total of twenty-two such women in 1983.

Nyinba women have trouble marrying for the same sorts of reasons found in many other societies. Among these are physical unattractiveness, physical handicaps, ill health, or a reputation for sexual laxity or laziness or a bad temper. A woman also may be handicapped by her clan membership or by the economic standing of her parents' household. This is why being left over reflects so badly upon the woman and her family.[9] Some women choose to stay home and wait, and all who have done so have married eventually—although to poor households or widowers or men considered less desirable for some other reason. Other women do not wait; they find husbands from other communities and leave. For Nyinba women, emigration through marriage probably is the best way out. This is because they lack marketable skills, and those women who have left on their own have tended to lapse into prostitution. This is why nine out of the fifteen women who left the community during this period reportedly did so in the course of marriage to outsiders. By contrast, only one out of the nineteen cases of male emigration was attributed to marriage with an outsider.[10]

The second most common reason given for emigration was the search for Shangrila. In 1967, approximately twenty-five Nyinba sold their lands and possessions in order to leave Humla to seek a "hidden place" (*sbas-yul*) in eastern Nepal, what we know through our popular literature as a Shangrila. They acted under the guidance of a charismatic lama, a refugee from Tibet. This minimillenarian movement seems to have arisen largely in response to the Chinese takeover in Tibet, which led to major political upheavals and radical social changes. The situation deteriorated during the Cultural Revolution and threatened trading relationships between Tibetan groups and virtually all the communities along Nepal's northern borderlands. In Humla, these problems came at a time when trading profits were declining in the middle hills. It is foretold that in times of great adversity such Shangrilas will open their doors to people with the foresight to find them, and for Nyinba, the 1960s brought greater economic adversity than they had known for generations.

Similar searches for Shangrilas sprang up all over Tibetan-speaking Humla at this time. Small groups of people set out under the leadership of various lamas to high glaciers which had been identified as possible sites in Tibetan texts. However, the time apparently had not yet come; in any event, all Humla attempts failed, and most Nyinba returned to their vil-

[9] This excludes nuns, and it is no accident that households which have a handicapped or unattractive daughter and who are concerned about their prestige will educate her to be a nun, rather than risk problems in arranging her marriage.

[10] This is a freedman who joined a low-status household of another Tibetan-speaking community in Humla as an uxorilocal spouse, or magpa.

lages a year or two later. Fortunately, they were able to buy back their lands and possessions and they soon returned to their normal lives. Several people died along the way, and several others settled permanently in urban areas such as Kathmandu. One of the searches by another Humla group from Trugchulung uncovered a habitable site nearby to the west, and this became a focus for new settlement in the 1980s.

The events surrounding the search for Shangrila show what a negative impact emigration can have upon poorer households and those suffering problems of viability. Nine of the people who were involved in the emigration came from these sorts of households. In two cases, the departure of young, hardworking adults pushed the household over the edge into extinction. In a third case, the household was extremely wealthy in land, and fellow villagers helped the younger people along until they grew up and were able to restore their household to a position of strength again. The remaining households are doing more or less well, depending upon the number of workers they now have and the extent of their landholdings and other resources.

The 1980s find Humla people in difficult economic circumstances once more. Profits in the southern segment of the salt trade continue to worsen, while unpredictable government policies make the Tibetan segment of the salt trade extremely volatile. Adding to their problems have been the recent series of bad harvests. These events have prompted new group migrations, this time for purely secular reasons. Now the focus of attention is the unoccupied land found by Trugchulung villagers at the foot of Mount Saipal during their earlier search for a Shangrila. These villages' economic situation was far more precarious than that of most Nyinba to begin with, and in the mid to late 1970s a number of Trugchulung families moved to this area to begin new lives as nomadic salt traders. A few Nyinba followed; some found it less promising than they had hoped and returned home. Three of the seven Nyinba listed in table 10.10 as having migrated in search for a better living, are still at this site, as is a married couple from a well-to-do trongba household who went in 1982 and still may return home. The four other Nyinba who are said to have emigrated to secure a better living now reside in India and are employed in menial jobs.

As might be expected, most people emigrated in young adulthood—in their twenties or early thirties (table 10.11). Women tended to leave earlier than men, with the exception of one young freedman boy who emigrated with his father. This is because most women leave to marry, and women's preferred ages for marrying are the late teens and early twenties. Ordinarily Nyinba do not emigrate with young children. Young couples leave before children are born, and men dissatisfied with polyandrous marriages

Table 10.11 Age at the Time of Migration

	Male		Female		
Migrant's Age	Citizen	Freedman	Citizen	Freedman	Total
Less than 19	0	1	3	0	4
20–29	5	1	6	2	14
30–39	3	0	1	0	4
40–49	1	1	0	0	2
50 and above	1	0	0	0	1
Age unknown	5	1	1	2	9
Total	15	4	11	4	34

Table 10.12 Dates of Migration

	Male		Female		
5-Year Period	Citizen	Freedman	Citizen	Freedman	Total
1960–64	3	1	0	0	4
1965–69	6	2	4	2	14
1970–74	1	0	4	0	5
1975–79	3	0	1	0	4
1980–83	1	0	2	0	3
Date unknown	1	1	0	2	4

can leave any joint children they may have behind with their brothers and common wife.

Over time, the rate of emigration seems neither to have increased nor decreased (table 10.12). There seems to have been just a steady and very small trickle of people out of the Nyinba community during the past twenty-five years. Except in the period of the late 1960s, an average of only one person left each year, and overall, the loss of population averaged approximately .1 percent per year. The present period may also witness higher rates of emigration, but at the time I left Humla it was too soon to tell—most of the moves still were regarded as exploratory. If the migrants return, they later will see their experience as a youthful adventure. If they do not return, the Nyinba community may lose individuals from economically marginal households and individuals whose departure will bring formerly stable households to conditions of inviability.

It is likely that these patterns of migration will change in future. Ever since the establishment of schools in Humla in the 1970s, Nyinba parents have been educating their children, mostly boys and a few girls. Some chil-

dren have won scholarships for further study in Kathmandu, and a few very
wealthy households are paying for private schooling there. If these children
stay on in urban centers, and I think some will, the community will lose the
people who could contribute most to its future.

Traditionally, emigration served as an outlet for members of economically marginal households, for individuals who were not content to remain
in the closed Nyinba world, and for women who could not find marital partners in a strictly polyandrous system (despite the high sex ratio also found
in that system). It permitted the community to continue with a membership
of economically effective trongba who could maintain their community obligations, plus an economically marginal population of former slaves, later
freedmen, who supported themselves by working for the wealthiest households. These facts contribute to the Nyinba citizen-landholders' image of
themselves as a community largely of equals. Although there are major
status gulfs between freedmen and citizen-landholders, and lesser divisions
between members of new clans and old, we do not find economic disparities as great as those which divide rich and poor in the neighboring
Nepali-speaking high-caste villages.

In closing the chapter, I should return to an issue raised at its outset: the
rationale and consequences of pressures against emigration. Obstacles to
immigration in a group facing resource constraints have an obvious com-
monsense logic. By this logic, however, obstacles to emigration would
seem to be self-defeating. Were more Nyinba to emigrate, it would drain
off surplus population, alleviate pressure on resources, and provide an outlet for disgruntled brothers in polyandrous marriages. Despite this, Nyinba
take exception to emigration, exert pressures against it, and speak ill of
emigrants. Moreover, individuals largely choose to stay on even when their
economic opportunities are limited. The reason is that decisions of this
kind rest not only on objectively measurable material advantage. For
Nyinba, rich and poor alike, emigration is intrinsically problematic, for it
means a life spent apart from kin and community. Individuals measure the
success of their lives in manifold ways, as framed by an encompassing
sociocultural system. For one example, a major goal for most individuals is
trongba betterment. This demands family concordance and household
unity as well as the appreciable expansion of landholdings. It is a goal that
is future as well as present oriented, and it requires maintaining an undivided household and an intact estate from one generation to the next.

11
Conclusion

One reason given for this most odious custom is the sterility of the soil, and the small amount of land that can be cultivated owing to the lack of water. The crops may suffice if the brothers all live together, but if they form separate families they would be reduced to beggary. Filippo de Filippi, ed., *An Account of Tibet: The Travels of Ippolito Desideri of Pistoia, S. J., 1712–1727.* (1937:194)

Among various peoples polyandry has been traced to economic motives. It has been said that in Tibet it obtains "as a necessary institution. Every spot of ground within the hills which can be cultivated has been under the plough for ages. . . ." And not only does polyandry serve the end of checking the increase of population in regions from which emigration is difficult, but it also keeps the family property together. (Westermarck 1926:259)

These statements reflect prevailing conceptions of polyandry in the present as much as in the past. Polyandry remains a textbook curiosity explained primarily in economic terms; it continues to be seen as an exotic and rare adaptation to uncommonly difficult environmental circumstances. Accompanying these presumptions is a continuing concern with polyandry's origins and the forces for its persistence, that is, with external issues, rather than movement toward analyses of sociocultural systems and how they may shape and be shaped by polyandrous institutions. This is why Westermarck's early discussion still is cited. He argued that polyandry had to have a cause—which he was modern enough to conceive in synchronic terms—and he found this to lie in demographic and economic factors. Among these are sex ratio imbalances—which are better seen as the consequence of polyandrous regimes—and "economic motives," including resource scarcity, high dowry expenses, and prolonged male absences in pursuit of livelihood. Westermarck argued too that only extreme necessity could override "the natural desire in most men to be in exclusive possession of their wives" (1925:206).[1] Modern arguments continue to be phrased along similar lines. They focus upon polyandry's special adaptive advantages under conditions of scarcity and explain its persistence in terms of individual assessments of personal benefits achieved at the cost of sexual and reproductive sacrifice.

The problem is this: treating marriage and kinship systems as artifacts of economic or demographic exigencies and individual marital relationships as governed by material calculations impoverishes our understandings of these as social and cultural phenomena. Nonetheless, we find assumptions such as these in a range of anthropological approaches. Cultural materialism perhaps offers the most extreme example. In their most recent recension, Harris and Ross (1987) divide sociocultural systems into three sectors: "infrastructure," or modes of production and reproduction; "structure," or domestic and political economy; and "superstructure," or aesthetic, symbolic, and religious systems. Predictably, infrastructure is regarded as "more powerfully determinative" than the other two. Note, however, that kinship has no place in this scheme at all, unless it is presumed to fit somewhere between modes of reproduction and the domestic economy.

Reduction of kinship practices to presumptively prior domains of social life is a long-established position in British social anthropology, where it developed in the course of reactions against a dominant kinship paradigm. Leach, for one, argued that treating economic relations as prior could serve as a corrective against overemphases on societal equilibrium and presumptions of society as a moral order. In this view, kinship came to be squeezed out of the picture entirely, for Leach defined it negatively, that is, as neither "intrinsic" nor "a thing in itself," but rather "at every point in time, adaptive to the changing economic situation." Descent and affinity were simi-

---

[1] Westermarck, however, also possessed a broad grasp of the cross-cultural literature and recognized that none of these factors, alone or in combination, predicted marital form. As he concluded his discussion of polyandry: "I certainly do not maintain that my discussion of the causes from which polyandry has sprung gives a full solution to the problem. There are many peoples among whom the males outnumber the females or to whom polyandry would be useful on account of poverty or as a method of keeping property together or for other reasons, and who all the same never practise it. A paucity of marriageable women, for example, may lead to celibacy, prostitution, or homosexual practices, as well as to polyandry" (1925:206). I cite Westermarck so frequently here because he anticipated virtually every modern explanation of polyandry more than half a century ago.

larly defined as "expressions of property relations which endure through time" (Leach 1961 : 7–8, 11). Leach applied similar arguments to Sri Lankan polyandry, which he saw as a solution to the paradox of bilateral inheritance in a society where brothers are expected to co-reside. Polyandry, that is, was a way of reducing disparities between brothers and the sons of brothers, who otherwise would have separate property interests through their mothers and wives ([1961] 1968 : 109–12).

This approach contains its own paradox, for it discounts what is most obvious in the ethnographic data (Sahlins 1976 : 7–8; Fortes 1969 : 221–28). Whereas the people themselves cite kinship as a major factor in the patterning of social relationships, Leach stresses the observable political and economic effects of these relationships and links effects with cause. This is in itself a classic functionalist stance (Bloch 1973 : 76). Similar points can be made about Worsley's critique of Fortes's Tallensi materials, where he argues that "the particular forms which kinship relations will take . . . are largely determined by economic and historical forces" (1956 : 62–63). Or, as Beattie has generalized: "Kinship is the idiom in which certain kinds of political, jural, economic, etc., relations are talked and thought about in certain societies. It is not a *further* category of relationships" (1964 : 102; emphasis in original). In these views, kinship has no independent modality, kinship relations are seen as shaped by other factors, and kinship is no more than a way of talking about more fundamentally real aspects of social life and a highly effective way of rationalizing social cooperation. Exactly why people should select kinship as a primary idiom and see it as influencing behavior or why it should be so effective in motivating cooperation is left unexplained.

Similar presumptions have guided accounts of kin-group structure and its cross-cultural variations. Here I refer to arguments which find the explanation of kin-group size and composition to lie in the demands of the society's productive system, which is explained, in turn, by available resources (e.g., Pasternak 1976 : 87–112). This involves movement through an explanatory process that presumes social arrangements to be malleable and adapted, via a mediating economic system, to environmental givens. Descent groups, for example, are explained by residence rules (which bring particular classes of kin into association); residence rules are explained by subsistence patterns; and subsistence patterns are explained by resource type and availability. Accounts of domestic group size and composition follow a similar logic. Again the productive system is cited—with requirements for labor and its scheduling seen as particularly critical—and this system is explained by techno-environmental forces and state demands

for taxes or corvée labor.[2] All are variables which also have figured in explanations of polyandry.

Here I have given priority to people's own assessments of their circumstances—whether phrased in terms of what we conventionally assign to
kinship, political, or economic categories—and to the interplay between
evaluative processes and social behavior. I began with kinship categories
because Nyinba, like people of so many other small-scale societies, speak
of kin ties as pre-existent and as conditioning conduct, and because a majority of transactions occur between kin—or between those for whom the
absence of a kin tie is the significant fact. I then turned from internal fields
of structure to exogenous factors which have impinged on Nyinba social
life. This led in the end to interactions—between notions of kinship, cultural identity, and ethnic boundaries; between traditional systems of village
management and external political systems; between a polyandrous household system, the constraints of mountain agriculture, and regional economic and labor systems; and ultimately, to interactions between kinship,
domestic economy, and population dynamics.

For some, these concerns are irrevocably divided. Sahlins, for one, suggests that models of culture as the codification of pragmatic action and as
ordering practical experience are irreconcilable, and that anthropology can
do no more than oscillate between the "objective" logic of pragmatic action and the meaningful order, with dialogue and dialectic impossible between them (Sahlins 1976:55–56).[3] The problem is that to consider either
in isolation poses its own limitations and generates contradictions of its
own. Just as with materialistic explanations, the purely cultural account
risks overemphasis on systemic integration and stability.[4] While culture
may be seen as dominant over material conditions, it may come to be
treated as untransformed in the encounter. In short, the risk is of cultural
reductionism, of creating a symbolic variant of functionalism with neglect
of ambiguities, inconsistencies, and the tension between what Moore describes as indeterminacy and the processes of regularization and adjustment in social life (Moore 1978:39, 46).

Even so seemingly simple a question as why Nyinba men sometimes dis-

[2] General criticisms of these arguments have been presented in recent review articles (Kelly
1968; Yanagisako 1979:169–75). Analyses of residence, household formation, and household composition in the Nyinba case also illustrate the flaws in these presumptions.

[3] Elsewhere Sahlins speaks of a dialectic with practice and interactions of system and event
(1981:33).

[4] Fox (1985) has attempted to join cultural and materialist approaches. His resolution, however, privileges social over individual action and event over structure, thus reinforcing other
antinomies dividing anthropologists.

solve their polyandrous marriages is not easily resolved with any sectarian theoretical approach. Earlier accounts of polyandry placed the answer in assessments of opportunities and the balance of material advantages. This answer, however, fails to explain why Tibetan polyandry is fraternal. Were material concerns dominant, the strongest and brightest Nyinba men would group together in polyandrous unions and would leave lazy, cantankerous, and handicapped brothers to fend for themselves. The fact is that men stay together with brothers who are sickly and troublesome and say they do so because of the obligations associated with fraternal kinship. The fact too is that there is no better way to account for their actions. At the same time, kinship obligations are moderated by other forces, which similarly are subject to cultural evaluation. Thus we find that marriages seem more likely to be dissolved when additional land is available, but that decisions about what constitutes adequate land and an adequate standard of living seem to be culturally and socially conditioned. This is suggested in the effects of social status on partitioning—the fact that immigrants and freedmen have dissolved their polyandrous marriages more frequently and live on their own with lesser means.

Kinship and Closure

For Nyinba, community closure is rationalized in terms of kinship and the distinctive qualities of ru heredity and is expressed in diverse ways: through dress and other material markers of ethnic identity and through language. Nyinba men traditionally wore a topknot seen nowhere outside of Humla and significantly different from the styles worn by other Humla Tibetan men. Women's clothing is the most elaborate and finely detailed of any to be found in the region and differs in style from that found elsewhere in Nepal or Tibet. House styles and the layout of Nyinba villages are unique in ways obvious to passers-by. Finally, the Nyinba dialect—nearly unintelligible to other Humla Tibetans—provides a context for formulating ideas and idioms peculiar to Nyinba culture and for expressing ethnic uniqueness. All these differences involve variations in detail which might be small, but they are not small matters. They serve to identify Nyinba wherever they go and display Nyinba villages as distinctive.

Closure also is reinforced in the policies of endogamy and in the status preoccupations associated with it. The emphasis on marital exclusivity is more extreme among Nyinba than other Humla Tibetans, who themselves may be atypical among Tibetan peoples in this regard. Goody has found a common logic in endogamy among European and Asian societies—as associated with strategies for maintaining status and, correlatively, associated with dowry, the practice of gifting substantial property to women upon their marriages: "In-marriage . . . is a policy of isolation. One reason among others for such a policy is to preserve property where this is transmitted through both males and females, to encourage marriages with families of 'one's own kind' and thus to maintain property and prestige" (1976:21). Nyinba society provides a partial exception to this. Marriage within the community and attempts at status enhancement through marriage are major preoccupations for reasons of prestige, but not property, and dowries are kept minimal.[5] Moreover, people pay as much attention to descent credentials as household wealth in choosing spouses, and most place greater emphasis upon status than upon finding affines who might be helpful in mundane pursuits. Goody is quite right, however, about the outcome: a policy of isolation and exclusion against the outside world.

Sociocultural dynamics and facts of local history have contributed to the making of a community whose membership is largely closed and whose external political relationships are narrowly circumscribed. The sanctions on migration have meant little assimilation of outsiders and the necessity to accommodate people born as Nyinba in approved social identities within the community. Because there are limited marital opportunities for women and because single women are an embarrassment to their parents, women less likely to marry are less likely to be reared to adulthood. Because emigration is so strongly sanctioned, brothers are likely to remain at home, which means cooperating in the household's marriage, the rights and obligations of both shared and individuated parentage, and contributing to a diversified household economy. Were polyandry less attractive, more brothers might partition or emigrate. Were partition and emigration more acceptable, brothers might try less hard to keep their marriages, families, and households together.

Culturally, closure might have a certain reality, but it is achieved only by an illusion. That is, the kinship calculus is seen as closed, but it also encompasses regular means of reforming and transforming the clan identities of new immigrants. It does this so slowly and imperceptibly that progress must be measured in generations. And despite present-day constraints on migration, some people continue to enter the community, and more manage to leave.

Closure and isolationism, nevertheless, have been seen as causes of polyandry. As Westermarck, citing F. Drew and E. F. Knight, states: " . . . geographic isolation hindered emigration. . . . which is not a feasible relief to over-population for a people like the Ladakhis, who, accustomed to

---

[5] Sizable dowries would be inconceivable, because they would defeat one of the overriding goals of the household system: the conservation of property within a unified trongba.

high elevations, succumb to bilious fever when they reach the plains"
(Westermarck 1925:188). Here geographical determinism joins other explanations for polyandry. The idea of Ladakhis prevented from emigrating
to the Indian plains by high mountains and fear of bilious fever seems im-
probable, yet we can find it reproduced in present-day discussions. Thus
Crook and Crook (n.d.:25) argue that the people of the Zanskar valley,
which lies south of Ladakh, are too isolated to emigrate. Obviously Zanskar
was not too isolated to be settled in the first place, nor has its isolation kept
Zanskaris from wide-ranging travels or ordinary Europeans from reaching
there in the course of trekking holidays.[6] If anything, polyandry and the
low rates of population growth associated with it facilitate constraints on
emigration. High caste Nepali groups in Humla may voice similar objections to emigration, although they are less able to inhibit it (cf. Campbell
on Jumla 1978:81). These of course are groups which are mostly monogamous, rarely polygynous and never polyandrous.

Regulation and Village Size

Regulation of village size is a matter of collective assessments based on an
array of considerations, and the goal is to maintain an effective village internally balanced in section memberships. This is managed case by case,
through the climate of opinion toward partitions, decisions to extend assistance to households in need, enforcing rights of trongbat heirs versus
allowing occupations, and also through realignments in trongbat and reorganizations of village sections when member households partition or
become extinct. Excessive losses of households threaten traditional ceremonial life and leave villages less able to defend themselves against en-
croachments on their pasture and farming land. Unchecked partition poses
risks of impoverishment and compromises the ability of households to
meet traditional village obligations. Nyimatang already has several households with such small memberships and shares of property that they had to
be forgiven many of their obligations. These concerns may seem a small
matter too, but Nyinba take great pride in the high standard of living of
their community as a whole and in their ability to sustain a rich ceremonial
life, one which most other Humla Tibetans can no longer afford.

Attempts at regulation may be only partial, and partition may occur
more frequently than villagers say they wish—and occur frequently enough
to outweigh the effects of occasional household extinctions and support
a low rate of growth. The marked contrasts between Nyinba and other
Humla communities mark its salience, however, and Nyinba see the expe-

[6]For a popular account of life in Zanskar, see Peissel (1979:47, 54).

riences of their Humla neighbors as proof of the dangers of unchecked partition. Within direct view are the high-caste villages of They and Teyshel, located lower down on the hillside, and the Tibetan-speaking community of Tsang, further east in the same valley system. No more and no less than Nyinba, these villages are subject to rigid resource constraints and a fixed agricultural base. Despite this, all have grown greatly over the past century. Members of these villages now live on fractionated shares of land; most are exceedingly poor, and they have no choice but to accept employment as casual laborers with their Nyinba neighbors or emigrate elsewhere.

Rapid population growth and a declining standard of living are the prevailing situation in Nepal. Most middle-hills and highland villages face increased pressure on already-scarce agricultural land, loss of forests, soil erosion, and a declining standard of living. These changes have been so rapid and dramatic as to be apparent within the brief span of anthropological investigations and have become the dominant concern of a number of studies. In his account of the Gurung, a Tibeto-Burman-speaking people of the central and western hills, Macfarlane charts the common dynamic of population growth, expansion of resource base, intensification of productive techniques, and environmental degradation:

> For many centuries the Gurungs were wandering bands of shepherds who also practised hunting and a certain amount of slash and burn agriculture. By the middle of the nineteenth century they were also traders over the mountain passes to the north and beginning to be famed as army recruits. During the following century, population pressure forced them to establish villages lower down the slopes, where wet rice could be grown, but herds and flocks could no longer be grazed. They now have permanent fields which they plough instead of hoeing. (Macfarlane 1976:293)

> The . . . most important change now taking place throughout Gurung villages . . . is the transition from an economy where land is plentiful and labour is the limiting factor in production to the reverse situation. (Macfarlane 1976:32)

Gurung population growth—the doubling time now is under forty years—has led the move into marginal, less-productive agricultural lands. Expansion of agriculture has meant a diminution of forest for fodder and hunting and of pasture for grazing herd animals. The effects of this transition upon the local diet are predictable. What sustains many Gurung is income from external employment as mercenaries in foreign armies.

A similar trajectory has been sketched by Fricke for a village of Tamang, another Tibeto-Burman-speaking group, in eastern Nepal:

> Since their arrival, the Tamang have not only expanded into all parts of the territory containing arable land, but have also modified their agriculture toward greater diversity and intensity of production. It is likely that the original settlers in Timling practiced slash and burn agriculture in conjunction with heavier reliance on the pastoral economy than the present population. . . . More recently, however . . . land quality has begun to decline; the possibilities for exploiting new resource frontiers within Timling's bounded environment have been exhausted. Additionally, political events beyond the control of the village have closed the potential for intensifying trade and other relationships to the north. Thus, the latest resource frontier for each household is the cash economy in which labor can be sold. (Fricke 1986: 193–95)

Thus far the Nyinba have been able to keep village growth at a moderate level and to support an enviable standard of living in one of the poorest regions of the country. Most Nyinba live in large, comfortable houses well-equipped by Nepalese standards; most have fine jewelry and other valuables. People of middling and higher incomes enjoy varied diets—varied that is, for a high-altitude remote area—with wheat, barley, millet, and imported rice alternating with the staple buckwheat. The reasons for this difference are to be found in Nyinba culture and social structure, which meet in a distinctive way the environmental constraints faced by all middle-hills and highland Nepalese groups. The critical factors appear to be polyandry, minimization of numbers of married women, household unity, and policies of village regulation, added to which are restrictions upon immigration and the formation of new households. A long-standing assumption in the literature has been that polyandry is implicated in low population growth. This is one of the classic issues in the study of Tibetan society, and it has been central to other studies of Nepalese Tibetans.

Functionalist and Homeostatic Models: The Tibetan Case

Assumptions about population in Tibet are based on impressionistic evidence, and the most complete data we have derive from research completed on ethnic Tibetans living within the borders of Nepal.[7] One study that focused on population issues was carried out in Limi, a narrow, high-

---

[7] Assumptions that Tibetan societies had stable or even declining populations were based upon anecdotal evidence (Goldstein 1981:723). In the absence of census data, it is impossible to come to any conclusions about population dynamics in traditional Tibet, and matters are complicated further by regional variations and variations between different occupational and social strata of the population.

altitude valley located four days' walk northwest of Nyinba. Limi is geo-
graphically and socioculturally closer to Tibet than Nyinba is, it may be
longer settled—it probably has existed for over seven hundred years—and
it is smaller: in the mid 1970s the population totaled under eight hundred
people. Goldstein, Limi's ethnographer, describes patterns of recent change
that differ in significant ways from the analysis of polyandry presented here.

> Over the last twenty-five years, Limi has experienced major eco-
> nomic changes and undergone a dramatic expansion in population.
> Unlike so many other groups in Humla and Nepal, Limi people
> benefitted from the Chinese takeover of Tibet. First, nomadic
> herdsmen who fled Tibet via Limi could not take their animals any
> farther south and had to sell them to Limi villagers for a fraction
> of their value. Second, Limi people were able to retain the right of
> pasturing their animals in Tibet in winter, although they had to
> move to a different site. Third, repression of religion in Tibet per-
> mitted Limi traders to acquire priceless Tibetan artifacts at low
> cost; some of these they placed in local temples, others they sold
> at great profit in India. In the past, many Limi villagers were poor;
> households were in debt for food loans from Nyinba agricul-
> turalists, and Limi women traditionally sought winter labor in
> Nyinba villages. Now they had become much wealthier and net
> creditors to Nyinba and other Humla Tibetans.
>
> These events changed Limi from a community whose house-
> holds maintained multiple economic involvements—agriculture
> predominantly and supplementary pastoralism, small-scale trade
> and traditional crafts—to one that had become increasingly re-
> liant on high profit, high risk trade. In the past, men engaged in
> diversified subsistence strategies, which was made possible by
> their large polyandrous households. Now they could and increas-
> ingly choose to work on their own. In Tibet, we find traders tend-
> ing to be monogamous (Aziz 1978:158), and in Limi, the move
> toward trade was associated with increased partition and more
> monogamous marriages. With more women married, the rate of
> population growth began to soar.[8] Thus in Limi the shift from an
> agriculture-based to a trade-based economy and from a polyan-
> drous to a monogamous marital system was accomplished within
> the space of a generation and was accompanied by changes in
> population dynamics. (Goldstein 1974, 1978b)

[8] In Limi, there was a far greater proportion of single women, who supported themselves by
working for their wealthier Limi neighbors during the agricultural season (see chapter 9, note
16) and by engaging in labor migration in winter.

Goldstein evaluates these changes through an adaptationist perspective and through an explicitly materialistic understanding of polyandry. He thus describes polyandry as a practice that developed in the context of resource limitations and as "part of a negative feedback process which operates to adjust . . . population size to resources" (1976:231) As he explains:

> When resources or economic opportunities . . . were scarce, fraternal polyandry was more strictly adhered to, but when such opportunities arose defections from polyandrous unions were common. This, in turn, produced an increase in overall fertility since unmarried females previously excluded from the reproductive pool now married. . . . This increased fertility and generated population pressure . . . leading to the reassertion of the conservative view of the opportunity costs of fission and stricter adherence to the fraternal polyandry alternative. (1978b:330)[9]

In the case of Limi, this is more a hypothesis than an argument, for detailed historical and ecological data are lacking. However, the basic assumptions and the view that polyandry is the regulative mechanism in a homeostatic system, mediating between resource availability and population processes, follows a well-established position in systems ecology. The guiding assumptions are these: that polyandry persists because it is adaptive, that such behaviors are directly responsive to changes in material circumstances, and that these processes are independent of actors' conscious recognition of the mechanisms involved or their consequences.[10] Similar arguments can be found in other studies of alpine cultural and social systems, no doubt in recognition of the balance that must be achieved between population and resources in these limited environments. Netting's (1981) study of a Swiss alpine community, where detailed historical and ecological data are available, provides another, recent example.[11]

[9]Crook and Crook (n.d.) develop a fuller argument along similar lines. In their model the prevalence of polyandry varies with the demand for labor, which in turn varies with the community's stage of agricultural development and the degree of its incorporation into a state system (which is presumed to add to the burden of taxes of various kinds).

[10]Durham (forthcoming, chap. 2) similarly argues that the beliefs governing marriage in Limi and Nyinba have "adaptive significance" and "seem to guide behavior in directions that are reproductively advantageous."

[11]The parallels extend to the treatment of marriage as a primary regulative mechanism and the description of the system in terms of homeostasis and an equilibrium model (Netting 1981:90). This, however, is an argument which has been criticized and which Netting subsequently refined (see Laslett in Netting 1981:ix; Netting 1984:226, 231).

Frameworks of Explanation: Structural Analysis

Nyinba society might serve equally well as an example of equilibrium achieved through social institutional measures. One need only make certain "simplifying assumptions" and "reduce the variables being considered" (Netting 1981:42), and the Nyinba case might make a smooth fit to models stressing systemic adjustments and reciprocal causality through negative feedback. Chapters 9 and 10 would have to be rewritten; the argument would have to be changed to show how population is responsive to resources and to emphasize the role played by changing resource availability—for example, through land reclamation, altered trading opportunities, village extinctions, and the like—or by changing economic productivity. Here as well marriage could be treated as the critical mechanism. Available marital opportunities for women would have to be shown as decreasing as economic conditions worsen and as increasing, through conjoint marriage and monogamy, as new opportunities open up.

Such an analysis would not only oversimplify, it would also direct attention away from some of the most critical facts of Nyinba historical experience. The reality of Nyinba social life over the more and less recent past is of social change as much as continuity and of population imbalance as much as stability. Some of the changes have defied full readjustment and have led to completely new arrangements. Slavery provides the most dramatic example. Population growth, however moderate, does not follow resource availability; it continues in apparent disregard of deteriorating economic conditions. We have seen how Nyinba have been pressured out of their lower-altitude, more-productive fields over the past two centuries. Their response has been to move up, to less-productive, higher-altitude land, which in turn has had the effect of reducing pasturelands and forests. Nyinba herding has suffered as a result, and people now have to travel farther for firewood. It is true that relatively more partition and the greatest growth have occurred in the new hamlets, which have access to vacant lands. This suggests that polyandry and partition are to some degree sensitive to resource availability. However family traditions seem equally implicated in hamlet growth, for six out of eleven hamlet partitions occurred among freedmen and immigrants. Hamlet dwellers also have to make do with much poorer land, and partition continues in the older villages, where the least land is available. At present, the salt trade is profitable enough to justify major investments of time and labor, but it has come to a standstill in the past and may do so again. Profits have declined radically over the past two generations and now must be achieved through increased efforts:

larger herds, more trading trips, and longer trading routes. The situation is one of more work for less profit in all economic spheres.

Coincident with these changes are continuities in social structure and forces for stability in social life. Thus we can find a village structure of seeming antiquity largely in place. This has been achieved through traditional practices of village management. For one example, Barkhang villagers added a third headman to the two appointed by the government, simply to represent the village's third section in external matters. Nyimatang's history offers an example of a village that reconstituted itself from the households remaining in two depopulated villages and those of the newer immigrants who had settled nearby. This reconstitution produced a village that conforms to the classic Nyinba template—and commemorates its diverse origins through the names of its sections and the identities of its household gods.

Thus we find stability and regulation as well as discontinuity and disorder. Equilibrium and functionalist models, whether socially or ecologically oriented, admit no such dualities. Both emphasize closure from the outside world and thus internal integration and independence from exogenous sources of change. Traditional ethnography treated societies as if they were closed—that is, isolated and self-contained—and neglected linkages to larger regional systems (cf. Keesing 1981:111). This may have been inevitable with the disciplinary emphasis upon microanalysis of single societies and reliance upon village studies. The problem is that analytical closure—a means of delimiting the subject of study—was mistaken for social reality. And the tendency of the subjects of study to emphasize their separateness further reinforced this view. If Nyinba emphasize their separateness, it is for a variety of reasons, among them substantiation of ethnic identity, and as part of a policy of keeping outsiders out and insiders in and also of keeping limited resources within the community—a culturally and socially salient policy with demographic ramifications.

The stress on equilibrium and functionalist integration in anthropology has meant a neglect of facts that fit the model poorly, a sacrifice of complicating details, and an emphasis on stability at the expense of social change. Leach has argued that this is unavoidable, that "conceptual models of society are necessarily models of equilibrium systems," even though "real societies never can be in equilibrium" ([1954] 1965:4). That is because models, which are inherently fixed, are incapable of describing a reality in constant flux and rife with contradictions (Gellner 1973:93–97), so that the changes and contradictions necessarily acquire fixity in the course of their description. Methodological difficulties aside, there is little justification for neglecting factors that manifest openness, ambiguity, imbalance, and change and emphasizing in their place examples of closure, consistency, balance, and stability. What I have tried to do here is provide an account that encompasses both, in order to better explore the cultural and social contexts in which polyandry occurs.

Polyandry and Domestic Life: The Value of Kinship

Nyinba are a community of kin, or more accurately, two semipermeable circles of kin, and kinship ties provide the fundament of intracommunity social relations. Notions of substance heredity rationalize this, by confirming the intrinsic nature of kin ties. Bone links collectivities of people in a system glossed as clanship; clanship determines political prerogatives and ritual participation and influences marital choice; blood crosscuts ties of clanship and provides a way of conceptualizing the integration of immigrants into the social and kinship universe.

For Nyinba, kinship is seen as providing the most reliable basis for trust, and this notion has effects on the patterning of interpersonal relations in households and in marriages. Household heads have more amicable relationships with their sons than with unrelated, in-married sons-in-law. Headwomen similarly find it easier to share power with their daughters than with unrelated daughters-in-law. This is one of the arguments for cross-cousin marriage, which brings uncles and aunts together with their nephews or nieces. Siblings also are thought to have less trouble as cospouses. This is why Nyinba try to arrange sororal polygyny and why they say that polyandrous marriage among men with identical parentage is easiest to sustain.

There is no way of distinguishing whether these are notions that frame experience or are interpretations drawn from experience, because each may influence the other. Thus sisters may make better co-wives because ideas about kinship and mutual trust have an impact on their behavior, and the success of their relationship may reconfirm opinions about the advantages of sororal polygyny. Equally, predicting the success of sororally polygynous marriages may support sisters' relationships. In any event, Nyinba notions about kinship and conduct are largely confirmed in observations of their behavior. As they suggest, men with different mothers and those with different mothers and fathers are more likely to marry conjointly, although this is not true of men with different fathers, something Nyinba also suggest.

We might expect fraternal solidarity to reach its acme in polyandry, a system of marriage in which siblings share spouses and children as well as property and work obligations. Despite what might seem self-evident, the prevailing understanding of polyandry has been a materialist one. In this view economic variables are held to play the determining role and individuals are presumed to assess their situations in terms of economic categories and to place the highest priority on optimizing resources. As we have seen, resource availability is only one of many considerations that Nyinba take into account when they decide whether to stay in polyandry or partition. Their decisions involve a composite analysis and incorporate elements drawn from kinship and politico-jural as well as economic domains.

Among Nyinba, polyandry restricts the numbers of fully reproducing couples and in this way appears to limit population growth. This is particularly important in a land of limited resources, such as Nyinba and most Tibetan agriculturalists face. However this consequence cannot be treated as polyandry's cause.[12] There are numerous examples of societies in similarly unfavorable environments that lack a system incorporating population-regulative mechanisms. At the same time, other societies have developed quite different practices with similar effects, among them the late marriage–delayed inheritance system of Europe and systematic infanticide in Japan (Hajnal 1965; Smith 1977). Nepalis, who are subject to the same constraints as Nyinba, deal with their population problem mostly by emigration, which has led them from west to east across Nepal.

Ethnographic analysis and Nyinba culture are in fundamental agreement on this point: economy is no more compelling of marriage, household, or family organization than any other feature of the sociocultural system is. No one sphere of social life—economic, politico-jural, ritual, or kinship—has priority over any other; none is in itself decisive. Yet the notion that kinship practices derive from or are reducible to environmental and economic necessity recurs frequently in critiques of kinship studies. Nonetheless, for Nyinba kinship is and must be treated as a structurally autonomous domain of social life, "symbolized in ideals of non-sexual love, of brotherhood, of equality in sharing, of giving without expectation of obligatory return, and, above all, of involuntary, perpetual and inescapable bonds of complete mutuality" (Fortes 1972:293).

[12] Ellen attributes much of the weakness of arguments that find serendipitous, equilibrium-maintaining responses to environmental exigency to: "the logical fallacy of demonstrating that certain practices have effects and then assuming that this is their purpose, either in the conscious minds of sentient human beings or in terms of some evolutionary dynamic. It is, of course, the fallacy of functionalism. Showing how things work is explaining neither why they came about nor why they persist" (Ellen 1982:193).

Appendix A
Weights and Measures

Monetary

1973–75	$1.00 = Rs 10.5
1982	$1.00 = Rs 13.1
1983	$1.00 = Rs 14.2

Volume of Grain

2 *mana* = approximately 1 liter
2 *mana* = 1 *tre* (*bre*)
20 *tre* = 1 *khal*

Measures of Area

1 *hal*, or plow-day = approximately 1,208 square meters
1 autumn *hal* = approximately 1,050 meters
1 spring *hal* = approximately 1,365 meters
1 acre = 4,047 square meters (or 43,560 square feet)

Appendix B
Sources of Data on Landholdings

The tax roll on which I have based my estimates of village population was compiled in 1868. According to prominent elders, this was the third such registration of households in Humla for tax purposes. Dates of the first two are uncertain; the third is said to have been instituted in 1852, although no records of this remain. (Other data suggest that the second such assessment may have occurred in 1836 [M. Regmi 1972:31–34].)

The 1868 tax roll consists of a list of household heads, described according to the convention: "X, Y's son." Under each name are a list of different types of taxes, together with the assessments for each in the old currency notation and the total tax obligation. This is followed by a brief list of taxes owed by the entire village: export taxes on falcons, musk, woven cloth, and so on. In 1889, this tax roll was updated with a list of new households. The only Nyinba village which acquired new households during this twenty-one-year period was Trangshod, where three more were added. According to household genealogies, all were created by partition.

I first transcribed these records in Kathmandu, although I later found copies in the homes of village headmen and in the district capital tax office. Barkhang headmen had penned in the names of current taxpayers next to those of the original household heads, who were their trongba predecessors. In the other villages, I asked the headmen to make a similar list. Because there have been no new assessments since 1868, successors to a given trongba owe what was paid over one hundred years ago, plus an increment of approximately 50 percent. In events of partition, the branch and main households each take on a portion of the tax, which they then pool and present to the headman–tax collector. In events of extinction, the inheritor is obliged to meet both its own tax obligations and those of the household which it has inherited. No further acquisitions of or transactions

in land were recorded until 1976, possibly because of their questionable
legal status (see M. Regmi 1972:30; M. Regmi 1976:chap. 10).

The Land Reform Act of 1964 provides a second source of data. The
purpose of the act was to put a ceiling on landholdings, and in order to find
cases of land held in excess, the government surveyed land ownership
throughout the country. This survey involved a careful field-by-field ac-
counting and also a house-by-house census to identify coparceners. I found
these data to be extremely accurate in listing lands held and household
membership at the time of the survey and was able to use them during my
second term of field research as a cross-check for migration, mortality,
dates of marriage, and so on.

Appendix C
The Nyinba Population

The data discussed here derive from a census taken between December 1982 and March 1983 from each of the 184 Nyinba households and from retrospective fertility histories collected from one married woman in each of 126 of those households. Junior and senior household women were approached alternately, so that fertility and infant- and child-mortality data come from women representing a wide range of ages. Thirty-four percent of those women were over fifty years of age at the time of the interview, 37 percent were between the ages of thirty-five and forty-nine, and 29 percent were between the ages of twenty-one and thirty-four.

Age and Sex Structure of the Population

Data on age and sex composition of the Nyinba population are presented in table A.1. Assessing ages here does not present the problems we find in other preindustrial populations, because Nyinba, like most Tibetans, mark their age in terms of a sixty-year calendric cycle. In this, each year is assigned a special animal and element name and is easily converted to a Western date. The only problem is that of overlap, for the Tibetan year begins a few weeks after the Western New Year. The result is that any person born in these interstitial weeks would give his birth year as and be assigned to the previous calendar year. This is not the case for small children, for whom age as well as year of birth is recollected and for whom I also have exact birth dates. All Nyinba know their birth year, because it is important for astrological calculations, and because it is thought to affect character and thus is considered in arranging marriages and establishing friendships.

Age-sex pyramids (see fig. A.1) graphically display some of the basic

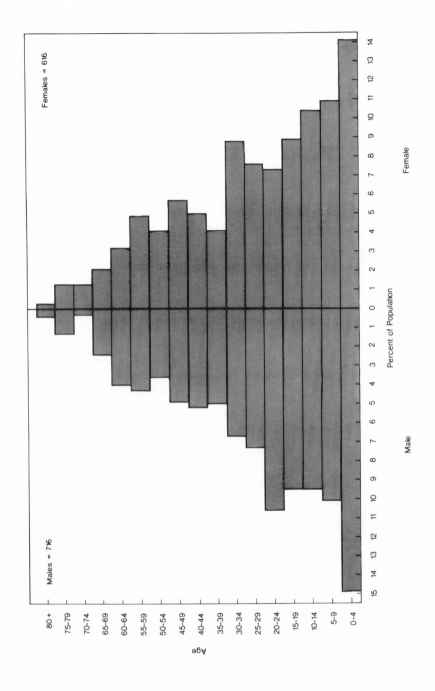

Males = 776

Females = 616

Male

Female

Percent of Population

Age

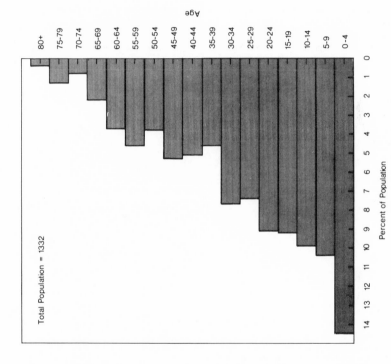

Figure A.1 Nyinba Age-Sex Pyramid, 1983

Table A.1 Age and Sex Structure of the Nyinba Population

| | Population in Interval[a] | | | | | |
| | Males | | Females | | Total Population | |
Age	N	%	N	%	N	%
0	21	2.9	26	4.2	47	3.5
1–4	86	12.0	61	9.9	147	11.0
5–9	72	10.1	67	10.9	139	10.4
10–14	68	9.5	64	10.4	132	9.9
15–19	68	9.5	55	8.9	123	9.2
20–24	76	10.6	45	7.3	121	9.1
25–29	52	7.3	47	7.6	99	7.4
30–34	48	6.7	54	8.8	102	7.7
35–39	36	5.0	25	4.1	61	4.6
40–44	37	5.2	31	5.0	68	5.1
45–49	35	4.9	35	5.7	70	5.3
50–54	26	3.6	25	4.1	51	3.8
55–59	31	4.3	30	4.9	61	4.6
60–64	29	4.0	20	3.2	49	3.7
65–69	17	2.4	13	2.1	30	2.2
70–74	2	0.3	8	1.3	10	0.8
75–79	9	1.3	8	1.3	17	1.3
80 +	3	0.4	2	0.3	5	0.4

[a] Population
Total	1,332
Males	716
Females	616
Sex Ratio	116

characteristics of population structure. A glance at the Nyinba pyramid shows a structure comparable to that of a number of middle-hills and high-land Nepalese groups, including the Gurung of central Nepal (Marfarlane 1976:282), the Tamang of eastern Nepal (Fricke 1986:49), and other Humla Tibetan-speaking populations (Goldstein 1976:225; Ross 1981:37). All stand intermediate between the markedly young populations found in many less-developed countries, whose age-sex pyramids have a very broad base and rapidly taper off to a narrow peak, and the older populations found in many modern Western countries, whose pyramids have a relatively narrow base and do not contract until advanced ages.

The Nyinba data also show substantial irregularities that might be expected for a small population subject to random fluctuations in rates of birth and death. These irregularities, however, may be the product of more than random fluctuations. As we can see, the pyramid shows a pronounced hollow between ages thirty-five and fifty-four, and this would be consistent with reports of high mortality during smallpox epidemics in 1939–40 and 1951. Epidemics undoubtedly have occurred many times, and together with political unrest and other events of exogenous origin, probably were a limiting factor on population growth among the Nyinba, as in so many other small-scale premodern populations (see Macfarlane 1976:305–6). This may be a factor in the remarkably low rate of growth between 1868, the date of the first modern tax lists, and the present. The eradication of smallpox, the increasing availability of modern medical treatments, and the moderation of other crises due to greater political stability and improved communications may be responsible for the apparently increased pace of population growth today.

The data on age composition and on infant and child mortality (see below, table A.3) can be used in attempts to fit the Nyinba data to model life tables and to frame estimates of present-day population growth. The "West" series of model tables constructed by Coale and Demeny (1983) have been found most satisfactory by a number of anthropologists, including those who have worked with Nepalese groups (Fricke 1986:112; see also Shryock and Siegel 1980:814). There are, however, special problems with the Nyinba data. First, there is the exacerbated female infant mortality; second, the fact that the population is not closed to migration; and third, the unusually low number of individuals aged thirty-five to fifty-four. If the latter does reflect historical events of epidemics, then Nyinba experience cannot be equated with that of the stable populations represented in model life tables, and any estimates derived from stable population theory may be subject to significant error. With these qualifications kept in mind, I should note that the greatest similarities, particularly for Nyinba of younger ages, exist for mortality levels 6 and 7 for females and mortality levels 8 and 9 for males in the West series of tables; both suggest an intrinsic rate of natural increase between 1 and 1.5 percent per year. These rates of growth would lead the population to double its size within forty-six and sixty-nine years.

Nyinba Fertility and Mortality

Table A.2 charts the general fertility rate during the period 1965–82, as derived from retrospective fertility histories for married women. As these data show, the rate of fertility is quite high, at an average of 235 births per 1,000 aged fifteen through forty-four (compare Goldstein on Limi [1981:725]). Morever, it is likely that this figure is an underestimate, for fertility rates seem to rise over time. Rather than a genuine increase in fer-

Table A.2 Annual Variations in Fertility, 1965–82

	N of Births	N of Women Aged 15–44	General Fertility Rate
1965	21	99	212.1
1966	20	106	188.7
1967	18	107	168.2
1968	28	104	269.2
1969	18	108	166.7
1970	25	109	229.4
1971	24	105	228.6
1972	27	104	259.6
1973	16	101	158.4
1974	33	103	320.4
1975	20	102	196.1
1976	24	98	244.9
1977	19	96	197.9
1978	35	93	376.3
1979	19	88	215.9
1980	26	84	309.5
1981	18	81	222.2
1982	24	78	307.7
Total	415	1,766	235.0

Table A.3 Infant and Child Mortality, 1965–82
(Age at Death in Months)

	Infant Mortality[a]		Child Mortality[b]			
	< 12	N of Births	12–23	24–59	12–59	N of Births
Males	198.0	202	26.8	80.5	107.4	149
Females	236.3	182	36.0	71.9	107.9	139
Total	216.1	384	31.3	76.4	107.6	288

[a] For children born between 1965 and 1982.
[b] For children born between 1965 and 1977.

tility, it is likely that numbers of children who were born and died in earlier years were "forgotten" and were not reported by their mothers. At the same time, mortality among infants and children is extremely high, as table A.3 shows, and more than a third of the children reported born did not live to see their fifth birthdays.

Glossary

The first spelling is that used in the text; the second, in parentheses, is classical Tibetan. See last paragraph of Preface.

Dagpo (bdag-po). Traditional landowners and slave owners who have full rights of citizenship in the community.

Dangri. Priest to local, village gods that possess spirit mediums, or dhamis (possibly derived from *jhankri* [Nep.] or *'brang rgyas* [Tib.]).

Gompa (dgon-pa). Temple households, occupied by lamas, or Tibetan Buddhist priests. These households are expected to provide ritual services to the village; in recompense, they receive use rights over land and payments in grain.

Kalyal. The name of the Thakuri (caste) dynasty that once ruled Humla, and present-day members of their clan.

Khangchung (khang-chung). Literally "small house." Refers to the small households that slaves occupied in the past and to freedmen who have failed to acquire full estates today.

Khyimdag (khyim-bdag). Household head. The term *khyimdagmo* is used for household headwoman.

Kudpu (skud-po). Youngest husband in a polyandrous marriage.

Magpa (mag-pa). A term of reference used for an individual's son-in-law and for a household's uxorilocally resident son-in-law.

Mukhiya (Nep. mukhiyā). System of hereditary headmanship instituted after the Nepalese conquest. The Tibetan equivalent, *gedpo (rged-po)*, refers both to headmen and respected elders.

Nyen (gnyen). Relatives that may marry, such as cross-cousins, and households and clans linked by past or present marriages.

Nyenpun (gnyen-spun). Relatives, including bilateral kin and affines.

Panchayat (Nep. **panchāyat**). Councils elected from the members of one or more villages which form part of a hierarchy of similarly constituted councils linking the district, the zone, and the nation.

Paral (Nep. **pariwar**). Family.

Pholha (**pho-lha**). Household gods shared by all the successors to a given ancestor-founder's estate.

Pun (**spun**). Children of a monogamous, polygynous, or polyandrous marriage and with qualifying prefixes, cousins through parallel sex links.

Ru (**rus**). Literally "bone." Heredity passed through bone—that is, patrilineally—which determines clan and stratum affiliations.

Rutsho (**ru-tsho**). Literally "bone," or "clan subdivision." Refers to a village section, which also may be known as *patti* (Nep.) or *yul* (Tib., literally, "village").

Shima (**gzhi-ma**). The status, akin to serfdom, which Nyinba held during the Kalyal regime.

T'ak (**khrag**). Literally "blood." Heredity through blood, that is, through women, which is seen as the basis for matrilateral kinship, affinal relationships, and complementary filiative ties to clans.

Thalu (Nep. **thrālu**). Literally "big man." Powerful men in Humla's hierarchy of patronage, the most powerful of whom are descendants of the former ruling Kalyal dynasty.

Trongba (**grong-ba**). Corporate landowning households that possess distinctive names, succession from free, founding households, and shrines to *pholha;* they act as full participants in village economic, political, and religious affairs.

Trongbat (**grong-'byed**). Literally "partitioned households." Households formed in a common partition who provide certain forms of mutual aid for one another and have the right to reinherit one another's property.

Tso or **Tsobo** (**gtso-bo**). Village-founder households (Nep. *nai*).

Yalba (**yal-ba**). Literally, "to fail," or "to disappear." Household extinction.

Yogpo (**g.yog-po**). Former slaves who were freed in 1926 and now constitute a stigmatized subpopulation.

Zurba (**zur-ba**). Adjunct households. Households created to provide minimally adequate support and independent residence for divorced trongba members.

Bibliography

Acharya, Meena, and Lynn Bennett. 1981. *The Rural Women of Nepal: An Aggregate Analysis and Summary of 8 Village Studies*. Kathmandu: Centre for Economic Development and Administration.

Allen, Nicholas J. 1976. Sherpa kinship terminology in diachronic perspective. *Man* 11:569–87.

———. 1978. Quadripartition of society in early Tibetan sources. *Journal Asiatique* 266:341–60.

Aziz, Barbara N. 1974. Some notions about descent and residence in Tibetan society. In C. von Fürer-Haimendorf, ed., *Contributions to the Anthropology of Nepal*. Warminster, England: Aris and Phillips.

———. 1978. *Tibetan Frontier Families*. New Delhi: Vikas.

Barnes, J. A. 1971. *Three Styles in the Study of Kinship*. London: Tavistock.

Beattie, J. H. M. 1964. Kinship and social anthropology. *Man* 64:101–3.

Bell, Charles. 1928. *The People of Tibet*. Oxford: Clarendon Press.

Bender, Donald. 1971. De facto families and de jure households in Ondo. *American Anthropologist* 73:223–41.

Berkner, Lutz K. 1975. The use and misuse of census data for the historical analysis of family structure. *Journal of Interdisciplinary History* 5:721–38.

Berreman, Gerald D. 1975. Himalayan polyandry and the domestic cycle. *American Ethnologist* 2:127–38.

———. 1978. Ecology, demography, and domestic strategies in the Western Himalayas. *Journal of Anthropological Research* 34:326–68.

———. 1980. Polyandry: Exotic custom vs. analytic concept. *Journal of Comparative Family Studies* 11:377–83.

Bishop, Barry C. 1978. The changing geoecology of Karnali Zone, Western Nepal Himalaya: A case of stress. *Arctic and Alpine Research* 10:531–48.

Bloch, Maurice. 1973. The long term and the short term: The economic and political significance of the morality of kinship. In Jack Goody, ed., *The Character of Kinship*. Cambridge: Cambridge University Press.

Bogoslovskij, V. A. 1972. *Essai sur l'histoire de peuple tibétaine ou la naissance d'une société de classes.* Translated by A. W. Macdonald. Paris: Librairie C. Klincksieck.

Campbell, James G. 1978. Consultations with Himalayan Gods: A Study of Oracular Religion and Alternative Values in Hindu Jumla. Ph.D. dissertation. Columbia University.

Caplan, Lionel. 1975. *Administration and Politics in a Nepalese Town.* London: Oxford University Press.

———. 1980. Power and status in South Asian slavery. In James L. Watson, ed., *Asian and African Systems of Slavery.* Berkeley: University of California Press.

Carrasco, Pedro. 1959. *Land and Polity in Tibet.* Seattle: University of Washington Press.

Carter, Anthony. 1974. A comparative analysis of systems of kinship and marriage in South Asia. *Proceedings of the Royal Anthropological Institute for 1973*:29–54.

———. 1984. Household histories. In Robert McC. Netting, Richard R. Wilk, and Eric J. Arnould, eds., *Households.* Berkeley: University of California Press.

Carter, Anthony T., and Robert S. Merrill. 1979. *Household Institutions and Population Dynamics.* Washington, D.C.: Agency for International Development.

Cassinelli, C. W., and Robert Ekvall. 1969. *A Tibetan Principality: The Political System of Sa sKya.* Ithaca, N.Y.: Cornell University Press.

Chandra, Ramesh. 1972. The notion of paternity among the polyandrous Kanet of Kinnaur, Himachal Pradesh. *Bulletin of the Anthropological Survey of India* 21:80–87.

Coale, Ansley J., and Paul Demeny, with Barbara Vaughan. 1983. *Regional Model Life Tables and Stable Populations.* New York: Academic Press.

Crook, J. H., and S. J. Crook. n.d. Explaining Tibetan polyandry: Socio-cultural, demographic, and biological perspectives.

de Filippo, Filippi, ed. 1937. *An Account of Tibet: The Travels of Ippolito Desideri of Pistoia, S.J., 1712–1727.* London: George Routledge and Sons.

Dumont, Louis. 1970. *Homo Hierarchicus.* Chicago: University of Chicago Press.

Durham, William H. Forthcoming. *Coevolution: Genes, Culture, and Human Diversity.* Stanford: Stanford University Press.

Ekvall, Robert B. 1968. *Fields on the Hoof: Nexus of Tibetan Nomadic Pastoralism.* New York: Holt, Rinehart and Winston.

Ellen, Roy. 1982. *Environment, Subsistence, and System.* Cambridge: Cambridge University Press.

Evans-Pritchard, E. E. [1940] 1969. *The Nuer.* Oxford: Oxford University Press.

Fisher, James F. 1986. *Trans-Himalayan Traders: Economy, Society, and Culture in Northwest Nepal.* Berkeley: University of California Press.

Flandrin, Jean-Louis. 1979. *Families in Former Times: Kinship, Household, and Sexuality in Early Modern France.* Translated by Richard Southern. Cambridge: Cambridge University Press.

Fortes, Meyer. 1953. The structure of unilineal descent groups. *American Anthropologist* 55:17–41.

———. 1958. Introduction. In Jack Goody, ed., *The Developmental Cycle in Domestic Groups*. Cambridge: Cambridge University Press.

———. 1959. Descent, filiation, and affinity: A rejoinder to Dr. Leach. *Man* 59:193–97, 206–12.

———. 1969. *Kinship and the Social Order*. Chicago: Aldine.

———. 1972. Kinship and the social order. Precis and reply. *Current Anthropology*. 13:285–96.

Fortes, Meyer, and E. E. Evans-Pritchard. 1940. Introduction. In Meyer Fortes and E. E. Evans-Pritchard, eds., *African Political Systems*. Oxford: Oxford University Press.

Fox, Richard G. 1985. *Lions of the Punjab: Culture in the Making*. Berkeley: University of California Press.

Fricke, Thomas E. 1986. *Himalayan Households: Tamang Demography and Domestic Processes*. Ann Arbor, Michigan: UMI Research Press.

Fürer-Haimendorf, C. von. 1964. *The Sherpas of Nepal*. Berkeley: University of California Press.

———. 1966. Unity and diversity in the Chetri caste of Nepal. In C. von Fürer-Haimendorf, ed., *Caste and Kin in Nepal, India, and Ceylon*. London: Asia Publishing House.

———. 1975. *Himalayan Traders*. London: John Murray.

Geertz, Clifford. 1957. Ritual and social change: A Javanese example. *American Anthropologist* 59:32–54.

———. 1965. Religion as a cultural system. In Michael Banton, ed., *Anthropological Approaches to the Study of Religion*. London: Tavistock.

Gellner, Ernest. 1973. *Cause and Meaning in the Social Sciences*. London: Routledge & Kegan Paul.

Giddens, Anthony. 1979. *Central Problems in Social Theory*. Berkeley: University of California Press.

Goldstein, Melvyn C. 1971a. Taxation and the structure of a Tibetan village. *Central Asiatic Journal* 15:1–27.

———. 1971b. Stratification, polyandry, and family structure in Central Tibet. *Southwestern Journal of Anthropology* 27:64–74.

———. 1974. Tibetan speaking agro-pastoralists of Limi: A cultural ecological overview of high altitude adaptation in the Northwest Himalaya. *Objets et Mondes* 14:259–68.

———. 1975a. Preliminary notes on marriage and kinship. *Contributions to Nepalese Studies* 2:57–69.

———. 1975b. *Tibetan-English: Dictionary of Modern Tibetan*. Kathmandu: Ratna Pustak.

———. 1976. Fraternal polyandry and fertility in a high Himalayan valley in Northwest Nepal. *Human Ecology* 4:223–33.

———. 1978a. Adjudication and partition in the Tibetan stem family. In David C. Buxbaum, ed., *Chinese Family Law and Social Change in Historical and Comparative Perspective*. Seattle: University of Washington Press.

———. 1978b. Pahari and Tibetan polyandry revisited. *Ethnology* 17:325–37.

————. 1981. New perspectives on Tibetan fertility and population decline. *American Ethnologist* 8:721–38.

————. 1987. When brothers share a wife. *Natural History* 96:3:39–49.

Goody, Jack. 1971. *Technology, Tradition, and the State in Africa*. Cambridge: Cambridge University Press.

————. 1972a. The evolution of the family. In Peter Laslett, ed., *Household and Family in Past Time*. Cambridge: Cambridge University Press.

————. 1972b. *Domestic Groups*. Reading, Mass.: Addison-Wesley.

————. 1976. *Production and Reproduction*. Cambridge: Cambridge University Press.

Gubhaju, Bhakta B. 1985. Regional and socio-economic differentials in infant and child mortality in rural Nepal. *Contributions to Nepalese Studies* 13:33–44.

Guillet, David. 1983. Toward a cultural ecology of mountains: The Central Andes and the Himalayas compared. *Current Anthropology* 24:561–74.

Hajnal, J. 1965. European marriage patterns in perspective. In D. V. Glass and D. E. C. Eversley, eds., *Population in History: Essays in Historical Demography*. London: Edward Arnold.

Hall, Andrew R. 1978. Preliminary report on the Langtang region. *Contributions to Nepalese Studies* 5:51–68.

Hamilton, Francis Buchanan. [1819] 1971. *An Account of the Kingdom of Nepal*. New Delhi: Manjusri Publishing House.

Harris, Marvin, and Eric B. Ross. 1987. *Death, Sex, and Fertility: Population Regulation in Preindustrial and Developing Societies*. New York: Columbia University Press.

Hiatt, L. R. 1980. Polyandry in Sri Lanka: A test case for parental investment theory. *Man* 15:583–602.

H. M. G. Nepal, Finance Ministry. *Tirja Lagat Record of Taxpayers of 1925–1946 B.S.* Department of Land Revenue.

H. M. G. Nepal, Land Reform Ministry. *Form Number Seven, Phant Wari;* and *Form Number One, Record of Tenants.*

Höfer, Andras. 1979. *The Caste Hierarchy and the State in Nepal*. Innsbruck: Universitäts Verlag Wagner.

Holy, Ladislav. 1979. *Segmentary Lineage Systems Reconsidered*. Belfast: Queen's University of Belfast.

Holy, Ladislav, and Milan Stuchlik, eds. 1981. *The Structure of Folk Models*. London: Academic Press.

Inden, Ronald B., and Ralph W. Nicholas. 1977. *Kinship in Bengali Culture*. Chicago: University of Chicago Press.

Jäschke, H. A. [1881] 1972. *A Tibetan-English Dictionary*. London: Routledge and Kegan Paul.

Jest, Corneille. 1975. *Dolpo: Communautés de la langue tibétaine du Népal*. Paris: Editions du C.N.R.S.

Kansakar, Vidya B. 1977. *Population Censuses of Nepal and the Problems of Data Analysis*. Kathmandu: Centre for Economic Development and Administration.

Keesing, Roger M. 1970. Shrines, ancestors, and cognatic descent: The Kwaio and Tallensi. *American Anthropologist* 72:755–75.

———. 1974. Theories of culture. *Annual Review of Anthropology* 3:73–97.

———. 1975. *Kin Groups and Social Structure*. New York: Holt, Rinehart and Winston.

———. 1981. *Cultural Anthropology: A Contemporary Perspective*. New York: Holt, Rinehart and Winston.

———. 1987. Models, "folk" and "cultural": Paradigms regained. In Dorothy Holland and Naomi Quinn, eds., *Cultural Models in Language and Thought*. Cambridge: Cambridge University Press.

Kelly, Raymond C. 1968. Demographic pressure and descent group structure in the New Guinea Highlands. *Oceania* 30:36–63.

———. 1977. *Etoro Social Structure*. Ann Arbor: University of Michigan Press.

Kihara, H. 1957. *Peoples of Nepal Himalaya: Scientific Results of the Japanese Expeditions to Nepal Himalaya, 1952–53*. Kyoto: Kyoto University.

Kopytoff, Igor. 1982. Slavery. *Annual Review of Anthropology* 11:207–30.

Krótki, Karol, and Harsha N. Thakur. 1971. Estimates of population size and growth from the 1952–54 and 1961 censuses of the Kingdom of Nepal. *Population Studies* 25:89–103.

Landon, Perceval. 1905. *Lhasa*. Vol 2. London: Hurst & Blackett.

Laslett, Peter. 1972. Introduction. In Peter Laslett, ed., *Household and Family in Past Time*. Cambridge: Cambridge University Press.

———. 1984. The family as a knot of individual interests. In Robert McC. Netting, Richard R. Wilk, and Eric J. Arnould, eds., *Households*. Berkeley: University of California Press.

Leach, Edmund R. 1961. *Pul Eliya, a Village in Ceylon: A Study of Land Tenure and Kinship*. Cambridge: Cambridge University Press.

———. 1962. On certain unconsidered aspects of double descent systems. *Man* 62:130–34.

———. [1954] 1965. *Political Systems of Highland Burma*. Boston: Beacon.

———. [1961] 1968. *Rethinking Anthropology*. London: Athlone.

Levine, Nancy E. 1976. The origins of *sTod-pa:* A Nyinba clan legend. *Contributions to Nepalese Studies* 4:57–75.

———. 1980a. Opposition and interdependence: Demographic and economic perspectives on Nyinba slavery. In James L. Watson, ed., *Asian and African Systems of Slavery*. Berkeley: University of California Press.

———. 1980b. Nyinba polyandry and the allocation of paternity. *Journal of Comparative Family Studies* 11:283–98.

———. 1981a. Perspectives on love: Morality and affect in Nyinba interpersonal relationships. In A. C. Mayer, ed., *Culture and Morality: Essays in Honour of Christoph von Fürer-Haimendorf*. Delhi: Oxford University Press.

———. 1981b. The theory of *ru:* Kinship, descent, and status in a Tibetan society. In C. von Fürer-Haimendorf, ed., *Asian Highland Societies*. New Delhi: Sterling.

———. 1981c. Law, labor, and the economic vulnerability of women in Nyinba Society. *Kailash* 8:123–53.

———. 1982a. Belief and explanation in Nyinba women's witchcraft. *Man* 17: 259–74.

———. 1982b. Social structure, fertility, and the value of children in North-western Nepal. *Contributions to Nepalese Studies* 9:1–19.

———. 1987. Caste, state, and ethnic boundaries in Nepal. *Journal of Asian Studies* 46:71–88.

Levine, Nancy E., and Walter H. Sangree. 1980. Conclusion: Asian and African systems of polyandry. *Journal of Comparative Family Studies* 11:385–410.

Lévi-Strauss, Claude. 1967. *Structural Anthropology.* New York: Anchor Books.

———. 1969. *The Elementary Structures of Kinship.* Boston: Beacon Press.

Linton, Ralph. 1968. The natural history of the family. In Morton H. Fried, ed., *Readings in Anthropology.* Vol. 2. New York: Thomas Y. Crowell.

Macdonald, Alexander W. 1980. Creative dismemberment among the Tamang and Sherpas of Nepal. In M. Aris and A. Kyi, eds., *Tibetan Studies in Honour of Hugh Richardson.* Warminster, England: Aris and Phillips.

Macfarlane, Alan. 1976. *Resources and Population: A Study of the Gurungs of Nepal.* Cambridge: Cambridge University Press.

March, Kathryn S. 1983. Weaving, writing, and gender. *Man* 18:729–44.

Miller, Beatrice D. 1956. Ganye and Kidu: Two formalized systems of mutual aid among the Tibetans. *Southwestern Journal of Anthropology* 12:157–70.

Moore, Sally F. 1978. *Law as Process.* London: Routledge & Kegan Paul.

———. 1986. *Social Facts and Fabrications: Customary Law on Kilimanjaro, 1880–1980.* Cambridge: Cambridge University Press.

Nag, Moni, Benjamin N. F. White, and R. Creighton Peet. 1978. An anthropological approach to the study of the economic value of children in Java and Nepal. *Current Anthropology* 19:293–301.

Nakane, Chie. 1967. *Kinship and Economic Organization in Rural Japan.* London: Athlone.

Nepal, National Planning Commission. 1984. *Population Census—1981: General Characteristics Tables.* Vol. 1—Part 1. Kathmandu: Central Bureau of Statistics.

———. 1985. *Intercensal Changes of Some Key Census Variables, Nepal 1952/54–81.* Kathmandu: Central Bureau of Statistics.

Netting, Robert McC. 1981. *Balancing on an Alp: Ecological Change and Continuity in a Swiss Mountain Community.* Cambridge: Cambridge University Press.

———. 1984. Reflections on an alpine village as ecosystem. In Emilio F. Moran, ed., *The Ecosystem Concept in Anthropology.* Boulder, Colo.: Westview Press.

Netting, Robert McC., Richard R. Wilk, and Eric J. Arnould. 1984. *Households: Comparative and Historical Studies of the Domestic Group.* Berkeley: University of California Press.

Orlove, Benjamin S., and David W. Guillet. 1985. Theoretical and methodological considerations on the study of mountain peoples: Reflections on the idea of subsistence type and the role of history in human ecology. *Mountain Research and Development* 5:3–18.

Ortner, Sherry B. 1973. Sherpa purity. *American Anthropologist* 75:49–63.

———. 1978. *Sherpas Through Their Rituals.* Cambridge: Cambridge University Press.

———. 1981. Gender and sexuality in hierarchical societies: The case of Polynesia and some comparative implications. In S. B. Ortner and H. Whitehead, eds., *Sexual Meanings.* Cambridge: Cambridge University Press.

Parry, Jonathan P. 1979. *Caste and Kinship in Kangra.* London: Routledge and Kegan Paul.

Passin, Herbert. 1955. Untouchability in the Far East. *Monumenta Nipponica* 11:27–47.

Pasternak, Burton. 1976. *Introduction to Kinship and Social Organization.* Englewood Cliffs, N.J.: Prentice-Hall.

Pasternak, Burton, Carol R. Ember, and Melvin Ember. 1976. On the conditions favoring extended family households. *Journal of Anthropological Research* 32:109–23.

Paul, Robert A. 1982. *The Tibetan Symbolic World.* Chicago: University of Chicago Press.

Peissel, Michel. 1979. *Zanskar: The Hidden Kingdom.* New York: E. P. Dutton.

Peter, Prince of Greece and Denmark. 1963. *A Study of Polyandry.* The Hague: Mouton.

———. 1965. The Tibetan family system. In M. F. Nimkoff, ed., *Comparative Family Systems,* pp. 192–208. Boston: Houghton Mifflin.

Pignede, Bernard. 1962. Clan organization and hierarchy among the Gurungs. *Contributions to Indian Sociology* 6:102–19.

Quinn, Naomi, and Dorothy Holland. 1987. Culture and cognition. In D. Holland and N. Quinn, eds., *Cultural Models in Language and Thought.* Cambridge: Cambridge University Press.

Radcliffe-Brown, A. R. 1929. A further note on Ambrym. *Man* 35:50–53.

———. 1952. *Structure and Function in Primitive Society.* London: Cohen & West.

Rana, Chandra Shumshere. 1925. Appeal to the People of Nepal for the Emancipation of Slaves and Abolition of Slavery in the Country. Kathmandu. Reprinted in *Regmi Research Series* 4 and 5 (1972–73).

Rauber, Hanna. 1982a. The Humli-Khyampas of far western Nepal: A study in ethnogenesis. *Contributions to Nepalese Studies* 8:57–79.

———. 1982b. Humli-Khyambas and the Indian salt trade: Changing economy of nomadic traders in far west Nepal. In P. C. Salzman, ed., *Contemporary Nomadic and Pastoral Peoples: Asia and the North.* Studies in Third World Societies. Williamsburg, Va: College of William and Mary, Department of Anthropology.

Regmi Research Ltd. 1971. Miscellaneous Documents on Jumla, 1834–1846, and Regulations for Jumla District 1844, A.D. *Regmi Research Series* Vol. 3, no. 3 and no. 9.

———. 1976. Adoption and Inheritance. *Nepal Law Translation Series* Vol. 16. Kathmandu: Nepal Press Digest.

Regmi, Mahesh C. 1972. *A Study in Nepali Economic History, 1768–1846.* New Delhi: Manjusri.

———. 1976. *Landownership in Nepal.* Berkeley: University of California Press.

Rhoades, Robert E., and Stephen I. Thompson. 1975. Adaptive strategies in Alpine environments: Beyond ecological particularism. *American Ethnologist* 2:535–51.

Rivers, W. H. R. 1924. *Social Organization.* London: Kegan Paul.

Róna-Tas, A. 1955. Social terms in the list of grants of the Tibetan Tun-huang chronicles. *Acta Orientalia Academiae Scientiarum Hungaricae* 5:249–70.

Rose, Leo E., and Margaret W. Fisher. 1970. *The Politics of Nepal.* Ithaca: Cornell University Press.

Ross, James L. 1981. Hindu and Tibetan Reproduction and Fertility in Northwestern Nepal: A Study of Population, Ecology and Economics. Ph.D. diss., Case Western Reserve University.

———. 1984. Culture and fertility in the Nepal Himalayas: A test of a hypothesis. *Human Ecology* 12:163–81.

Sahlins, Marshall. 1974. *Stone Age Economics.* London: Tavistock.

———. 1976. *Culture and Practical Reason.* Chicago: University of Chicago Press.

———. 1981. *Historical Metaphors and Mythical Realities.* Ann Arbor: University of Michigan Press.

Scheffler, Harold W. 1966–67. Ancestor worship in anthropology. *Current Anthropology* 7:541–51; 8:505–9.

———. 1972. Systems of kin classification: A structural typology. In Priscilla Reining, ed., *Kinship Studies in the Morgan Centennial Year.* Washington, D.C.: The Anthropological Society of Washington.

Schneider, David M. 1968. *American Kinship: A Cultural Account.* Englewood Cliffs, N.J.: Prentice-Hall.

———. 1976. Notes toward a theory of culture. In Keith H. Basso and Henry A. Selby, eds., *Meaning in Anthropology.* Albuquerque: University of New Mexico Press.

Schuler, Sidney. 1978. Notes on marriage and the status of women in Baragaon. *Kailash* 6:141–52.

———. 1981. *The Women of Baragaon.* Kathmandu: Centre for Economic Development and Administration.

———. 1987. *The Other Side of Polyandry.* Boulder, Colo.: Westview Press.

Sharma, Ursula. 1980. *Women, Work, and Property in North-West India.* London: Tavistock.

Shryock, Henry S., Jacob S. Siegel, and Associates. 1980. *The Methods and Materials of Demography.* 4th printing (rev.). Washington, D.C.: U.S. Government Printing Office.

Smith, Thomas C. 1977. *Nakahara: Family Farming and Population in a Japanese Village, 1717–1830.* Stanford: Stanford University Press.

Srivastava, Ram P. 1958. The Bhotia nomads and their Indo-Tibetan trade. *Journal of the University of Saugar* 7:1–22.

Stein, R. A. 1972. *Tibetan Civilization.* Stanford: Stanford University Press.

Stenning, Derrick J. 1958. Household viability among the Pastoral Fulani. In Jack Goody, ed., *The Developmental Cycle in Domestic Groups.* Cambridge: Cambridge University Press.

Stiller, Ludwig F. 1973. *The Rise of the House of Gorkha: A Study in the Unification of Nepal.* New Delhi: Manjusri.

Strathern, Andrew. 1972. *One Father, One Blood.* London: Tavistock.

———. 1973. Kinship, descent, and locality: Some New Guinea examples. In Jack Goody, ed., *The Character of Kinship.* Cambridge: Cambridge University Press.

———. 1981. "Noman": Representations of identity in Mount Hagen. In Ladislav Holy and Milan Stuchlik, eds., *The Structure of Folk Models.* London: Academic Press.

Strong, Anna Louise. 1960. *When Serfs Stood up in Tibet.* Peking: New World Press.

Tambiah, S. J. 1966. Polyandry in Ceylon—with special reference to the Laggala region. In C. von Fürer-Haimendorf, ed., *Caste and Kin in Nepal, India, and Ceylon.* London: Asia Publishing House.

Tucci, Giuseppe. 1955. The secret characters of the kings of ancient Tibet. *East and West* 6:197–205.

———. 1956. *Preliminary Report on Two Scientific Expeditions in Nepal.* Rome: Rome Oriental Series.

Turner, Ralph L. [1931] 1966. *A Comparative and Etymological Dictionary of the Nepali Language.* New York: Frederick Ungar.

United Nations. 1980. *Population of Nepal.* Country Monograph Series No. 6. Bangkok: Economic and Social Commission for Asia and the Pacific.

Verdon, Michel. 1979. The stem family: toward a general theory. *Journal of Interdisciplinary History* 10:87–105.

Vinding, Michael. 1979–80. Marriage systems of the Thakaalis and related groups of the Bodish section of Sino-Tibetan speaking peoples. *Folk* 21–22:325–343.

Watson, James L. 1980. Slavery as an institution: Open and closed systems. In James L. Watson, ed., *Asian and African Systems of Slavery.* Berkeley: University of California Press.

Westermarck, Edward. 1925. *The History of Human Marriage.* 5th ed. Vol. 3. London: Macmillan.

———. 1926. *A Short History of Marriage.* London: Macmillan.

Wilk, Richard R., and Robert McC. Netting. 1984. Households: Changing forms and functions. In Robert McC. Netting, Richard R. Wilk, and Eric J. Arnould, eds., *Households.* Berkeley: University of California Press.

Worsley, Peter M. 1956. The kinship system of the Tallensi: A reevaluation. *Journal of the Royal Anthropological Institute* 86:37–75.

Wrigley, E. A. 1978. Fertility strategy for the individual and the group. In Charles Tilly, ed., *Historical Studies of Changing Fertility.* Princeton: Princeton University Press.

Wylie, Turrell. 1959. A standard system of Tibetan transcription. *Harvard Journal of Asiatic Studies* 22:261–67.

Yanagisako, Sylvia J. 1979. Family and household: The analysis of domestic groups. *Annual Review of Anthropology* 8:161–205.

Zhabs-dkar sna-tshogs-rang-grol. 1975. *Snyigs dus 'gro ba yongs kyi skyabs mgon zhabs dkar rdo rje 'chang chen po' i rnam thar pa.* Portions translated by Matthew Kapstein. New Delhi: M. M. Offset Press.

Index

Acham, 220, 225
Acharya, Meena, 232 n
Added man (nonfraternal polyandry), 161
Adjunct household, 7, 108–9
Adoption: disapproval of, 163, 163 n; legal,
  for *magpa*, 116
Adultery, 148, 151, 165
Affinal relationships, 118, 161; and tradi-
  tional food exchanges, 220
Age, and animal calendric cycle, 285
Agriculture: annual cycle of, 210 (fig. 9.1),
  211; intensification of, 206; men's and
  women's work in, 206–9; mountain, 252
Alliances, marital, 30, 122
Altitude, of villages, 22, 211
Ancestors, 27–28, 32
Ancestress, ritual importance of, 31, 48,
  210
Aziz, Barbara N., 127, 158, 160, 165 n,
  169, 170 n

Bajura, 220
Barkhang, village structure, 194–97
Barren women: in polygynous marriages,
  146, 148–49; in second marriages, 163,
  181; status of, 119
Beattie, J. H. M., 267
Beef-eating, caste consequences of, 66, 258
Behavioral ecology, 5
Bender, Donald, 126
Bennett, Lynn, 232 n
Berkner, Lutz K., 140

Berreman, Gerald D., 4
Bhotia (Tibetan), as term of abuse, 258
Bhutan, 184
Bishop, Barry C., 92 n
Bogoslovskij, V. A., 38 n
Bon religion, 48
Buckwheat, as staple grain, 212–14
Butter, sales of, 226
Byansi: and Humla Bura, 24; as traders,
  219

Caste: and ethnic Tibetans, position of, 25,
  66, 92; in Humla, 24, 90 n; and Tibetan
  ranking system, 66–67
Cattle herding: limitations on, 226, 233;
  work of, 227
Ceremonies: annual cycle of, 209; importance of, 271
Change, models of, 16–17, 277–78
Children: in households, position of,
  122–23; in partition, 151, 169, 175, 177
Clan: exogamy, 41, 195; gods, 47–48;
  membership and civic entitlements,
  42–43; names, 28, 40–41; and village
  populations, 45. *See also* Descent;
  Strata, social
Climate, 24
Closure: dimensions of, 258, 269–70; illu-
  sion of, 270; theoretical assumption of,
  277
Commensality, 42, 64
Conjoint marriage: definition of, 6, 144;

Nyimatang, village structure, 197–98
Nyinba and Tibetan society, 19–20, 28–
  29, 39–40, 65, 100, 171, 258
Nyingmapa Buddhism, 22, 160
Nyin Yul Tshan Zhi, 21

Orlove, Benjamin S., 211n
Ortner, Sherry B., 76n

Pal clan, 46, 54, 199
Panchayat councils, 43, 85, 94, 95, 97
Parentage and partition, 174–75. *See also*
  Partition; Polyandry
Partition: children in, 151, 169, 175, 177;
  disadvantages of, 125; disapproval of,
  183–84; and family realignment, 176–
  78; and fraternal equity, 179–80; in
  Hindu joint family, 183; incidence of,
  243, 245; influences on, 184, 239–40,
  257; and mergers, 251–52; and Nepali
  law, 121; and occupations, 250; and
  property division, 178–80; and resource
  constraints, 155, 185, 269, 272, 276;
  among social strata, 276; in Tibet, 121;
  timing of, 182–83; and village structure,
  30, 49
Pasternak, Burton, 132
Pastureland: as collective land, 22, 97; diminution of, 276
Paternity: assignment of, 167; certainty,
  concerns about, 167; importance of,
  5–7, 150, 168; and kinship, 169; and
  partition, 179; in Tibet, 167, 169
Pholha, 27, 47–48, 102–3, 198
Polyandry: advantages, perceptions of, 9,
  32, 159; and androcentric biases, 4; economic rationales for, 4, 158–59, 169–
  70, 265, 269, 279; eldest brother's role
  in, 5, 165–66, 170; and emigration,
  270–71; father-son variant of, 160; and
  fraternal equity, 152; homeostatic models
  of, 275–76; incidence of, 144; and marital flexibility, 163; as marriage, 150; nonfraternal, 161; norm of, 143, 146–47,
  157; and population, 273–75, 279; and
  sacrifice, for men, 4, 170, 266; and sexual preferences, 165, 170; and sibling
  group size, 7, 147–48, 152, 154; in Sri
  Lanka, 154n, 267; in Tibet, 100, 158,

160–61; and wealth, 8; "wife-bringer,"
  role of, 165–66. *See also* Conjoint marriage; Marriage; Polygynous polyandry
Polygynous polyandry, 144, 149; and sons'
  conjoint marriage, 152–54
Polygyny, 8; mother-daughter variant of,
  160; nonsororal, 147, 163; sororal, advantages of, 6–7, 149, 154, 176
Population: age and sex structure, 286–88;
  concerns about, 32–33; growth of, in
  Humla and Nepal, 241–42; growth and
  crises in past, 289
Potatoes, 212
Property: household and individual, 101,
  104; and explanations of polyandry, 100,
  267; slaves as, 70. *See also* Dowry
Prosperity, of Nyinba, xiv, 206, 273. *See
  also* Wealth
Pun, 7, 51–52, 120, 127, 147
Purang, West Tibet, 27, 217–19

Rana, Chandra Shumshere, 68, 79n
Raskot, 220, 225, 228
Reflexivity, 11, 17, 34, 45
Residence, 128, 267
Retirement, 116, 117, 119, 123
Rig, 39
Ross, Eric B., 241
Ross, James L., 266
Rongba, 19, 258
Ru: and descent, 38; concepts of, 37–39,
  64, 67; priority of, 58, 59; and social
  ranking, 39, 42–43, 63–64
Rutsho, 46, 99

Sa, symbol of, 46, 48
Sahlins, Marshall, 268
Saipal, Mt., 24, 218 (fig. 9.3)
Sakya temples, ruins of, 25
Schneider, David M., 40n
Section founder, household of. See *Tso*
Section system, 99–100; changes in indi-
  vidual villages, 194–201; foundations of,
  189–91. See also *Trongbat;* Village
Servants, 227, 228
Settlement patterns, 188–89, 198, 199
Sex ratio, 74–75, 288
Sexual relationships, in marriage, xiv, 6,
  150–51, 164–65, 170, 176, 179, 181